Seeking Arnolds

Finding Family, Muted History, and a Guardian Angel

Indulis Pommers

TABLE OF CONTENTS

PREFACE

This book project started as a family history meant for my imme-diate family and their progeny. As a young boy, I knew little of my Father, Arnolds, since he died when I was two, but as I matured, there rose a grow-ing interest to discover him. That search then piqued my interest in the history surrounding his time and place, or broadly speaking, World War II and Latvia. The era is fascinating and the study became a mild obsession: many books were read, museums visited, events googled, videos watched, trips made, and many questions were asked of relatives who lived through this time. Here, I record some of the results of this passion.

My original intent, then, was to give my downstream family a sense of where they came from, of their ancestors and the experiences that shaped them, and still influence to some degree all of us and our descendants. Many geographic particulars have been included, and for a selfish reason. I have received gifts of meaningfulness and pleasure by visiting many of the places where my parents and family lived their story: important loca-tions in the homeland of Latvia, such as Gulbene, Cesis, Riga, Daugavpils, and Liepaja; Berlin, Hamburg, Waren, Soltau, Mele, and Bad Rothenfelde in Germany, to where the family fled; and the neighboring countries of Estonia, Lithuania and Russia, whose histories often intersected and influ-enced my people. Google Earth and hard-copy maps have filled visitation gaps to carry me away to those holy sites of suffering of the imprisoned and deported Latvians, sites that were buried by time and prejudiced report-ing. It is my hope and expectation that my future family will appreciate this history…but, most importantly, that at least one of my progeny will have this same intense interest, tying family history into places where that history happened - perhaps visiting these same places - and will get that same pleasure I have been granted. This as-of-yet-unknown relative is my idealized target audience.

As the book architecture developed, mission creep extended my efforts well past only a memoir of family. Context was needed to better tell the story. Thus the account grew to include the history of Latvia; the chilling events in the Neighborhood; the Latvian diaspora of 1944, as lived by my immediate family; and the tragic circumstances of those Latvians who did not flee. I was also given the personal account of a relative, Rita, who had been swept up in the Soviet deportation of 1941, survived the Gulag, and left behind a memoir of her experiences which is translated and published here for the first time.

Scattered throughout will also be particulars about me and my family, as befits the original family history focus of the narrative. Parts of this may be of no interest to the casual reader, so feel free to skim or skip those passages, without guilt. Also sprinkled in are quantifications of history, details of life and survival, reflections on the human condition, viewpoints on governance and its consequences, and other musings. All this makes for a book with many twists and turns and some overlaps, and for this, please forgive me - but some elements bear repeating under different contexts to drive points home.

You may notice some sense of outrage seeping through my writings. Guilty as charged! For most of my younger years, the fate of our families stuck behind the Iron Curtain was unknown. I could not understand this injustice. People were afraid to write, truth could not be spoken, and the Communists lied - big lies, as they are still doing (witness Covid and Chernobyl) - and hid their atrocities. Unfortunately, it still seems that the record of Communist behavior, with as many as 40 million having been slaughtered in Russia and another 70 million, largely innocents, killed in

Red China, is all too little appreciated. None of the perpetrators has been brought to trial, and in fact many of these villains are still viewed as heroes within their own countries and by Communist sympathizers throughout the world. The Nazis - National Socialists - were very properly brought before the Nuremberg trials, convicted and punished, and that murderous philosophy has virtually been eliminated; its few champions are subject to international scorn and opprobrium. Not so with the Communist philosophy and its socialist relatives. So, to me, it's important to shine additional light on this portion of history, to help expose a moral wrong.

A warning: the early events of my family history and their surroundings make for dark reading. While people of that time and place certainly lived some joy and happiness - love, marriage, children, celebrations, laughter, friendships and so on - the dark forces that enveloped them ended up a smear on everything else. This was the burden on adults; children were ignorant and somewhat shielded, living innocent lives filled with the typical fun of childhood. For grown-ups, the fear of losing everything, the terror of a relentless monster hunting for you, the inability to protect and be protected, the constant, daily unknowns, all pressing on innocent people… this had to dominate the feelings and behaviors, and this gets reflected when describing the times. You may have to shield your children until they are prepared to handle these bitter tales.

To end on an upbeat note, I will chronicle a beautiful set of experiences that point toward the possibility that Guardian Angels exist! It feels strange to note this because I am not traditionally religious, a spiritualist or mystic, and indeed have a strong skeptical core. Yet events with extremely low probabilities while searching for my Father did happen, with such a shocking intensity and frequency that the use of the term "Guardian Angel" seems justified. Others have seen it clearly as God at work; or maybe the term "Invisible Hand" applies; or perhaps it's simply fate and circumstance - but things happened outside of my ordinary expectations. Over the years, I finally placed all this under the Guardian Angel label, finding it both explanatory and very comforting. May this be of some interest, and perhaps enlightenment and joy, to you.

CHAPTER 1
FINDING ARNOLDS

"Coincidence is God's way of remaining anonymous"

- Albert Einstein

I have no memories at all of my father, Arnolds Pommers. Growing up, he sort of didn't exist for me, since I was 1 year and 11 months old when he passed on November 7, 1948. This empty hole was actually reinforced by having, starting at age 7, a father-figure, my stepfather Aleks Siraks. My mother Anna spoke little to me of her past life with Arnolds. Some of this was to avoid memories and reminders of difficult times, and some was to keep herself and me forward-looking and appreciative of Aleks. After all, he was taking on financial and other fatherly responsibilities for a child not his own, with the natural lessening of the biological imperative. But as I matured, married Sue, and had a family of my own, the role of my biological father became more important and my need to understand Arnolds a bit more began, and then grew.

1.1 FIRST CHAT

That first moment of insight remains very vivid. It was January in the mid-1980s when I flew to San Diego, California to attend a Simulation Society conference. My distributor in the area had arranged for a room in Rancho Santa Fe, a beautiful inland suburb. I was sitting on the small patio, eating a sandwich, when I felt Arnolds' presence. He was hovering just overhead, although I couldn't see him…and said that I should visit him, although I heard no voice. It was disquieting, yet not scary at all, but a sensation I had never had before, and would have not believed in, had I not felt it. After those few seconds had passed, I resolved to find Arnolds.

Several photos exist of Dad's funeral. A key one was of his gravestone, a large vertical monument, 3 or 4 feet high, engraved with the name, birth and death dates and places. The Latvian inscription "Milestiba Nekad Nebeidzas" ("Love Never Ends") was carved into the large stone burial slab set in the ground directly in front of this headstone. Other slabs and their associated headstones were next to his. After returning from the San Diego trip, I asked my mother Anna where the cemetery was located. She said it was in Soltau, Germany, near the main road from Soltau to Hamburg, on a small side road, in the Wolterdingen area, with a train track next to it. Armed with this minimal description and photo of the gravestone, I began my search for Dad a few years later.

1.2 GUIDES ARE SENT!

It was in the spring of 1990 when I flew from London, where I had been on a business trip, to Hamburg, Germany. The next morning, on Thursday, March 22, I drove south toward Soltau. I kept my eyes peeled as I neared the target area some 50 miles south of Hamburg, and soon saw a small sign for Wolterdingen. Almost immediately, on my right, visible through a leafless spring forest, was a small cemetery. I slowed down, wondered if this could be it, but then resumed driving straight down the road, based on the disqualifiers of not yet being in Soltau, plus the visibility of the cemetery from the main road, versus it supposedly being on a side road. About a half-mile further there was a road sign - "Entering Soltau" - and I pulled off on the shoulder. Perhaps that small cemetery was worth checking out? So I waited for traffic to pass, did a U turn, and went back, taking a left onto the side road, Soltauer Str., and 2 quick right turns into the cemetery parking lot. A railroad track crossing then became visible just ahead; this immediately raised my hopes that I had found the right spot.

The parking lot was tiny, with room for maybe 10 cars. The cemetery itself was also small, perhaps 200 X 200 yards. Only one car was parked in the lot. I got out of my car and walked to the single cemetery entrance, a small gate between fencing. As I walked up to the gate, an elderly couple was approaching from inside the cemetery. We met - exactly - at the gate. Five seconds earlier or later, they would have been strangers that you might wave to, or not even acknowledge due to distance. But the timing was absolutely precise.

We had to talk. I held the gate open as the couple stepped through, and they said, in German, "Guten Tag" (good day) to me. I responded "Guten Tag" to them. They stepped through the gate, looked at me, thanked me for holding the gate open, and then said, "Sie ist nicht Deutsche" (you're not German), and "Vas volen Sie heir"? (what are you doing here?). Since this area is well out of normal tourist haunts, their curiosity was reasonable. I replied in broken German that I was looking for my father who was buried somewhere around here. They asked, who was your father? I replied "Ein Lettish DP" (a Latvian Displaced Person), whereupon the man asked "Sprechen Sie Lettish?" (do you speak Latvian?), and I replied "Ja". He then said, and this is an exact quote seared into my memory, "Tad runasim Latviski!" (then let's speak Latvian!), in Latvian, which is shocking. There are perhaps 2 million Latvian speakers in our world of 7.5 billion people - and what are the odds of running into one at that exact time, at that exact place, a thousand miles from Latvia?? Mere circumstance? Strange, but at the moment, it seemed perfectly normal. Only later that night did the incident strike me for the statistical oddity that it was, or for the sheer supernaturalness of it.

But there's much more. Further conversation revealed that the gentleman, Gabrielle, had known my father and knew exactly where he was buried - I was at the right Cemetery! Gabrielle had also been a Latvian

DP at that same Wolterdingen Camp where we had lived in 1948, and had married a local German girl, Hildegard, and stayed in the area (Note: it's possible that my guide's names were Vilis and Erica; my personal documentation has become sketchy over time and I apologize and feel horrible about this possible inaccuracy. My later local acquaintance, Waldemar, who you will soon meet, said with great certainty that the guides were Gabrielle and Hildegard). Gabrielle then said "You would not have found the grave", and walked me a hundred feet to Dad's grave…and it was easily apparent why I would not have found it alone. The huge 4 foot monument that I was looking for, as portrayed in the photo, had been replaced by a 1' x 1' stone plaque flat in the ground, with Dad's name on it, but covered by low evergreen bushes that had crept up and almost obliterated the gravesite. The explanation was that the large upright gravestone was simply a cheap concrete marker (which explained a mystery to me - how could my penniless Mother have afforded a huge granite monument?) - which had crumbled over time. For years after World War II no one had paid attention to foreigners' graves. Cemeteries were crammed with local casualties, and Germany was more concerned with food, medicine and shelter. Many years later, after Germany had minimally recovered, the nation began replacing these crumbling concrete monuments with flat stone plaques wherever possible. I salute them for this.

To be finally standing next to Arnolds was a highly emotional moment. Tears flowed. The grief for a life cut short at 40 years, of a father unknown, of a son unknown to the father, all gushed out. My hosts waited respectfully by, and then invited me to view the remnants of the Wolterdingen Camp - a bit down this side road, just past the Soltau-Hamburg road, on the left. After cleaning up Dad's site, laying down some wildflowers, and "touring" the graveyard, we left to see the old Wolterdingen Camp.

(Note: As an important aside, this Cemetery also has monuments to commemorate the massacre of 269 prisoners - mostly Jewish - on April 12, 1945. They were being transported by rail from the nearby Bergen-Belsen concentration camp in an effort to hide Nazi atrocities as the War was winding down. The Allies were bombing German trains, and one raid hit such a train in Wolterdingen, with many inmates escaped in the tumult. They were hunted down and murdered by a combination of locals and German troops, and the monuments in the Cemetery are in remembrance of these victims. So, very sadly, this was the site of many tragedies besides our personal one.)

To continue - after a short ride we arrived at the old Wolterdingen Camp. There were still the remains of buildings, cellar holes, foundations, and paths where my family and I had lived in 1948. We actually stood on the road where Arnolds' funeral procession passed from the Camp to the Cemetery - I have a photo - so this was also breathtaking. My hosts then kindly invited me to their home, which was just a few miles toward Hamburg on the main road, on the right side - where we chatted, ate, and parted company. Upon leaving, they gifted me with two souvenirs, decorative plates of Soltau. Gabrielle and Hildegard were wonderful people, and primary players in this most amazing, miraculous happening.

1.3 SECOND CHAT

On the same trip, but later in the day, I took a short detour to Bergen-Belsen, the notorious concentration camp liberated by the Allies in 1945. The grey spring weather and the total lack of other visitors added to the melancholy of the place. I paid my respects by walking around the burial mounds and their body counts and contemplated man's horrors visited on man. My memories remain vivid: I observed closely the trees surrounding the main camp, which were either witnesses or their offspring to the suffering and carnage. On the camp's edge, near the trees, I scooped a handful of soil, which was sandy but with black grains scattered throughout, presenting a well-deserved malignant impression. There was also a monument to young Anne Frank which commemorates her passing at this site, multiplying the sadness.

Next I drove south and spent the night at a hotel in the city of Osnabruck. For the second time, I had a sense of Arnolds' presence, this time hovering over the foot of my bed, toward the upper right corner of the room. I felt him wordlessly approving of my trip, but "saying" that his true grave was not exactly where the replacement gravestone I had just discovered was located! Years later I discovered that he was right. This turned out to be yet another "miracle" in my search for Dad. More on that later. This second appearance, again, was not at all frightening and seemed quite normal and ordinary. It was only later that the wonder, questioning and mystery registered to me, and added to my emerging Guardian Angel theory.

Osnabruck was the larger regional city near the site of the Melle Baltic DP Camp in which my family had lived, and where I spent my first days. I had been born in nearby Bad Rothenfelde, and the strange circumstances of my finding the exact birthplace, described later, again added to the wonder and mystery of my search for the past.

1.4 WALDEMAR APPEARS

Skipping forward in time to June 2013, yet another happening occurred. I had wanted to take my wife Sue to Arnolds' gravesite - it had been 23 years since I had found it - and combine that with a driving vacation to Berlin and Northern Germany. I had also queried my dear cousin Kitty about different places where our extended family, prior to my birth, had stayed in or passed through while fleeing through Poland and north Germany in the last days of WW II. One of the localities where they stayed, long enough for the kids to briefly attend school, was named Varen (or Waren). It was supposedly well northeast of Berlin, on a large beautiful lake, but by my calculations this "Varen" was probably in what is now Poland, and my search through old maps yielded nothing. Nonetheless, later in our tour, Sue and I did make a hotel reservation in Waren, Germany, situated on Lake Muritz, taking comfort in the similarity of names. Later clarification revealed that this village was exactly where our family had stayed so many years ago! Perhaps this was a small example of an Invisible Hand or Guardian Angel at work? But I digress - back to bigger miracles.

Sue and I had started this trip by flying to Berlin, renting a car, and driving some 150 miles to Bad Fallingbostel, a village near Wolterdingen, where we had a hotel reservation. The objective was to find again Arnolds' grave, and show it to my wife. My hope, also expressed to Sue, was that the gravesite was somehow tended and not overrun, and that it could remain neatly tended into the future. The thought was to hire a person or group to keep the site proper. It seems that the odds were against this - we arrived in the area late on a Saturday after flying all night, were to leave on Sunday, spoke halting German, and knew no one in the area. These were not the best circumstances for locating landscaping help in perpetuity.

We checked into our hotel and immediately drove out to find the Cemetery. This proved more difficult then we'd thought. I drove through Soltau and started heading north toward Hamburg on the main road. The Cemetery should have been near the corner of another small inter-section, on the left, several miles out. But it seemed to have disappeared. We drove perhaps 10 miles out and finally turned around, knowing that the Cemetery was much closer to Soltau. I wondered whether this was even the right road that we were on, or if the road I took 23 years ago was now parallel, unmarked, perhaps unused. But as I drove back toward Soltau there appeared a tiny sign, low and partially hidden by foliage, at an intersection that said the magic word "Wolterdingen". Upon turning right, suddenly the Cemetery appeared. Since this was summer and the corner forest was heavy with two decades of growth and greenery, Dad's Cemetery was now invisible from the main road, whereas my first trip had been in the spring and I could see it through the leafless trees. As we pulled into the parking lot, there was one car there, but we never saw the owner and the car soon disappeared. Locating Arnolds' marker also proved difficult because of the overgrowth of low bushes, but Sue finally found it after we consulted old photos and triangulated. I cleared the area up, being disap-pointed that there had been virtually no maintenance, tarried a bit, uttered some silent thoughts to my Dad, and then did a short walk around through the Cemetery. As we were returning to Dad's gravestone to say our final goodbyes, there appeared a man walking very slowly perhaps 10 feet from the grave. We had to have an interchange - the timing was again precise. So... "Guten Tag" - "You're not from here, what are you doing here" - me pointing, "That's my father's grave" - and a conversation ensued, in broken German and English, about the DP camps and our families. That's how we met Waldemar. His family had fled from Prussia, as I recall, during World War II - a horrible, undertold escape - and had been resettled in Wolterdingen. His parents were buried in Arnolds' Cemetery. Waldemar still lived in the area, and knew and identified Gabrielle and Hildegard as the guides that had miraculously led me to Arnolds' grave decades ago. We three again walked through the Cemetery together, paying our respects both to Waldemar's parents, and Gabrielle, who had died in 1999.

Waldemar invited us to his home. We accepted, and followed him and his bicycle to his house, perhaps a half mile away. That's why Waldemar's appearance at the Cemetery seemed so magical - there was no car, no sound, and no one visible in the entire Cemetery, but suddenly there he stood, a few feet away from Arnolds. At the house, we chatted as best we could about family and history, and a good bond quickly developed between us. As we were getting ready to leave, Waldemar simply said "I will tend your father's grave site for you".

So it had happened again! What I wished for on this trip, and had no reason to hope for and no plan to execute, miraculously happened via a person being right there at exactly the right time. Had we found the Cemetery immediately - or, once on the grounds, had we quickly found the gravesite - the precise timing of the chance encounter would've been thrown off. There would have been no conversation and nothing new would have happened. I can't explain it, but it again might suggest that my Guardian Angel was again working the Invisible Hand to bring son and father closer.

Waldemar and I then started writing letters to each other. He has been good to his word, sending photos of the neatly tendered gravesite, with beautifully planted flowers. We planned to meet up again. Unfortunately, in 2016 Waldemar, well into his 80s, had taken ill, according to a relative. There were doubts that he would be able to maintain the grave site, and perhaps no one else would step in to fill his shoes…though part of me felt that his relatives would continue the task, out of respect for Waldemar's pledge.

1.5 DAD WAS RIGHT!

Another miracle of sorts happened on my third visit, again with Sue, to Dad's gravesite on October 11 and 12, 2016. How many miracles can one expect? We spent two days and one night at an Inn in Wolterdingen. Originally, the plan was to meet Waldemar and his family, but his illness had taken hold and we could not get together. We had just finished a Danube River cruise, a land trip to Prague, and a flight to Hamburg, leaving me with a bad cold which restricted our touring plans in the Wolterdingen area. A visit to the gravesite revealed it to be well tended, and we paid our respects. So even in illness, dear Waldemar had seen to it that his pledge to help me was discharged! I also spent more time observing the railroad track in the tiny Wolterdingen station, just a few hundred feet away, which was how and where my Dad's body had been returned to us so many years ago.

The next morning was rainy and we were preparing to go back to Hamburg but I wanted to stop one more time at the Cemetery, since there was the possibility that this could be the last time. I went out alone in the wet weather, looked at the small replacement plaque for Arnolds, and wondered if this marked the exact site of his burial spot, remembering Dad's questioning words that I felt 23 years ago in the hotel room in Osnabruk, immediately after the miracle of site discovery. Originally, the large concrete monument was at the head of the stone slab under which Dad rested. Now, the replacement plaques were placed on either side of the one remaining slab, so one could not tell which plaque was associated with which slab. In fact, that single slab was considerably closer to Dad's neighbor's new replacement memorial plaque, so I had always assumed that those two items were associated, and that Arnold's slab marking his exact burial spot was simply gone. Nonetheless, I bent down over this single remaining slab, which was mottled, overgrown with moss, and severely faded by the elements of 60+ years. There was no evidence of any chiseled writing on the slab. For some reason, I started scraping the moss and growth with my fingernails, and soon felt slight grooves on the surface of the stone, below the moss. In a controlled frenzy, I kept scraping until a chiseled phrase was revealed: "Love Never Ends"! This was the phrase in the 1948 photo of his slab...so now I knew exactly where Arnolds lay. He had been right again. My assumption that he was sleeping in line with his new flat headstone was incorrect; he was buried several feet away, and his slab had survived and the neighbors' slabs had disappeared, instead of vice-versa. I had been guided to the proper place, and my fingers had been directed to scrape, and keep scraping, until the illuminating words were revealed.

These occurrences have remained a source of peace and joy in my life, and have provided a continuing connection to a father known only in this way. Recounting the story still gives me chills. Now on to the rest of the story.

CHAPTER 2

LATVIA - A CONDENSED HISTORY

Before delving more deeply into the family saga, here is the broader history of Latvia that provides context to the fate of its inhabitants. Individuals, families and cultures are both shaped by their history while in turn also shaping it. World views, reactions to circumstances, choices of political and economic systems, religious feelings and so on of the members of a culture are passed on through generations - not uniformly, not in an unchanging fashion, but as influencing factors. Thus my family and tribe can be better understood by looking back. One clear lesson is that you do not want to be a small country between large nations often at war with each other! That is a geographic recipe for disaster. But it's not a choice, is it?

2.1 PREHISTORY; BALTIC TRIBES ARRIVE

As the ice retreated from the area that is now Latvia toward the end of the last Ice Age around 12,000 years ago, hunters followed reindeer herds north and explored this new area. They found a flat, marshy, heavily forested coastal plain in a northern climate at the same latitude (57/58 N) as mid-Hudson Bay, Canada or Sitka, Alaska. A thousand or so years later, the first permanent settlements appeared. Around 4000 BC Finno-Ugric tribes appeared, having traveled west from Asia, and remained in the area.

Between 3000 - 2000 BC new tribes arrived, the Balts. They spoke a different language then the earlier Finno-Ugrics, and had migrated from the south. Their Baltic language had twin roots in the Proto-Indo-European language which serves as a foundation for about half of the world's population, plus Sanskrit, an even older language. Thus Latvian and especially Lithuanian are considered to be the oldest languages of Europe. This early Baltic culture was part of the "Corded Ware" culture which encompassed a large part of North, Central and East Europe, between the Rhine and the Volga Rivers, and is also descriptively called the "Single Grave and Battle Axe" culture.

Genetic studies of the Corded Ware populations reveal a strong DNA component related to the earlier Yamnaya culture, which derived from the steppes north of the Black Sea. Baltic cultural integration with the existing Finno-Ugric peoples appears to have been mostly peaceful. Thus the Latvian ethnical heritage has a biologic match of about 50% with the Yamnaya; in comparison, Germans are at 75% and southern Europeans at 25%. The Yamnaya genetics yielded people who were overwhelmingly dark-brown eyed, dark-haired and with moderately light skin color, though usually darker than the average modern European. A small subset of the Yamnaya heritage derived from the Mal'ta-Buret' culture, originating around the Angara River, west of Lake Baikal in Siberia. This group is genetically related with Siberians and native Americans, featuring some mongoloid features and a darker skin, and is only found in Northern Europeans. This mixture is called "Ancient North Eurasian".

As a personal aside, I have always had a fascination with central Asia, finding it an area of mystery, with relatively little revealing literature to penetrate the secrets. So when I discovered these ancient biologic ties between some Latvians and Central Asians, my interest seemed validated, with a long line bridging the millennia. My relatively swarthy complexion might point to Asian influence, so perhaps my search had very deep roots that I could somehow feel. Very satisfying!

These various people settled into agricultural lifestyles and around 500 AD clustered into several groups with distinct, though related, identities. The Balts became four identifiable groups: the Curonians, Semigallians, Latgalians, and Selonians. Curonians occupied south west Latvia along the Baltic Sea and pursued coastal lifestyles, including piracy; Semigallians and Selonians were agriculturalists respectively in the west and east of lands south of the Daugava River; Latgalians were in the north east. The adjoining Finno-Ugric neighbors split into the Livonians, Estonians, and Vends. My ancestors, located in the Gulbene area in the north east of Latvia, would have most likely been Baltic Latgalians, with some Livonian overlap. A commercial study of my genetic history has yielded, unsurprisingly, a 97.4 percent Eastern European component, concentrated in a swath including Latvia, central Lithuania and western Russia; a 1.7% Scandinavian component; and a larger than average (77th percentile) Neanderthal DNA component. My Mother's distant ancestry traces back to the western Caspian Sea area, and is part of a large ancestry grouping. My Father's grouping, however, is fairly rare in Europe, and springs from indigenous Siberian peoples.

The area of present day Latvia became a trading crossroads. This was fueled by the existence of a large navigable river, the Daugava (Western Dvina in Russian) connecting inland Russia to the Baltic Sea, plus the existence of a desired object, amber. Amber is the resin of pine trees, compressed over thousands of years into a jewel-like consistency that polishes well and at times has been very popular. There is evidence that the Greek and Roman empires traded for amber with the Baltic tribes, and there was an "Amber Road" to facilitate this. At times in the Middle Ages, amber was worth more than the perennial value leader, gold, and by law could not be possessed by ordinary peasants - it was reserved only for nobles and clergy. I have read that the major reason for this value was that occasionally amber has insects and other flora and fauna trapped in it, perfectly preserved, a snapshot of life from millions of years ago. The ancients took this one step further, concluding that indeed amber was the source of life itself - thus creating an inflated and mystical value to this biologic jewel.

2.2 1200s - 1600s: RELIGIOUS WARS; GERMANS AND RUSSIANS

Around 1200 AD, with increasing trade throughout the area, German traders brought with them Christians who wanted to introduce their faith to the 150,000 inhabitants of the area. Religious wars, funded by the Pope in Rome, began. The first was called the Livonian Crusade. In 1228, it resulted in the Livonian Confederation, a group of disjointed territories encompassing much of present-day Latvia and Estonia, and under direct rule of the Pope. The city of Riga was officially established in 1201 by Bishop Albert of Riga, who spent decades trying to subjugate the pagan tribes. Riga became, and still is, the major city in this part of the Baltic, and remains the capital of Latvia. It presently has a population of over 600,000, or about a third of the Nation.

Warfare throughout the region continued through the 1200s. The first Crusaders in the area, the Livonian Brothers of the Sword, joined forces with the larger Teutonic Order centered further south on the Baltic coast. Livonians were subjugated by 1207; Latgallians by 1214; Couronians and Semigallians by 1290. Many of these last two tribes moved to present-day Lithuania during these times. Bringing Christianity to these pagans was a blood-soaked 100 years struggle, and these ancient Baltic peoples were the last pagans of Europe. When these religious wars ended, the Germans were the singular force in the area. Riga and the area of Latvia became part of the Hanseatic League, a confederation of German-dominated city-states around the entire Baltic Sea that focused on "free" trade among the members. Also during this time, just to the east in Russia and Ukraine, and south and southwest to Poland and bits of Germany, the Mongols were conquering and settling in the lands, but Latvia was basically untouched by this invasion. Perhaps the forests of the Baltic states were a check on the horse culture of the Mongols, who much preferred the steppes.

Latvian life outside of Riga remained focused on agriculture, with small private landholdings providing a decent life for the peasants. The former local "kings" held positions of privilege and imposed taxes, including a 10% tax to the church and labor requirements, but there were too few hereditary nobles and German overlords to really subjugate the populace.

In the 1500s and 1600s, things changed. The German overlords evolved into a class of barons with huge estates, and took total control of the locals who lived there. Thus serfdom, a form of slavery, took hold on the land. As the barons became more rapacious, the taxes grew higher and work requirements by the peasants for the manor was increased to 75% of their working week. Since serfs would try to flee to manors that they thought had better living conditions, or escape to Riga or even other countries, a law was passed in 1494 that tied the serfs to the land. With this, there was no escape. The march towards slavery had ratcheted up a notch.

The Lutheran Reformation spread from Germany and by about 1550 most Latvians had converted to Lutheranism, with the exception being that easternmost part, the present-day region of Latgale. The Catholic-based Livonian Order thus lost its power and dissolved in 1561, but the landowners remained and, feeling vulnerable, asked for protection from the Polish and Lithuanian empire just to the south and east. The concern was that the Russians would fill the void, and indeed they tried. The result was a Livonian War (1558 - 1583), pitting Ivan the Terrible of Russia, who invaded Livonia, against the Polish-Lithuanian state and the remnants of the Livonian Order. A complicated series of land trades by the hereditary nobles then began, further fracturing the area. Ultimately the south and west areas of present-day Latvia - then Courland and Semigallia - remained in Polish and Lithuanian hands, along with Riga. Our ancestors' area around Gulbene remained under Russian domination. But in 1583, Poland annexed Livonia and merged it into their possessions to the south of the Daugava River, thus encompassing most of modern-day Latvia.

2.3 1600s - 1800s: SWEDEN AND RUSSIA

The Polish-Lithuanian empire and Sweden fought a war between 1600 and 1629, and Sweden, ruled by King Gustav II, won. It took possession of most of Latvia by 1621. These times are remembered as being good for Latvians. The Swedes were relatively kind rulers. Serfdom was abolished and education and career opportunities were expanded, including the establishment of first University in the area, Dorpat, in what is now Estonia.

Russia under Peter the Great came back in force during the Great Northern War of 1700 and fought with Sweden, and won. By 1710 Estonia, Livonia (northern Latvia) and Riga were in Russian hands, and 80 years later all of Latvia was Russian. Latvia was again devastated by this War, and the horror was multiplied by the outbreak of the Plague which reportedly killed 75% of the inhabitants in the worst hit areas. Livonia was soon re-titled as "Vidzeme", which translates into "the middle land", and was ruled in a peculiar fashion. Peter the Great allowed the old German barons to regain the rule they had lost during the Swedish times. These barons then swore allegiance to the Russian leaders, starting with Peter the Great in 1721, up to Alexander II in 1881. In exchange, the Russians allowed the German barons to maintain German as the language of law and commerce; keep their financial and business systems; keep their estates; retain Lutheran as the official religion; and reverse Swedish laws, to reinstate serfdom on the Livonian peasants, who are my direct ancestors. My Mother's family tree, researched and compiled lovingly by my first cousin, Ievina, has the first entries cited during this time - "Janis", born around 1720 in Litene Manor, and "Juris", born in 1732 in the Vecgulbene Manor. As Serf/Peasants, they had only one name - last names were added later.

Under the reign of the German barons and Russian Czars, with the exception of the Swedish times, Latvian peasants lived in serfdom, a form of slavery. Serfs could be punished, tortured or beaten for any reason, supposed or real. Women were subject to sexual servitude, a form of rape, with no recourse or defense. If a master was sadistic, life could be unbearable. In Russia, nobles were also in effect serfs of the Czar - he or she had total control of them, and they of their serfs. Serfs could be sold and only had rights granted by "their" noble, with no guarantees. Periodically rebellions would happen. Strangely enough, given the brutal history of Russian Soviet behavior later, it was the Russians who forced liberalization of the Latvian serfs on the German barons. In 1804 laws were passed in Livonia so that serfs could only be sold along with the land they occupied, a great step up from simply selling people. Other liberalizations occurred, including the first attempts at freeing the serfs, permitting them land ownership, and allowing land inheritance. But these changes were opposed by the barons and the advances were choked by new laws in 1809. In the mean-time, Estonia to the north and Courland to the south of Livonia were also having status changes decreed by Russia. Small groups of serfs were to be emancipated yearly, and were granted personal freedom but no ability to own land, which had to be rented from the German barons. There were also restrictions on moving into towns, which were largely populated by German and Jewish peoples.

2.4 1800s: NATIONAL STIRRINGS

In fits and starts, with different timetables in the different parts of modern-day Latvia, the peasant serfs gained freedom. In Livonia, my ancestral region, major changes happened in 1850. Serf peasants were allowed to rent or buy land for the first time, though 75% had no money and were forced de facto to labor a number days per week for the benefit of their German landlords as the way to pay off the land price. In 1861 serfdom was officially abolished in Russia by Alexander II. By 1864 credit possibilities were extended to peasants, and this accelerated land purchase to the point that within 40 years about 90% of Livonian peasants owned their own land. It was during this time that my family, both paternal and maternal sides, acquired their land from their German barons. So it was these laws and the availability of credit that created a prosperous farming class, with options for the children to get educated, and work in other than farm-based activities.

As serf emancipation grew along with education possibilities, a Latvian National Awakening began. In the 1820s and 30s the first Latvian newspapers appeared written in Latvian, not German. By the 1850s a nationalistic trend appeared, aligned with other such trends throughout Europe. The focus was literary and cultural, pushed by young intellectuals who rediscovered ancient Latvia's pagan religious beliefs, folklore and music, all in the rapidly growing Latvian language. There was a political side also, which began to call for a nation run by Latvians to be formed, to the great displeasure of the German land barons and their Russian masters.

Later in the 1800s, Czar Alexander III decided to reduce the German influence on his Latvian territories. He began a policy of Russification around 1890 which made Russian the official language of commerce and law, replacing German. My Grandparents would have been affected by this. The emerging Latvian language was banned, and schools could no longer teach in Latvian. This put serious brakes on the nationalist movement and drove it underground.

At about this same time a new political group was organized by Latvians, called the "New Current". It had a revolutionary core, not surprising considering the centuries of serfdom and repression of Latvians by the Germans and Russians. Its leftward leanings were broadly in line with another nearby leftist movement - Russian Marxism. These two movements joined in Latvia and became the Latvian Social Democratic Labor Party. The early leader was Peteris Stucka, who became the major Latvian pro-Soviet Communist leader when they swallowed Latvia early in World War II. His name is reviled by most Latvians to this day, synonymous with "traitor", although his early politics had noble objectives.

2.5 1900 - 1920: WW I; WAR OF INDEPENDENCE

1905 marked a serious unrest against Russian and German baron authority in Latvia. Armed insurrection resulted in hundreds of casualties to Latvians in Riga. Parishes throughout the Country elected scores of self-governing local administrators, and violence against the German barons escalated. Hundreds of baronial manor houses were put to the torch, with loss of German life. This budding revolution was put down by a combination of Russian troops and German mercenaries, brutally. Over 2500 Latvians were executed; another 2500 people were exiled to Siberia, a harsh punishment, often fatal; and some 5000 were exiled to the friendly western nations. To put this in perspective, that would be like 330,000 Americans executed, 330,000 sent to a harsh exile, and 660,000 gone to a better exile. This is based on the Latvian population at the time being about 2.5 million, and the US population now being about 330 million, a multiple of 132 (with variations up to 170 based on population changes).

World War I began in 1914 with Germany declaring war on Russia. There were immediate clashes in Latvia, and by summer of 1915 Latvia was fully engaged in the War. Russia conscripted 32,000 Latvians, among them being my maternal Grandfather. These were also the approximate chaotic times in which my parents were born. The Courland peninsula in the southwest of Latvia was totally evacuated by Russian orders, with some 500,000 (US equivalent today, 66 million) people relocating north and east to the Vidzeme part of Latvia and to Russia proper; only about 250,000 remained in Courland. The deported people were forced to leave their properties and possessions which were then destroyed by retreating Russian armies under a scorched-earth policy. Many of these exiles stayed in Russia and became ardent Bolsheviks; others returned around 1920. Later Riga was 50% evacuated, along with the moving of most of its industries into Russia. Although Courland and Riga suffered the most, all of Latvia was devastated. The population dropped from 2.6 million to 1.6 million - the equivalent of today's US losing 127 million people, shrinking from 330 million to 203 million people in a few years! - and to this day Latvia has not recovered the loss of Latvians in the nation. Imagine that magnitude of loss, of human displacement and suffering. Farms, crops and livestock were also destroyed. Those who survived and stayed often went hungry and lived in desperation. These were the conditions for my parents and our family just one generation ago.

As German troops were overrunning Latvia, a volunteer native force, the Latvian Riflemen, was formed to help Russia drive out the Germans. The Riflemen played a key role in the reversal of the German tide, but in February of 1917 the Communist revolution broke out in St. Petersburg, Russia, resulting in the execution of Czar Nicholas II and his family and the establishment of the Communist state. Interestingly, some of the Czar's executioners were Latvians and Lithuanians - with unconfirmed reports indicating that they were the majority of the murder squad. After some serious infighting in November 1917 between the White (moderate) and Bolshevik (radical) Communists for control of the revolution, the Bolsheviks won. During this time the Red Latvian Riflemen - that sub-set of the Riflemen who believed deeply in the promise of Communism - were a powerful force. They participated in many battles against the Whites, and had a reputation as being absolutely the most brutal and fearless of the Bolshevik troops, with legendary status to their enemies. Critically, the Red Latvian Riflemen elevated and kept Vladimir Lenin in power, serving as his personal guard in these early years when he and the Communist movement were barely surviving. Other prominent leaders also had their protection. Furthermore, they guarded the most important strategic sites in Moscow and other key cities, and were called upon to quell several rebellions that would have overthrown the infant Bolshevik movement. Lenin acknowledged their singular role, saying that without the Riflemen's support, the revolution wouldn't have ended successfully. In these early Communist years, Latvians displayed an oversized role, fulfill-ing many positions of Communist power and authority. Upon victory over the Whites, the Bolsheviks immediately sued for peace with Germany and

Russian participation in World War I ended. The Germans now effectively owned Latvia.

Through the chaos of these times in Latvia there emerged a variety of attempts at self governance. Provisional land councils, formed democratically by local inhabitants, lobbied both Germans and Russians for increased local autonomy, often simply wanting a greater voice within a Russian or German confederation. For a few months between 1917 - 1918 the "Iskolat" movement, heavily influenced by Bolshevism, ruled Latvia. But with the Brest-Litovsk treaty of March 3, 1918 ending World War I, Latvia was basically a German possession.

Another democratic force was rising during this time, the Latvian National Council. It lobbied Western governments for recognition, as well as friendly politicians in Germany, plus Russia. When Germany acquired "rights" to most of Latvia following World War I, the Council declared to the world that a Latvian state should be established. On November 11, 1918 the British Empire recognized the Council as the government of Latvia. Germany then also recognized the independence of Latvia.

But the Russians were not done. The Bolshevik faction of the Communist Party wanted to reclaim Latvia for Russia, and attacked. Many of the "Russian" soldiers attacking were actually Latvians from the "Red" sect of the Latvian Riflemen army. Thus, it had trappings of a civil war. On January 13, 1919 the Latvian Socialist Soviet Republic was established in Riga. This was a Bolshevik organization, loyal to Russia, and headed by a hardened Communist mentioned earlier, Peteris Stucka. The usual Bolshevik behavior began - class warfare, expropriation of private property, and execution of successful Latvians and German nobles. Someone 1000 people were murdered, and the disruption of food pipelines to the cities condemned many innocents to starvation. In Riga alone nearly 10,000 people starved to death (the US equivalent would be 2 million).

Meanwhile the Provisional government of Latvia and its small army enrolled German forces still in the area, and together they captured Riga on May 22, 1919. This force then terrorized and executed Communist sympathizers. It was again a bloody time in Latvia.

The time being described here, between 1918 and 1920, is known as a Latvian War of Independence. It was a complex set of events involving invasions, counter-invasions, and foreign nation involvements, but ultimately resulted in a free Latvian nation. After the combined German-Latvian forces captured Riga from the Bolshevik Latvian Socialists described earlier, a separate force of Latvians, aided by the Estonian Third Division, defeated the Germans on June 23, 1919 at the Battle of Winden. The Germans then pledged to leave Latvia. However, the retreating Germans re-formed and attacked Riga, only to be attacked in turn by the Latvians who, with the critical aid of British seapower, drove the Germans out. This chapter ended with a combined force of Polish and Latvian troops driving the Russians out of Latgale, the easternmost province of Latvia. Peace was finally near, along with true Latvian independence.

I have visited the major Cemetery in Riga that serves as the final home for Latvian soldiers who died in the War for Independence. It was a sad and sobering visit, and I recall my anger at the unfairness of the circumstances that led to their deaths, and the broader unfairness of the geopolitics of Latvia. My people were always vastly outnumbered and out-supplied, fighting against overwhelming odds. These individual heroes knew the odds were against them but fought for a free Latvia with all they had…and gave all they had.

2.6 1920 -1939: FREE LATVIA!

The Latvian-Soviet peace treaty was signed on August 11, 1920. Russia gave up all claims, forever, to Latvia, without reservation. (How did that work out? And how has that worked out for many national treaties with Russia, including the recent events in Ukraine? Shame!). On January 26, 1921 the Allied Supreme War Council formally recognized Latvian independence, and membership in the League of Nations was granted on

September 22, 1921. The USA was late in recognizing independence but did so in July of 1922.

Elections were held during this time and the form of Latvian government took shape. The Country was still devastated - the population had fallen from 2.6 million to 1.6 million (a US equivalent of 330 million down to 203 million), and Riga fell from 500,000 to 250,000 people (US equivalent of 103 million down to 51.5 million) - and there were many political parties. A parliament, called the Saeima, based on proportional representation from the various parties, was created. It was tasked with choosing the Nation's executive leadership, the Prime Minister and the President. Several problems developed soon. With many parties representing many special interests, fractionalization occurred and it was tough to get majority agreement on anything. Also, the major party, the Social Democrats, basically refused to participate in the government. They were a hard-left Bolshevik-oriented party that - typically - wanted all the power for themselves, and when they could not get other parties to vote with them they simply abstained from governance. Feelings between them and the other parties, like the center-right number two party, the Farmers Union, were seriously strained. The Social Democrats were viewed, with much reason, to be agents of the Soviet Communists; for example, they displayed the Communist red flag and adopted the Internationale as their anthem, instead of the Latvian flag and anthem "God Bless Latvia".

While this parliamentary strife was going on, Latvia's borders were being settled. Russia got a slice of eastern Latvia; Estonia got some of northern Latvia in exchange for their help in the revolution; Lithuania got some coastline on the Baltic; and Latvia received some lands and compensation from some of these parties. This resulted in some net loss of Latvian population to these other countries, but these borders have survived to this day.

Despite the parliamentary troubles, actions were passed to get the Country going. Banking and currency systems were started; social programs for unemployment etc. were created; the education system was strengthened; tax structures were implemented; land was distributed from the German baronial holdings to landless peasants; and trade with other countries was developed, consisting largely of dairy products and forestry goods exchanged for manufactured goods, with England being the biggest partner. Also during this time Latvia achieved the highest rate of secondary education in the world, demonstrating the culture's love of knowledge, as well as music and the arts.

In 1934 the parliamentary chaos and the continued threats of the Communist-inspired Social Democrats resulted in a coup by Karlis Ulmanis, the Prime Minister. It became a mild dictatorship and some civil rights and press rights were suspended. No blood was shed, and no repressions or executions occurred. My parents and a majority of Latvians, especially those in the countryside, became very supportive of Ulmanis and found him to be a fair, strong and popular leader. They saw him as a hero who risked his life to confront the Latvian Bolsheviks, and thereby literally saved Latvia from destroying itself.

Then came World War II.

2.7 1940 - 1950 : RUSSIANS, GERMANS, USSR; ATROCITIES, DIASPORA

Latvia's horrors began with the signing of the Molotov - Ribbentrop Pact between Russia and Germany on August 23, 1939. This was supposed to partition Eastern Europe into spheres of influence between the two socialist powers, but it also allowed each free rein to meddle in their smaller neighbors' affairs. The Soviets threatened to invade Latvia under the guise of needing to establish a buffer zone to keep German potential advances at bay. Having no choice, an agreement was signed allowing 25,000 Soviet troops into Latvia. Russia then pressed its advantage and in early summer of 1940 accused Latvia and the other Baltics of a conspiracy to help Germany, demanded that unlimited Russian troops be admitted, and that the government be modified to suit Soviet sensibilities. Vastly outnumbered (2 million people versus 170 million), alone and helpless, Latvia acceded and the Soviet occupation began there on June 17. A new "election" was held in mid-July 1940, and the results were published in Moscow 12 hours before the election results were in! Surprisingly, the Communist Party won! It declared Latvia to be a member of the Soviet Union on August 5, 1940. Prime Minister Ulmanis was summoned to Moscow, arrested, tortured, and send to the Siberian Gulag where he, like so many other millions, perished. Other Latvian leaders suffered similar fates.

Deportations of "class enemies" and other undesirables soon began throughout the Baltics, along with arrests, torture and execution. In the year from June 1940 to June 1941, over 130,000 people from Latvia, Estonia and Lithuania were deported out of the 6 million total population of these 3 countries. Of these, about 35,000 (US equivalent 5 million) were Latvians. This includes 15,424 Latvians arrested and deported just during the few days of June 13/14/15 of 1941, a week prior to the German re-invasion that ended the atrocities; about 40% of these people died. In total, by the end of the Stalin era in 1953, another 150,000 Latvians had been outright killed, imprisoned, or deported (a US equivalent of 22 million), for a total approaching 200,000 lives. It was also during this June 1941 period that several of our family disappeared, and my parents, aunts, uncles and cousins were scheduled for deportation, but saved by good fortune and the German invasion which began soon after.

German troops began to steamroll through eastern Europe on their way to Moscow on June 22, 1941, and occupied Riga by July 1, 1941. The rest of Latvia was quickly taken, with the Russians being routed back into Russia with horrendous losses of men and material. In contrast to the murderous Soviet Communists, the Germans were viewed by most Latvians as saviors and they acted like saviors - unless you were Jewish, Gypsy, or a Communist. These residents were rounded up brutally, put in concentration camps, and often murdered. Most Latvians did not know of the killings - they were told the victims were being sent to Israel or Madagascar - and it was hard to believe that industrialized murder was happening. As an aside, Allied soldiers were also shocked when they learned of conditions and activities in concentration camps when they overran them at the end of the War.

Overall, the Germans and their collaborators murdered about 65,000 people in Latvia, mostly Jewish, plus 20,000 brought into the country from other Eastern European countries. Although the actual atrocities were overwhelmingly committed by Nazi Germans, there were some enthusiastic Latvian participants in the slaughter. Specifically, the Latvian "Arajs Commando", with 500 members, hunted and delivered over 25,000 of these victims to the German butchers on November 30 and December 8 1941; these delivered people were shot into mass burial pits in a forest near the Rumbula train station near Riga. This is the tragic site of the largest Holocaust killing field in Latvia, and this was in addition to murders in smaller cities in the prior months. The Latvian participants in these horrors were tried and punished.

There were particularly hard feelings by some Latvians toward Jews; many early supporters of the bloody Communist ideology were Jewish, and Jews were overrepresented in Latvian Communist leadership that wrought horrors on so many Latvians, and racial reprisals certainly happened. This was all seriously accelerated by Nazi claims that the scourge of Communism was a Jewish plot, and that Jews were responsible for any and all plights befalling Europe in this era. Ironically, Latvians were also clearly overrepresented in the early Bolshevik movement, and both groups later became especially singled out to become victims of the Communists. One of Stalin's last murderous orgies, just before his death, was the Doctor's Plot, largely targeting the Jewish-Russian population. To modern sensibilities, this joining of tribe to certain ideologies is not well received; but in the WW II era it was viewed as real and obvious.

Generally, Latvians fared well under German occupation as described elsewhere in this book. If Latvians kept their noses clean they would mostly be okay, although about 7000 resisters were arrested to face varying punishments. As the war progressed, German advances into Russia stalled near Moscow and other cities, largely due to poor planning for the unexpected winter campaign of 1943-1944, and soon the Soviets pushed back. By October 13, 1944 Russians had re-taken Riga, and Latvia again was under Soviet control. Various Latvian guerrilla groups - the "Forest Brothers" - fought the Soviets as they had fought the Germans, but the odds against them were overwhelming. So the next brutalization of Latvia by the Soviets began. It was during this time, 1944, that my family joined 200,000 other Latvians (the US equivalent would be about 30 million people) in fleeing to the West, with some reports giving the number as high as 250,000. Thus by the War's end, another 200,000 Latvians had been killed or had disappeared on top of the 200,000 who had fled, plus the Latvian soldiers killed while fighting for both the Russian and German Armies. This population loss of 20% was devastating to the Nation; it would be like 66 million people disappearing from America.

The Soviets reintroduced their repressive behaviors with total control of every aspect of everyday life. Private landholding and farming were basically illuminated, with collectivization of agriculture becoming the norm. A centrally planned economy was reintroduced, with decrees substituting for free markets - and is always the case, the economy started to fall apart and an illegal, parallel black market emerged to provide the needs of the people. There was total repression of free thought, enforced by thousands of spies who were recruited both as volunteers, true believers, and via force and terror. People would disappear; torture was the common way of gaining confessions for crimes; crimes were typically thought crimes, unprovable, which demanded confessions. When the ill-advised central planning goals were not met, the blame was placed on "wreckers", who were quietly subverting communism and promoting capitalism, and they were to be eliminated or "liquidated". Though the war was over, a new and greater misery reigned.

During this second Soviet invasion, Latvians continued to be imprisoned, exiled or sent to Gulag work camps to labor as slaves and often perish. At the height of the new terror on March 25, 1949, 43,000 Latvians (US equivalent 7 million) were arrested and sentenced to Siberia. At that time, arrests occurred throughout all three Baltic nations in a carefully planned operation targeting "Kulaks" - successful farmers - and people thought to be especially patriotic to their former countries. As these people were expelled, hundreds of thousands of Russians were sent to replace the disappearing Latvians and occupy their homes. Upon the death of Stalin on March 5th, 1953, liberalization from the reign of terror almost immediately occurred. Though the Gulag prison system remained, it shrank and conditions for most prisoners improved. By 1959 Latvians comprised only 62% of the population of Latvia, with 400,000 Russians having arrived, while hundreds of thousands of Latvians had left. The Russianization of Latvia, including the language, accelerated. It was truly a captive nation.

2.8 1950 -1991: CAPTIVE NATION, CONTINUED

During 1960s and 1970s the various Soviet dictators (Khrushchev, Brezhnev, Chernenko, Andropov) left a mixed legacy of repression and liberalization. Latvia, like the other components of the Soviet Union, remained repressed, stuck in a gray Communism of slogans and dogma having little bearing to reality. Latvians were second-class people in their own country. Since a decent infrastructure had been created during the free years, the Soviets enlarged industrialization of the country with oil and food processing plants, and electronic, chemical, and machinery factories. More Russians also entered, many becoming permanent residents. While Latvians comprise 77% (about 1.5 million people) of the total population in 1940, that number was reduced to 52% (1.4 million) in 1989, and 60% (1.4 million) of the 2.4 million total population in 2005. In 2019, the population was down to 1.9 million, with the young and educated leaving for opportunities in other countries.

Significant changes began in the mid-1980s under the Soviet Union leader Mikhail Gorbachev, and the US President Ronald Reagan. Reagan presented the case publicly for the removal of the yoke around the necks of Soviet citizens and the Captive Nations behind the Iron Curtain - "Tear down the Wall...!" - while engaging the Soviets in an arms race that their flawed economy could not support. Gorbachev was also a different Soviet premier; he recognized that their socialist system was intrinsically flawed, and that a change was needed for survival. Thus he was a somewhat willing partner in the dissolution of the Soviet empire. Though still not appreciated by most Russians, he was a hero to the Captive Nations who started to believe that they might again see freedom.

Popular political grass-roots organizations began to appear throughout Communist Eastern Europe. A mass demonstration in the 3 Baltic nations was held on August 23, 1989, the 50th anniversary of the Molotov-Ribbentrop Pact that had enslaved the Baltics. A human chain, people holding hands for 400 miles from Tallinn, Estonia through Riga, Latvia and ending in Vilnius, Lithuania, was formed. It symbolized the need for independence, and the publicity of this peaceful protest got the world's attention. Other actions in other countries, such as the overwhelming greeting of the Pope in Poland, had helped get the word out; freedom was demanding a hearing.

On May 4 1990 the Latvian "Parliament", somewhat freely elected by Gorbachev's liberalization, declared Latvia to be free. After some bloodshed by fervent Communists in Riga in January 1991, and a failed coup in Moscow in August 1991, Latvia became free again on September 6, 1991.

Sue and I were with my Latvian cousins Ievina and Maija in North Conway, New Hampshire when the official announcement of Latvia's freedom was first aired on TV during a lunch stop. The joy was massive! These two lovely ladies had taken advantage of the Soviet Union's recent liberalization to visit and see their relatives who had fled Latvia for the first time since 1944, and we were all blessed to be together for such an emotional event.

2.9 1991 - PRESENT: FREEDOM, AGAIN

The newly-freed Nation had much to surmount, and has many tough problems to this day. It is a small country with a huge historically antagonistic neighbor, Russia. In a fight, Latvia would lose without foreign help. The radical change of systems from Communist/Socialist to Democratic/ Capitalist resulted in a dislocation that made things worse for the people in the short term, while promising better times to come in the future. Over time, that is politically dangerous; people typically respond more to the immediate than to the future. Latvia had been devastated by 47 years of Communist rule. Much of the infrastructure was decrepit, and more importantly, the peoples' culture and mores had been turned upside down. Personal responsibility, personal ambition, and personal striving had been viewed as capitalist deviations, and were largely buried; economic rules were not understood; politicians trained in the old corrupt Commie system often maintained power and knew only corruption; state assets were "bought", i.e., stolen, by the Communist bureaucrats who had run them. This left little for the ordinary citizens, who experienced this as their first, unpopular glimpse of dog-eat-dog capitalism. It all seemed unfair and very wrong. Furthermore, there remained a 30% Russian population that did not speak Latvian and resented their new status as foreigners in this land in which they had been the masters. Although some of these Russians loved Latvia, many others, especially those with military roots, maintained ties with their Russian motherland, creating a destabilizing situation. So much to overcome!

On the other hand, some old Latvian characteristics re-appeared and began to flourish. The Nation's strong musical tradition strengthened again with massive Song Festivals, drawing thousands of participants and viewers in a musical orgy free of politics. Midsummer Night celebrations (St. John's Day or "Janu Diena") accelerated with even more carefree and joyous behaviors, featuring young men leaping over bonfires to display their virility and attract the attention of garlanded lady friends. There has been a resurgence of interest in the old pagan religions and gods, such as "Perkonis", the Thunder God, and resurrection of the "Dainas", millions of four line poetic songs conferring insights and wisdom of the ancients. Freedom also allowed world exposure for some exceptional Latvians, such as the Conductor of the Boston Symphony Orchestra, and many professional basketball and hockey players.

Latvia has joined the International Monetary Fund, the United Nations, NATO, and the European Union. Its security concerns are somewhat alleviated via NATO. The Country gave up its currency, the Lats, for the Euro. There is foreign investment, a banking system, and financial stability brought about by belt-tightening to manage the debt and remain creditworthy. This was hard on ordinary Latvians as pensions and wages shrank, taxes and collection procedures increased, while prices for necessities went up. But conditions are slowly improving - besides foreign investment, the old hard-working cultural traits are being rediscovered, which will result in positive national gains. Unfortunately, many young people are leaving to other parts of the European Union where there are better opportunities. 25% of working age Latvians have left between 2000 and 2017. Of graduates of Universities between 2000 to 2009, fully one-third had left the country by 2014. The worker - retiree ratio is also trending poorly; in 2013, there were 3.3 workers per retiree, but that is expected to drop to 2 by the year 2030. Hopefully, some of these émigrés will gain knowledge and capital and bring it back to Latvia and seed it for future success.

CHAPTER 3

A ROUGH NEIGHBORHOOD

While Latvia was for the first time a free nation between 1920 and 1940, there was serious turmoil in the neighborhood, with direct effects on Latvia lasting to 1991. The primary mover was a socialist/Communist Russia residing next door. So during Anna's, Arnolds' and Aleks' free years as Latvians, nearby threats abounded and cast worry over them. The events described below were happening only about 40 miles away from our family, and although they were not directly affected until 1940, news of the nearby horrors would have seeped over the border. I want to describe conditions in these contiguous areas for several reasons. First, because of the ultimate effects on my people; second, because that history has been somewhat muted to many people of the free world; and third, in response to my moral outrage and the resulting desire to give additional exposure to all those innocents who suffered and perished, often silently, in this neighborhood. Warning - this chapter will be brutal. Although world history is full of scary chapters, the time documented here is especially murderous, made more terrifying by the randomness and widespread nature of the horrors. War between groups is always awful, but the combatants typically know who is on what side, and innocents can flee as recognizable danger approaches. A differentiator in this 1920 through 1990 timeframe is that for most, there was no escape. The horror surrounded them, and most of the victims were innocent.

3.1 EARLY COMMUNISM

Russia and its possessions, often including the Baltic nations, was a difficult place under the Russian Czars. They were absolute rulers, ordained by religious beliefs, and the vast portion of their subjects were serfs - a form of slavery - people tied to the land owned by nobles. Their destiny was hard work, few rights, starvation if crops failed, and enforced conscription to fight in wars. Any protesters or rebels were punished severely or summarily executed; and punishment was often banishment to the cold, wild and largely uninhabited expense extending thousands of miles north and east, called Siberia, either as exiles or as forced labor prisoners. The Russian prison system has long, deep roots.

Not surprisingly, this system of governance sowed the seeds of rebellion. In October 1917, in St. Petersburg, Russia, open revolution broke out by elements of the military who took control of the City, arresting and later executing Nicholas, the last of the Romanov Czars, and his family. Meanwhile, in Germany, Vladimir Lenin, a disciple of Communist Manifesto author Karl Marx, saw the turmoil in Russia as an opportunity to implement the Communist philosophy. It was supposed to be the rising up of the "proletariat" - the common working person - against the "bourgeois" - the ruling class. First, there would be socialism, defined as having the means of production owned communally by workers, with fairness of compensation and social justice. The next inevitable step would be Communism - where the state owned all means of production such as businesses and utilities, and services such as education and medicine, administered by a "Party" reporting to "The People". The ruling philosophy was defined as "To each according to their needs, from each according to their ability". After the horrors of serfdom, this idealistic message sounded really good to many people. Lenin and the early Communists believed that the triumph of Communism over Capitalism was historically inevitable; it would sweep the planet. This would create Paradise on Earth. It was morally such a wonderful concept that anything advancing the idea would be good, even if it was forced upon or even murderous against those who opposed this ideal. Theoretically, the first Communist revolutions were expected to happen in industrialized nations, such as Germany or England, and not in a backward agricultural nation like Russia. But in the chaos of the Russian Revolution, Lenin saw opportunity for the Communist credo, and as a charismatic leader filling a leadership void, he struck.

Again, it is ironic that some of the peoples that provided disproportionate and important early support for Lenin were Jews and Latvians - groups that were later especially targeted by Lenin's successor Stalin and his Communist henchmen. Jews in Russia had been a subjugated minority, with restricted property and employment rights, and subject to physical violence and bloody raids by Cossacks, a tough political/ethnic/quasi-military group who operated with the blessing of the Russian state. Latvians had been subjugated by German barons and their Russian Czar masters as serfs, also with miserable lives. So there is no surprise that Jews were strongly overrepresented in the early Communist movement, and this identification was used as justification later by the Nazis for the Holocaust - the "rationale" being that Communism was the spawn of Eastern semi-Asiatic hoards that would wipe out civilized Western Europe and Germany. Interestingly, the Communists created Birobidzhan in Siberia, the only Jewish Autonomous State besides Israel. Latvians were also overrepresented in the early Communist movement (examples are Aleks' 2 sisters; the founder of the deadly Kolyma /Magadan Gulag complex; the chief theoretician of the Communist Party, etc.). An armed military group - the Latvian Rifles - were given credit by Lenin for literally saving the Communist revolution.

In the chaos of these revolutionary times, Russia sued for peace with Germany to end their participation in World War I; Latvia fought against overwhelming odds, with significant third-party help, to obtain its freedom from Russia and the German barons; and a brutal war broke out between two Communist factions. The Mensheviks, or Whites, planned a slow, nonviolent transition to Communism in Russia, followed by world domination, while the Bolsheviks, or Reds, wanted a fast move to Communism, with elimination of anyone who was too slow to adapt, using whatever means necessary. Battles between these two groups were bloody and hateful. It is not surprising that the more brutal group, the Bolsheviks, won. Lenin was their leader, and this godless Communist philosophy, aimed at establishing radical democracy for full freedom of all workers, soon elevated Lenin to a godlike, dictatorial status.

In 1924 Lenin had a stroke and soon died. There ensued a power struggle between his lieutenants, and Joseph Stalin (Stalin = "Man of Steel" - his real name was Joseph Djugashvili - his nickname was "Koba"), a native of Georgia SSR, won. He was the most brutal of the contestants, so again the outcome was not a surprise.

Stalin had been a seminary student who dropped out and joined the early Communist movement. The Czars sentenced him for revolutionary activities and he was sent to Siberia three times, from where he easily escaped. He learned that Siberian prisons and places of exile were too lenient; if he got his turn to rule, he would make Siberia virtually escape proof. He did. Stalin was also rumored to have been an informer on his revolutionary buddies, and survived the Czar's Secret Police by being a turncoat. His most accurate description is "psychopath".

Stalin started to consolidate his power by eliminating all possible competitors - by prison, exile, or execution. Plans were drawn up to communalize agriculture, industrialize Russia quickly, build infrastructure to modernize the Russian Empire, and make fuller use of the extensive natural resources found in Siberia. Stalin set out to accomplish all this rapidly by forced collectivization and the conscription of slave labor. As a side benefit, any potential enemies of the state, real or imagined, would be liquidated.

Dwell on this term "liquidated" for a moment. It was not used by accident. As cited in the works of different Russian authors of the time, it's a chilling word. It means to take another human being with whom you might disagree and turn them into a liquid, to put them into a blender. This is an example of the class hatred that the Communists had for others...not just kill, but liquidate.

3.2 THE UKRAINE: FAMINE AS POLICY

In the 1920s mass arrests started in Russia. These began with the targeting of the early Communist supporters who would be most likely to challenge Stalin. 1929 was an especially brutal year with the beginning of "dekulakization", the elimination of prosperous farm owners as a class. The prison/forced labor system, called the Gulag, began to quickly metastasize into what became a cancer infecting all parts of the nation.

This program of mass collectivization of agriculture was accelerated between 1931 - 1934, especially in western Russia, Kazakhstan, and most emphatically in the area that is now the nation of Ukraine. All those stubborn, successful individual farmers - "kulaks" - had to be collectivized or eliminated quickly for Communism in agriculture to take root. The results were disastrous. All food and food materials were declared to be state property; deliveries of such goods were made to central collection points and recorded; and enforcement was via farm-by-farm brutal inspections by the Chekists, KGB-type police thugs.

With private possession of food having been made illegal, those peasants following the law began to starve. Their legal food allowances slowly killed them. If the Chekists found non-starving peasants, they were arrested, tortured, deported or killed, because it was clear that they had food - otherwise, they would be starving! The Ukraine was ringed by troops and the news of the starvation was repressed as much as possible. Neighboring nations, however, started to see the horrors just outside their boundaries, and these countries, Latvia included, became terrified as a general rule of the Soviet Bolsheviks.

Ukrainian peasants were not permitted to enter the cities, whose residents did get enough of a food ration to keep them alive. So the countryside became devastated. The dead and the near dead were everywhere, wandering about, eating pets, insects and grass. Cannibalism, typically a strong human taboo, became widespread. Family members would eat other family members, ghoulishly waiting for the weakest to die, and sometimes helping them along. Groups of cannibal youth roamed the countryside, often accelerating the death of near-dead strangers so that the next meal could be had. Mass insanity ruled.

The death toll from this enforced and planned famine - called the Holodomor, or "death by hunger" in Ukrainian - is hard to define because records do not exist. Evidence of the crimes was covered up, destroyed, or altered. On the low end, death estimates are 3.5 million. Figures of 5 - 7 million are often cited and justified (at peak times, there were 25,000 deaths per day, or 17 per minute). Many historians cite a figure of 11-12 million, which was also the toll referenced by a direct witness, the Ukrainian wife of a physician I knew in Massachusetts. The highest number was 15 million, published by the historian Robert Conquest.

Whatever number is used, the horror was immense and compounded by those who survived but were never again "normal"; by the millions of fetal abnormalities and children crippled in various ways; and by the lack of publicity, to this day. There was some early literature about the Ukrainian famine (first, "Harvest of Sorrow" by Conquest, and later "Imperium" by Kaczynski, and "Red Famine" by Applebaum), but these events have been largely ignored by the Western media while openly suppressed by Communist-Leftist nations and their media. The story is not a good reflection of Socialist-Communist behavior and has been shamefully minimized.

Some of the conspiracy of silence by the Western media bears harsh comment. A fair portion of the US public through the approximate 1920 -1960 time period had Socialist and Communist leanings. Contributing factors included the Great Depression, the gap between rich and poor, and the bad working conditions of many minority, rural, and urban Americans. These same leanings were evident in almost all European nations. Many citizens were seeking a better political way, with good reason. The stories coming out of the Soviet Union - pure propaganda, but believed by many to be the salvation - painted a rosy picture of happy people, laboring under humane conditions for their own communal welfare, equality for all, with no cruel bosses and industrial barons clouding this beautiful picture. Any news countering this fiction was labeled as slanderous by the Soviet authorities and by their apologists in the West.

Thus, when the New York Times dispatched a supposedly great journalist, Walter Duranty, to report on the conditions in the Ukraine, the writing was severely falsified. The Soviets guided Duranty throughout the Ukraine, cleaned up the dead bodies before his arrival, set up "Potemkin" (staged) villages with false fronts, populated by well-fed, happy looking peasants, eating, drinking and dancing. The guides brazenly lied, explained and justified everything to a willfully blind Duranty. How do you miss evidence of millions of dead? He undeniably did.

For this fake reporting, the New York Times and Duranty received a Pulitzer Prize for journalism! The fiction of a wonderful Soviet Union, well fed, kind, a just society led by a remarkable "Uncle Joe", as Stalin was referred to by his apologists and supporters, was enhanced and perpetuated. In 1942, Stalin was even named Time Magazine's Man of the Year! These are among the most shameful episode of western journalism, though other examples in more recent history abound.

Another example that lends credibility to the "muted history" cited in the title of my book is the 1986 documentary "Harvest of Despair", based on Conquest's previously cited research. This program was to be run on PBS, which at first refused to air it, but then, after pressure from William F. Buckley, permitted it to be shown on Buckley's "Firing Line" TV show - but with stipulations that competing perspectives on the Ukrainian famine also be shown! Imagine a program on the Holocaust having to present the Nazi perspective on the industrialized murder of Jews and others as a condition of getting air time! I still remember this incident and the outrage I felt…

3.3 RUSSIA: THE GULAG GROWS

Besides the starvation policies in Ukraine and the greater Neighborhood of western Russia, Stalin was busy expanding the Gulag. "Gulag"- an acronym meaning "Main Administration of Camps" - was a huge prison camp network with tentacles throughout the Soviet Union. The first Communist Gulag camp was in the Solovetsky Islands in the White Sea above the Arctic Circle, well to the north of St. Petersburg, in a former monastery. One of the first major Gulag work infrastructure projects was the Baltic-White Sea Canal. 200,000 prisoners (an official number, realistically much greater) hacked out, by hand, a canal to connect the Arctic Sea to the Baltic - but in the haste to make quota, the canal was too shallow to have any meaningful impact on transportation. Many died there; the canal is littered with the bones of political prisoners who died by starvation, overwork, accident, or at the hands of brutal guards and professional criminals who were mixed in among the politicals as a control mechanism. The range of mortality figures is vast: officially, 12,000 died digging the canal; Anne Applebaum cites 15,000, with apologies for relying too much on official data; Solzhenitsyn gave a figure of 250,000, which calculates to a death rate of 125% of the official number of workers!

From these beginnings, the Gulag rapidly metastasized. The cancer metaphor, originating with Aleksandr Solzhenitsyn, is very illustrative. Besides arrests of possibly politically unreliable persons, quotas of prisoners-to-be were handed down from the Central Soviet authorities. The numbers were often based on labor needs for the Directorates to meet their centrally directed objectives (examples: this year we need X million cubic yards of spruce logs for export to generate Y million rubles; we need Z million tons of nickel ore; we quickly need a railroad line to connect M Mine to P Port, so we can bring the nickel to market; we need to dam R River to create a Hydro Electric Station to make electricity to operate the machinery in mining sites, etc.).

The ruling Politburo, under dictator Stalin, would create these plans, and then order prisoners to be created in the right numbers and have them shipped as slave labor to execute the plans. As the orders flow downward, regions and municipalities would get their orders from the top ("arrest 5000 enemies of the people next month, and shoot 200 of them - then the others will "confess" to their crimes"... to be shipped off to different campsites). This type of activity, with peaks and valleys, happened every month from 1921 until 1953, when Stalin died, after which it significantly slowed down.

Some of these prisoners were simply arrested and shot on the spot. Others were arrested, tortured in jails, forced to confess to made-up crimes, and sentenced. The most common crime was the supposed violation of Article 58 and its many subsections, which amounted to crimes against the Socialist state - and these could be merely thought crimes, with no actions or evidence, which is why the signed confession, the result of horrible tortures often over extended periods, was so important to the Soviet legal system. Yet others were simply arrested and dispatched to work camps, to be informed of their crime and sentence at some future point. Many others, especially women and children, were exiled to remote areas in Siberia, working as slaves on collective farms, denied any civil rights such as writing letters to their families. Some deportations had entire families dropped into the wilds to survive the best they could...or not. Prisoner conditions also varied widely. After a brutal transport by train - thousands of miles in cattle cars, with only a hole in the floor for personal relief, lacking food or water, weakened by rampant illnesses such as dysentery and typhoid, and a consequent high death rate - prisoners arrived at transit stations where they would be sorted and shipped to their final destinations to labor for the State.

Typically, in solidarity with the camps of the Holocaust, there would be a sign over the camp entrance: "Honest Labor: The Road Home!" Some camps had milder conditions than others; often survival of the inmates depended on the relative kindness or sadism of the camp commander. Pure luck also mattered. If you want the wrong place at the wrong time, it was fatal.

3.4 HELL ON EARTH

There were many ways to die, or worse, in the Gulag… by design.

Overwhelmingly, political prisoners were the majority of the unfortunates. They were purposely mixed in with professional bad guys - thieves, murderers, rapists etc. - and politicals would easily be killed, maimed or raped by professionals during a theft of food, goods (like a spoon, food bowl, or shoes), or work output. The true criminals typically banded together and operated as street gangs, making the individual political prisoner - especially if newly arrived - literally helpless. Some especially gruesome tales involve gang bosses using political prisoners' lives or body parts as bets in their card games. Since criminal gangs also threatened the camp rulers, they often had free reign to do as they pleased. Many innocents lost their lives this way.

The work itself was deadly. Mining, the very common activity, used rudimentary equipment, had no safety provisions, and was often a death sentence. Most surviving miners developed silicosis from dust in the mines, and died later in life. Those unfortunates sentenced to the mines of Kolyma/Magadan, in the far north east of Siberia, viewed it as a death sentence. Kill rates there were exceptionally high. (The founder and most prominent camp commander there was Edvards Berzins, a Latvian!). At Kolyma, one might survive if they had an ancillary role; but if you were a straight miner with a pickax and cart, your life was typically very short. Interestingly, as reported by many survivors in their chronicles, the prisoners who survived the best were devoted religious believers.

Logging was another common prison task, using primitive saws and axes, with no safety concerns. As in all Gulag work, quotas or norms were assigned, and if you could not deliver your norm, you were typically denied rations or forced to stay at work until you did. This often resulted in death - there would be a downward spiral where the denial of food made you weaker, which made it impossible to do the hard labor, which allowed others, especially the hardened criminals, to steal your work, which resulted in less food, and so on. You would often be buried where you dropped, unless it was winter - then your corpse would be stacked and buried in the spring.

Road and railroad construction was the assigned task for millions of prisoners. One Siberian road, still called the "Road of Bones", claimed 1 million lives while being built - about 1 life per yard of road. The dead were simply integrated into the road itself, since digging new grave holes into the tundra was of no use to the State.

The extreme climate conditions were also killers. Many Gulag sites were above the Arctic Circle, so working in extreme cold alone would be fatal. Added to this, rations were barely adequate in the best of times, and the clothing was wildly inadequate. Losing fingers and toes to freezing was common, which could lead to your being of less value to the state, which was then justified in giving you less food - and the fatal spiral would begin. In the sub-arctic summer, mosquitoes and blackflies would be a severe, daily torture. In fact, one of the ways of punishing prisoners was simply to tie them to a tree: death by mosquito! The first reported incidence of this was in the Solovetsky Island Monastery Camp; later, there were many additional such reports. Besides the temperature, wind and snow, geographic extremes were also killers. Prisoners working in fish camps in the wild northern rivers of Siberia had inadequate boats, and drownings were frequent. Forced marches to worksites might involve fording icy streams etc., causing hypothermia on top of malnutrition to jumpstart the fatal spiral. It was an unimaginably brutal world.

Guards and the mechanics of prisoner work life were also killers. The guards were indoctrinated into showing no mercy for the enemies of the people they were guarding. In fact, showing even slight compassion might indicate capitalist leanings by the guard and he might become a prisoner himself under the broad provisions of Article 58. Also, if a prisoner escaped or disappeared, the assigned guards would probably be arrested and become prisoners. Some of the camp rules were also deadly; on the march from the prisoner barracks to the worksite - which might be 10 miles or more - standing orders were "one step to the right or left and you will be shot". Imagine being half starved, exhausted, sleepless, sick, marching to a horribly demanding job, and then marching back, maybe in -20° F conditions - and if you stumble, take a sideways step to catch yourself - you are executed. So guards were careful not to violate camp rules because of the cost to themselves. This also allowed psycho-sadistic guards to flourish. Normal people would find it impossible to function in these conditions.

Any illness could easily be fatal. Typhoid, dysentery, and vitamin deficiency diseases such as beri-beri, pellagra and scurvy were common; pneumonia, TB, flu and other viral respiratory infections abounded. Medical help was often nonexistent, at best meager. If you were not genetically equipped to get well on your own, you would simply die.

The widespread horror that primarily affected women was rape. It was endemic. Almost all women were subjected to it, in various forms. Sometimes it was simply opportunistic rape, one on one. Other times it was gang rape by a horde of criminals. Many of the worst of these incidents happened aboard ships full of female slaves in the North Pacific, bound for Magadan/Kolyma (they had typically departed from Vladivostok, the eastern terminus of the Trans Siberian rail). These ships were freight steamers, and the typical load of 3000 prisoners were stuffed into a cavernous hold below deck for the 1 week journey. There were several barrels, sloshing and overflowing, for bodily functions, and perhaps some water and food. The accounts of these voyages read like a trip to Hell, and rival the tales of slave ships centuries earlier sailing from Africa to the New World. Many more men were transported this way, but it was of course the women who had the common experience of rape. When researching this, the details literally made me sick. When writing about it, I had to stop for a few hours to collect myself. If you want a quick introduction to some of the horrors that occurred on these slave transport ships hauling their human cargo to the port of Magadan, gateway to the vast network of the Kolyma camps, hit the internet - and be prepared. How has much of the world not heard of these events?

To finish this aspect, another common form of rape gave the appearance of being consensual - where women became available to men who had something they needed, like food, protection, and medicine, to keep them living for a bit longer. In the Gulag literature, it appears that almost all women were subjected to at least one of the debasing horrors of rape. Many rape victims especially thought that death would have been preferable to life in the Gulag, and some of them and other tortured souls did act on that sentiment. Suicide was common.

Mothers giving birth to children was thus a fairly common occurrence. In some locations and at some times the mothers had limited access to their children, housed nearby while the mothers slaved away; but all too often the kids were removed and sent to childrens' Gulags to start working early in their lives under horrible conditions to further the Communist dream...or nightmare. Orphans, and there were many, were always warehoused this way. This was one of the darkest aspects of the infernal system.

3.5 NUMBERS; PEAKS

Let me try to put all this in perspective, so here is an attempt to quantify the Gulag. "Attempt" is an intentional word; the true numbers will never be known, and there is a huge disparity, depending on the source. Communists cooked the books, lied, manipulated data, used tricks to lower the counts, and so on. What should be counted is also tricky. There were so many categories that clarity is impossible; a few examples will illustrate the difficulties. Those who were executed in prisons or died by torture were often not recorded. Transport deaths were not counted. Wasted prisoners who died soon after release were off the books. Many prisoners were listed as dying of natural causes - this was a favorite. How do you account for the millions of exiled people, and their shortened lives? Or the prisoners released into Red Army death brigades, and their replacements - how are they counted?

The Gulag system had several major transit points, where prisoners were collected, stored, sorted, and sent on to their brutal work destinations. There were more than 50 major work camps or directorates, each having an average of 8 smaller camp networks around them, for a total of about 400 labor colonies, and those spawned thousands of individual sites totaling about 30,000. According to historian Anne Applebaum, a minimum of 18 million citizen-prisoners probably passed through these camps between the early 1920s in the mid 1950s. Add to this another 4 million POW's plus 700,000 special detainees and 6-7 million people in exile camps. This totals up to about 30 million souls, and that is probably a very low estimate. Officially, about 2.8 million died, with death rates varying from 25% in the peak World War II years to 2.5% in better years. Many historians cite a number of 10-12 million deceased; some French historians cite 20 million; Shalimov, author and victim, cites 3 million deaths just in the single Kolyma Camp network; V.D.Hanson cites 30 million as being the mortality figure caused by Stalin, which also includes the millions who died in the 1932-33 dekulakization with its millions of deaths; 40 million is cited by many historians as the broad toll of Soviet Communism; and Solzhenitsyn gives a number of 66 million as Stalin's total. What a range, with so many ways to view the mortality.

By any count, the mortality data of the Gulag was extreme, and so many uncounted were permanently altered, came out weak and sick, and passed before their time. Their families also lived shortened lives due to the hardships caused by being related to an enemy of the people, and the constant heavy stress. Russia seems to mostly want to bury this past, and only a few small groups, especially the Memorial Society, peek into this history, with still significant risks on their part. So from that perspective, the truth is largely buried. Unfortunately, the West seems only mildly interested in this history. I believe that these documented horrors represent a stain on Socialism and Communism that many left-leaners in the Western world would prefer to downplay, especially members of the entertainment, education and media complexes. These lefties do not support the horrors, but view them as an aberration caused by a nut case, Stalin, and truly believe that the world would be a better place with this alternate to capitalism. But to me, this is criminal; I hear the screams of the millions of innocents, dying brutal deaths: remember me! Remember me…

Historically, there were times of terror of special note in Russia and its captive nations. 1929 was brutal. 1937-1938 is known as the Great Terror. Nighttime raids by the secret police to arrest people terrorized both the arrested and those waiting to be arrested. It could be for no reason - to fulfill slave or execution quotas from Stalin - or due to jealousies, feuds, informers seeking to curry favor, etc. - followed by imprisonment, often torture to extract confession, and execution or transport to the Gulag for too often a slow death. In the Ukraine, Kazakhstan and western Russia, the great famine occurred from 1931 to 1933. In the Baltics, June 1941 was brutal. In 1949 another huge wave of arrests peaked. In between, there were always repressions, disappearances and generalized terror, but these dates represented apexes. It was so bad in the Neighborhood that Russians who survived often remembered the World War II years as the good years: the German terror had an understandable source, and you could identify it, and do something about it. The War made sense to common people, but the terrors did not.

3.6 EXILED PEOPLE AND CULTURES

Besides Gulag camps of different types, exile was the other main form of terror in the Neighborhood. This was often applied to women and children, separated from their husbands and fathers, and then sent away to distant lands as workers to advance the socialist cause. Most often, those deported and exiled ended up working virtually as slaves on communal farms and factories in remote areas. Details will be addressed later. In deportations of the late 1940s, more families, with the males, were taken and dumped in inhospitable places to start new communities. Orphans had their own special camps and places of exile.

Frequently entire cultures were exiled, such as the Chechens, the Ingush, and the Kalmyks who lived just west of the Caspian Sea. The best known of these unfortunate nationalities were the Crimean Tatars. An especially poignant story for these people happened right after World War II. Several hundred thousand Crimean Tatars had fled during the War to the protection of the British Army to escape the Russians, similar to my parents and many Latvians. The Russians wanted them back, and the British decided to comply. As these Tatars were railroaded out, women threw their babies out of the train windows, believing that this would give their offspring the best chance at a decent life if found, or even if they died from the fall, they were better off than if they went back to the Communist hell. Let that sink in. After being returned to the Russians in 1944, all the Crimean Tatars - estimates range from 200,000 to 400,000 - were exiled to Uzbekistan, thousands of miles away, except those who were executed; and 260,000 Tatars were finally allowed to return to Crimea starting around 1985. No wonder this group hates the Soviets, and were especially fearful of Vladimir Putins' recent annexation of their homeland in the Crimean Peninsula of Ukraine.

So this is some of the brutal history that surrounded my family, even as Latvia was free of the Communist menace between 1920 through 1940. This is what the Latvians suspected, and then knew, and finally suffered as the 1900s progressed. The motivation to flee this horror was very real and about as horrible as one could imagine - in fact, much of the world would not believe it, sort of parallel to the disbelief in the Holocaust. To understand my family, you need to understand this nearby, muted history of the Neighborhood.

The chapters that follow will present my family history in several phases, combined with exploration of the three conditions that composed the totality of Latvians' options during the times of post-1941 Russian domination. First, those who fled: my family history will be used to illustrate the story of those hundreds of thousands of Latvians who escaped and resettled in other nations. Second, those who stayed but were taken: stories of Latvian women and children who stayed in Latvia but were taken by the Russians, followed by the fate of taken Latvian men. Third, the lives for those who stayed and were not taken will be described. Finally, the memoir of family cousin Rita Jaunzems, a Gulag inmate, is published here for the first time, in her own translated words.

CHAPTER 4

MOM: THE EARLY YEARS

The stories of the three major adults in my life - Anna, Arnolds, and Aleks - are so intertwined that telling their tales in an understandable format is tricky. I will start with Mom's early biography first; then my Dad's; then their lives together which includes the family escape from Latvia, their lives in the camps of Germany, and for my Mother, her landing in America with me in tow but no husband. Input for this is based mostly on Mom's memories plus that of other extended family, but obviously with no recollections from my Dad. Aleks was on a different historic vector, so his early life is his own tale as he related it. Then, after some historic detours, I pick up the story of Mom and Aleks becoming a family in America, which eventually leads to my and wife Sue's memoir to complete our family history.

4.1 FAMILY AND HOMESTEAD

My Mother, Anna Aleksandra Nogobods, was the youngest of three children - Arturs and Helena were her siblings - born to Berta Alide (Jaunzemis) and Voldemars Nogobods on 11/10/13. Birthing happened at home, a farmstead named "Veckisi" (or "Vec Kisi", pronounced "Vets Chi'shi"), which as of this writing still exists, but only as a signed bus stop ("Kisi") on road P36. Google Earth shows it clearly. The town of her birth was Vec Gulbene, meaning Old Gulbene, part of the village of Gulbene (pronounced Gul'-ben-eh). The homestead was about a mile from Vec

Gulbene center. Gulbene is in northeastern Latvia, 30-40 miles away from both the Estonian and Russian borders. It has a population of about 7000 within a municipality of 30,000 people. The village name is derived from "Gulbis" (stork) - a loved and legendary bird in Latvia - which builds huge nests, often mates for life, and returns to the same nest every year after the seasonal migration.

The family lived on their farm, encompassing 60 hectares or about 150 acres. Their house was next to a very low hill named Doblu Kalns (Clay Hill), surrounded by fields, woods and gardens. Based on my cousin Kitija's written remembrances and her father Arturs' memoir, at the back of the property was Kristalice Upite (Cross Bay Creek), a small tributary of the Pedeze River, a lovely stream several miles away. The sides of the property were delineated by two smaller creeks, Kisupite and Skolas Upite. Doblu Kalns has an interesting legend; Kitija's great great grandfather supposedly buried bars of gold in a metal box in this hill upon his return from Russia after serving in a war, and despite extensive searching, it was never found.

The property had numerous buildings. The house had an entry hallway leading into the kitchen and informal dining area with a table and long benches on either side. Behind this was a "formal" dining room and then a living room, which also served as Berta's bedroom. To the right was a bedroom for Kitija's parents and her two sisters; to the left was a bedroom shared by Kitija and my Mother. Next to the house was a root cellar, which also functioned as a bomb shelter when fighting started. Adjacent to that was a storage barn, alongside a larger 2 story barn with farm equipment below and hay and animal feed above. A chicken coop, pig barn, large-animal barn with stalls for cows and horses, and outhouse completed the structures. The well was to the right of the house, away from the other buildings, with a sauna across the road. A large rock sat next to the driveway, and linden, birch, apple and oak trees, plus flower gardens, vegetable gardens, fences, meadows, woods and grain fields rounded out the property, which encompassed both sides of the main road. Farming was the family business and the land and homestead were the total source of wealth and income. Crops included rye, sugar beets, potatoes, carrots and other vegetables, plus hay for the cows and horses, and other livestock including pigs and chickens. Everybody participated in farm work, and although they were not rich people, they were comfortable, with decent food, shelter, and freedom.

According to my Uncle Arturs' memoir, his grandfather Andreis (March 8 1836 - March 28 1913) inherited Veckisi from his uncle, being the closest blood relative. Andreis had first married Estere Einenbauma (1842 - 1862), and they had 3 children; she died, and he re-married a 17 year old girl, Jule Skumstins (March 28 1850 - Oct. 1 1939), from the neighboring town of Litene. They produced 9 children, 6 sons and 3 daughters, and one of the sons, Voldemars, was my Uncle Arturs', Mother Anna's and Aunt Helena's father - my maternal grandfather. Uncle Arturs notes that he remembers his grandfather's passing at age 88 ; Arturs was 8 at the time. When my Grandfather Voldemars inherited the Veckisi homestead, he was already married to my Grandmother, Berta (Jaunzemis), from the nearby "Bodnieki" homestead, several miles further from town, and on the opposite side of the road. The family name, Nogobods, also mentioned somewhat rarely as Nagobods, is not a common name in Latvia, and has no meaning in the language that I could find. However, in Swedish "bod" is a shed or a shop and "noga" means exact or fastidious, so there could be a rough translation of Nogobods as meaning a "nice shop" or a "well constructed shed", so my suspicion is that the surname has roots from the Swedish times in Latvia.

I have visited the Veckisi site several times. The first time was with relatives in the early 1990s, and the big rock next to the driveway that the family often mentioned was still there, along with some bricks that lay around the barely visible foundation of the house. Nothing else was left to mark the spot where my Mother and her family lived their lives. Since that visit, it has become worse. There is now simply a cultivated field behind an electrified fence, with no sign at all of the homestead that witnessed so much that was dear to our family.

My Mom's sister, the oldest sibling, was Helena (B 1903 D?1980). She was a no-nonsense character who had three children, my first cousins Ievina and Maija, both of whom I got to know and love, and a son, Guntis, who died mysteriously in the Soviet times. He had disappeared (in the 1960s?), and was found under the ice of the Daugava River near Riga months later, leaving a wife and daughter, now a physician in Riga whom I have met. Ievina had three children, Gunta, Ilze, and Ugis; Maija had one daughter, Ineta, who we know well.

Mom's brother, Arturs, was a dear Uncle to me and with his wife Elza, also a distant blood relative of mine, brought up three daughters, all born in Latvia in the 1930s and 1940s. These are my cousins and closest family, Kitija ("Kitty") Treimanis, Inara Overfield, and Olita ("Lee") Meyer. Their husbands, respectively Janis (Latvian for John), Bill, and Neal (both Americans), all deceased, were also close to me and mine. Their children, respectively, are Ed and Rick, Sandy and Randy, and Jesse and Aaron. We all have remained as loving relatives, constrained only by geography.

Anna's mother, Berta Nogobods (1881 - 1955), was a hard-working, sober woman who handled life's unfairness with resolve and dignity. I knew her for seven years of my life - she fled Latvia along with Anna and Arturs - and often babysit me during my first seven years. She was the only grandparent I knew, and among my early memories is playing cards with her at Arturs' and Elza's home in Orchard Park, New York. She would cheat - in a humorous fashion - and really anger me when she won. Kitija remembers her as a very smart, hard-working women, but rather cool toward her grandchildren, in contrast to Elza, who warmly embraced all kids. Berta's maiden name was Jaunzemis (which translates into "new land"), and her siblings were the grandparents of other more distant cousins of mine: Andris and Vilnis Jaunzemis; Jakabs (deceased), Vija (deceased) and Margita; Zigurds Miezitis and his sister Mara (both deceased), and brother Juris.

Berta's husband - Mom's father - Voldmars (Dec. 23 1876 - Nov. 30 1920) was a farmer whenever he could be. He was drafted into the Czar's army in 1914 during WWI, served in St. Petersburg, Russia for 4 years and was promoted to Corporal. Then, according to Mom, he was being sent to Japan when some truce was announced and he was sent home (this is murky because the known Russo-Japanese War ended in 1905, before the beginning of WWI - but maybe there was preparation for another conflict that never materialized). All this, of course, was hard on the family which had to maintain the farm in order to survive - so Berta, the kids and probably the extended family had to work hard. One of Anna's tasks was to herd the cows, she recalled. Mom remembers the day when her father - whom she had hardly known - simply walked up the path to the house and reentered their lives. Anna was about five years old at the time, and he had left when she was one. According to cousin Ievina, Grandpa Nogobods was a hard worker on the farm, a trumpet musician in his spare time, and supposedly enjoyed parties and booze. He would play in a band on weekends and one night, on the way home from a gig in Gulbene, his horse's reins wrapped around the axle of the buggy. The horse jerked and speeded up, causing Grandpa to fall out of the buggy, which killed him. His body became entangled in the buggy apparatus and was dragged home as the horse continued to its customary destination, Veckisi. Grandma Berta found his dead body resting outside the front door. Anna was 7, Arturs was 12, and Helena was 15.

A moment of reflection...Anna was about 1 year old when her Father went off to war. He returned when she was 5. He died when Mom was 7. So he was around his youngest daughter for about 3 years, and Mom was aware of having a father for only 2 years of her life. How short and sad for both of them.

Berta, now a widow, had to keep the farm afloat again. This was soon after World War I and the country was still devastated. Men had been off to fight, many did not return or came back injured, and crops and livestock were often ruined from lack of supplies, farming implements and labor. Hunger again stalked the land. Latvia was newly free but no one had anything - you were on your own - with only family and friends as your support. So the kids all had to work full-time.

Anna during this time had been sent to public school for perhaps 2 to 3 years. This was the "Red School" in Vecgulbene Center - it's still there today - and I have been in it. The building was the former "Red Palace", officially converted into a school in 1924. It's across the street from the Vecgulbene Manor where the German barons of the 1700s and 1800s lived, and which has now been converted into a beautiful hotel and restaurant where we stayed in my visits of August 2014 and October 2019. I walked around the old Red School in 2014, and was flooded with thoughts of my Mother as a young child, walking these same grounds. The building seemed to be deserted, though in decent shape, so I tried a door. It was unlocked and I simply wandered through several rooms, halls and stairs, and found that this brief connection to Mom was a spooky joy. In October 2019 I again visited and was looking forward to entering the school, but it was, sadly, mostly in ruins. But back to Anna's time - though the Red School was perhaps only 1 mile from Veckisi, it was a boarding school and Anna would stay there for a week at a time. She told me that she would get a loaf of bread - probably Latvia's popular hearty black bread - as her ration for the week. Again, food was very scarce and bread was the staple meal for most people. Mom was a good student but soon after the death of her father she had to quit school and stay home and work on the farm with her mom and siblings. Thus she ended up with about a third grade education.

Mom also shared with me several supernatural stories that she remembered from her childhood. In the area there lived an older woman who had the gift of the "Vardi", or The Words, and Mom saw her mutter these holy utterances to miraculous effect. Once, a barn caught on fire - this may have been the Veckisi barn and pigsty ignited from lanterns in the barn, according to cousin Kitija's recollections - and this seer spoke the "Words" and the fire rapidly died down. Another time, a cow had been bitten by a snake, the poisonous Common European Adder, and its leg had swelled up severely. "Vardi" were employed to immediately reduce the swelling and save the cow from further damage. In this same vein but later in life, Mom claimed predictive dreams, with an example being watching her brother wade into a lake, turn, wave and continue despite her pleadings to come back - and Arturs died the next day. My cousin Kitija also dreamed of my Father's passing the night before that tragedy. Perhaps there was something in the Gulbene water?

Anna's older sister Helena was a teacher and for a while taught in Cesvaines, a town 25 miles from Gulbene. The school was located in a beautiful old baronial castle - I have seen it several times - and Anna stayed there with her sister for a while. So Mom boarded in several different places in her younger years - at the Red School, at Cesvaines, and at Veckisi homestead - while also having a checkered parental situation, with her father mostly gone and then dying young. That is an awful lot of change for a young girl to deal with, and as she aged, her shifting circumstances just increased. This had to have a huge effect on her world view.

Mom later wanted to be a nurse and started a nursing education. Apparently it was a separate track of study from the usual grade school and secondary education. The nursing school was, as I recall, in the city of Jekabpils, and Mom was then in her teens. This career goal was unfortunately sidetracked when she discovered that she would faint at the sight of blood, and thus she had to leave the school. I think her older sister then had a teaching job in Jekabpils and they lodged together. Anna then returned to Gulbene and helped work the family farm in the early 1930s. One of her primary tasks was herding the cows - a species called Latvian Browns. They were highly prized as being good milk producers with a high butterfat content. Dairy exports, especially to England, were a huge component of Latvia's foreign revenues during this time, so feeding, herding, and milking were important farm tasks. As is true of country people throughout time and place, Mom was very fond of her animals and knew their characteristics and how to deal with each creature. She had a horse who was exclusively hers for many years, named "Ojars" (pronounced Oh'-yars), and she was deeply attached to him. Ultimately Ojars was simply taken by Russians in the requisitioning of June 22 1941, since horses were still a primary source of transport during the War. Her sadness over this was profound, very visible as she told me the story. It was another loss in a lifetime of losses.

4.2 COURTSHIP

In the mid 1930s, during the best times of the free Latvian Republic, Anna grew fond of the son of a nearby large family, the Pommers. Apparently the feelings between her and my father-to-be Arnolds were mutual. The Pommers farm, named "Pomeri", was perhaps one half mile further out the same road (P36) from Vecgulbene past Mom's home at Veckisi.

My dear cousin Kitija remembers the courtship years between Anna and Arnolds. She recalls vividly that Anna was deeply in love with Arnolds, and what Anna wanted…she usually got! Kitija tells of hearing the squeaking of bicycle tires driving toward Veckisi in the evenings, a bit later in the courtship. This led to supposedly clandestine meetings between the young lovers in the Veckisi "kuts" (pronounced "koots"), the barn. During summers the young people often slept on the hay in the barn as a place to be cooler and perhaps escape from the communal living in the house, and gain some modicum of privacy. After a few years of this, Mom and Dad decided to tie the knot.

4.3 1940: RUSSIANS ARRIVE ; STRANGE TIMING FOR A WEDDING

On June 17 1940 the Russian Communists marched into Latvia as a result of the Molotov- Ribbentrop pact between Hitler's Germany and Stalin's Russia to divide Europe. Early in the morning of June 17, Russian troops and armored vehicles swarmed across the border. By 7 AM they were already visible on the roads around Gulbene. After that came convoys of army trucks, each with Red Army soldiers seated in rows of 4. Tanks then made their first appearance. All day the ground shook with the rumble of heavy vehicles, and over the next 3 days these troops and military vehicles branched out to all the side roads, making their crushing presence unmistakable. While this was going on, recon airplanes, marked with a huge red star, circled the area. The Gulbene airstrip, close to our family homes, was used in this effort.

The takeover was then consolidated and the process of "legitimization" proceeded. On July 21 an announcement of a new government was made to the Nation. Vilis Lacis, a long-time supporter of Communism, was named as the chief Minister, and he thanked the Russians profusely for saving Latvia. All Latvians were registered by the authorities so the vote for parliament representatives could be controlled. Everyone had to vote; people were forced into the voting booths, aided by overseers. There was a single list of candidates - no other choices were allowed. A Director of the Russian Politboro, named Maximov, arrived to direct the newly elected government toward proper ends. On August 5 Russia admitted Latvia into their official sphere as a Soviet Republic - after all, this is what the Latvians wanted and voted for!

Some changes were made in the countryside to gain some supporters for the takeover. Landless families were given about 25 acres of land, plus a starter set of farm tools, animals and access to leased farm machinery, all taken from their former owners. Instructions on farming process were also given. A bureaucracy was established to police this new order. Officials were recruited to oversee activities and report what was happening on their assigned farms to a secretary, who then passed the data to a county executive committee composed of trusted Communists. The level of detail was great; reports included all the individual farms activities, each day, including acreage plowed, planted, harvested, sown etc. Every bureaucrat was under extreme pressure to have numbers that looked good, so liberties were taken with the truth. These details of how Latvia was taken are representative of Communist behaviors throughout the Captive Nations of Eastern Europe.

At around this time, Anna and Arnolds had decided to get married. The timing of the wedding date is a fascinating mystery, being within a week of the Russians marching in. Had this date been long planned? (Cousin Kitija thinks it was, and also remembers being angry that Arnolds was taking Kitija's best friend, Anna, away!). Was it set suddenly in response to the Russian invasion, either as a means of protecting my Mother from unwelcome Russian soldiers' advances to an unmarried woman, or protecting Arnolds from being drafted for labor or armed service, or for some other reason? I don't know, and wish I had asked. But under any scenario, the mix of emotions for the wedding couple and guests must have been powerful - the joy of a wedding, and the fear of the future under a bloodthirsty regime, already showing its monstrous fangs.

The date of the ceremony was June 23, 1940 and the setting was at the Pommers' home. Communists had already closed the local Latvian Evangelical Church and - now restored and functioning as a church again - and converted it into a warehouse. Some 30 guests showed up and the ceremony was performed by a Minister in the main room, which I have visited several times. As part of the ceremony, Arnolds' mother presented a key to the house to Mom, symbolizing acceptance into the family and house. Cousin Kitija recalled that her mother, Elza, had to wait several years after her marriage to Arturs before getting a key to Veckisi, and that this resulted in some strained feelings for a while between my dear Mom and my dear Aunt Elza. Despite Grandma Pommers' handing the key to Mom, the early relationship between the two was rocky. Mom had moved in to the Pommers' house, and by custom was the lowest ranking household member, stuck with the most menial tasks. Later, the relationship developed and they learned to love one another.

My parents lived about one year - until June 1941 - under Stalin's Communist Russia, and survived. The times were very tense, with Latvians disappearing, being jailed, shot, intimidated, having their customs, work habits and worldview turned upside down. Anna, Arnolds, and the others stayed busy at work and on the farm and kept their heads down.

Anna recalls her first, chilling exposure to the Russian invasion, when soldiers of the Russian army came to the Pomeri door right around the time of the wedding. She was home alone when a patrol drove up, entered the house, and demanded food. This was a very frightening moment, since the Russian army had already well-earned a reputation for utter ruthless-ness - they were themselves treated with utter ruthlessness - resulting in rape, murder, looting and so on. It got even worse toward the end of World War II, to epidemic proportions, and much of that was fueled by vodka. Russians soldiers were expected to get blindly drunk so that they could carry out suicidal assaults and perform atrocities with their senses dulled.

So these Russians at Mom's doorway were armed, had bayonets at the ready, and demanded to be fed. My mother went to the larder to get food - they followed and watched every move - and then went to the kitchen to cook it. Again, they followed, with drawn bayonets pointed at her. Finally, after cooking, they made her eat some of it, to make sure she hadn't poisoned it. In her telling of the story to me, she said that despite the terrifying circumstances, she got indignant and was mad that she might be suspected of serving bad or poisoned food to anybody! One should never serve anything bad to a guest, whatever the situation. They ate and left, and Mom was scared but okay.

Conditions were very rough for all Latvians during this time. For example, cousin Kitija recalls that a poor Russian family was forcefully boarded with them at Veckisi during this first Russian occupation in 1940 - 1941. She would have to walk to school with the Russian boy, who would often beat her up on the walk. Not much could be done, since he was a poor Russian and thus entitled to act out on the Latvian landowners. Kitija's school was next to "Pamatos," meaning "Foundation", which was her mother Elza's family home, perhaps a half-mile away - but a long walk if you're being beaten. (As an aside, I have often visited and stayed with our relatives Aina, Vilis and family at Pamatos and spent many great hours there. The school is still there but evolved into a Russian defense plant, and now a sewing factory). To try to deal with their new circumstances emotionally and tactically, neighbors would quietly get together when it seemed safe to sneak out and have "what now?" meetings. The risk was that someone might turn them in to the Chekists either for reward or due to pressure, with severe consequences.

On Easter Saturday, 1941, during this first Russian occupation, part of Veckisi burned. Hay was ignited and the equipment barn and the pigpen were destroyed, along with the wagons and farm equipment. The horse and cattle barn were saved, along with the house. As Kitija recalls, lanterns had been placed at Veckisi and many other sites in the area by the Russian forces to serve as beacons for future bombing activities, if needed. One of these lanterns had tipped and ignited the haystack. Later that year, probably around June 23, 1941, as the Russians were leaving due to the German attack, a "depth" bomb hit Pomeri on the driveway between the house and barn. This would have been right around my parent's first anniversary - what a memorable gift! It may have been launched by the Germans or the Russians. Everyone was fleeing to the adjacent root cellar behind the house, seeking underground protection. Mom was the last one to dive in, and fortunately no one was injured. That root cellar still exists, and I have been there. Places like that are sacred sights to me; I imagine the feelings of relief that you survived the immediate bombing, and then the terror and desperation of being helpless, unable to do anything to protect you and yours. The dangers of those times came from many quarters.

About a year after the Russian takeover, the Germans were about to implement an all out assault to the east against the Russian occupied territories and Russia itself. This was "Operation Barbarossa" that officially began on Sunday, June 22, 1941. The Germans blitzkrieged into Latvia and were rapidly conquering territory, taking millions of Russian prisoners and winning all the battles. Riga was taken by July 1. The Nazi objective was to take Moscow by the winter of 1941 along with St. Petersburg - then called Leningrad - in the north, and Stalingrad in the south. As the Russians began their retreat, they decided to loot the captive nations including Latvia, Lithuania, and Estonia of their people and goods, so that there would be little of value left for the Germans.

CHAPTER 5

DAD: THE EARLY YEARS

5.1 FAMILY AND HOMESTEAD

Four farms southeast from Anna's home, Veckisi, and on the same road, the P36, lived my Dad and the others of the Pommers family. Built in the 1860s or 1870s after emancipation of the Latvian serfs by the Russian Czar, the house still stands and is occupied. Dad's farm was named Pomeri (or "Pommeri" and "Pomerpomeri", the name of the bus stop), and was composed of 150 acres situated on both sides of the road, like Veckisi and most of the other farms in the area. The Pommers surname originally was "Pomers", but one of the ancestors added an "m" for unknown reasons. This name had been granted for use by one of the ancestors after performing well as a soldier for a German baron from Pomerania, that part of northeast Germany and northwest Poland bordering the Baltic Sea. Literally, "Po" means "next to" and "Morze" translates to "Sea" in the Old Slavic language, so "Pommers" means "Land by the Sea". This is a bit ironic since Gulbene, where our Pommers family lived, is about as far from the sea as one can be in Latvia!

Pomeri was acquired by my family between 1861 and 1864 when the old baronial estates of the Germans were broken up by Czar Alexander II during the emancipation of Latvians from serfdom. The land was purchased by the Pommers and the house was probably built by my great-grandfather. The main house faced south and was a traditional one story dwelling with a kitchen, living room, several bedrooms, and an attic. Later several rooms were added in the back. A tiny room to the left of the entryway was my Parent's room after their marriage, and when I have been in it I can sense the emotions and quiet nighttime conversations that would have happened right there, both the good conversations of newlyweds and the hard discussions of losing babies, who to trust, how to flee, and so on.

Typical for farms, there were several buildings on the property. There was a large barn situated closer to the main road, a small barn for pigs and smaller animals, an outhouse, a root cellar, a small field barn, and a sauna. Access to the main road was via a U-shaped driveway. Down a sloping field to the east was the Krustalice Upite, the creek marking one of their property boundaries. A small pond was in the back of the house, behind the root cellar. I have visited Pomeri several times, each time an absolute thrill. The fact that it remains the best preserved house in the area, having been largely spared the destruction of the War, adds to the joy. Unfortunately, as of my last visit in 2019, the major barn had collapsed and its footprint is now just a small field.

Arnolds' parents were Otto and Louise Pommers (nee Bergis). My Mother described Otto as great person, pleasant and easy-going, with no significant downsides. He died of cancer after living a full life. When my Mother married Arnolds, she moved into the Pommers' house from Veckisi and assumed the traditional role as the lowest person on the family totem pole. Mom quietly clashed with mother-in-law Louise and they initially did not get along. Within a few years the relationship evolved and they learned to love one another. Louise apparently was also a very fine person but her loving qualities took some time to be revealed. She had cancer later in life, had surgery, and then developed a blood clot and died in her 70s. I know little else about these paternal grandparents, and would have loved to know the details of their lives, and to see if some of their characteristics had been passed on to me or my offspring. But there is no familiarity and to me they are merely names with minimal context. I so wish I had known them.

Otto and Louise had seven children. Emils was the oldest child. His wife was named Zenta, and they had one son, Janis, who died in Riga around 2002. I tried to track him down and actually had a phone conversation with him while staying in Gulbene during a trip to Latvia around that time. We set a loose appointment to get together, but he suddenly died. It would have been great to get his perspective on the Pommers' family, my aunts and uncles, the lives of other more distant relatives unknown to me, and reflections on his own life. I did learn that Janis married "Yalena", and they had a son, Herberts, who was perhaps 30 years old in 2002. Janis had then married again, for reasons unknown to me, to a lady named Gita, and they had a daughter, Eva, who was perhaps 25 years old in 2002.

Anna was, I believe, the next oldest child. She married Martins Purvitis who was not a native of Gulbene but settled there with Anna. They had a son, Maris, the only first cousin I knew on my father's side, and who I came to know well, especially in our later years. Maris eventually ended up living in Canada, and a humorous occurrence in his immigrant story will be cited below. The Purvitis family owned the movie house in downtown Gulbene, a small building that I have seen and currently is a bike and motorcycle shop. They were pleasant and kind people, and were especially appreciated because Pommers family members could watch movies for free! Aunt Anna, Martins, and Maris were part of the wagon train that left Gulbene together as the Russians approached for the second time in 1944, and they also ended up in the DP camps in Germany. Anna died in 1948 while at the Wolterdingen DP camp - the same camp my family lived in and where my father died, also in 1948 - of pneumonia. Her husband Martins died soon thereafter, leaving Maris as an orphan.

Next was Herberts Pommers. I know nothing of him except that he apparently died soon after the end of World War I, so he was still quite young.

Alfreds was the next by age. He was an attorney, married to "Lienite". They had no biological children but adopted two kids, one of them being Edita from Riga, who had at least one child named Helmuts.

My Father Arnolds was next. His birthday was December 6, 1907, and he died under questionable circumstances by a fall off a warehouse roof in Germany where he worked as a guard on November 7, 1948. Thus, he was only 40 when he passed, a life cut too short.

Following Arnolds was Ida. She fled with the others in 1944, lived in the same DP camps, and was admitted into Canada around 1950. Aunt Ida was a character, and the only aunt/sibling on my Father's side of the family that I actually knew as a young boy. My Mother kept our families apart, with only a few minor meetings, even though we lived relatively close by. Ida lived in Hamilton, Ontario, Canada and we at the time lived in Buffalo/Rochester New York, only a several hour drive. I believe this was part of Mom's tendency to minimize my knowledge and contact with the Pommers' side of the family, probably to make her second husband, Aleksandrs, more important in my perceptions. While I regret the minimal contact, I do not judge it harshly - my Mother was behaving from an innate survival mode.

In a great act of love and courage, Aunt Ida adopted cousin Maris when his mother and father died in Germany. She arranged for his passage from Germany to Canada and became his guardian until she died around the year 2000.

This trip by cousin Maris from Germany to Canada is a unique tale. He was 11 years old, an only child, newly orphaned, living in the DP Camps of Germany. Ida somehow arranged for him to board a trans-Atlantic ship which was to arrive in Montreal, Quebec, and then find and board a train ultimately bound for Hamilton, Ontario...all on his own! There was certainly help by the transportation employees, but I repeat, he was on his own. Although Maris was already bi-lingual in Latvian and German, he had no English language skills, which threw an extra curve ball into the undertaking. Somehow he arrived in Montreal safely and got on the right train. A gentleman seated nearby noticed Maris, looking tired and hungry, so this kind soul asked if he might want a hot dog. Maris quickly consulted his pocket dictionary and was shocked and disbelieving at the literal translation - so he refused the offer, despite his hunger, and became mildly depressed and questioning of the kind of culture that was adopting him, one that served dog meat, even though cooked. What a cute slice of the immigrant experience, always recounted with laughter, as seen through the eyes of a smart 11 year old.

Back to Aunt Ida - she was viewed by acquaintances, coworkers and relatives as a bit odd and marching to her own drummer. Apparently she had been a somewhat disordered personality for much of her life. In her younger years, she loved a good party, was popular with men, and smoked and drank. She never married and after arriving in Canada worked in a hospital kitchen in Hamilton, probably in a job well below her capabilities. Ida was an absolutely devoted guardian to cousin Maris - in significant contrast to her wild reputation. In her later years she became fully paranoid, and finally had to be committed. Maris stuck with her as she had stuck with him, and together they represent some of the best that "family" can be. Maris described how he would return from work and find Aunt Ida, in her later years, with the curtains drawn in the apartment, and the TV screen covered. She would warn Maris not to speak because the Communists were listening and watching from across the street - via the windows and TV - and would throw them into prison if they weren't careful. This level of paranoia continued and increased until there was no choice but to commit her. I wish I had known her better, and do fault my Mother a bit for keeping us apart more than necessary. I have paid my respects at her grave in Hamilton, and plan to visit there again to acknowledge her and cousin Maris, now buried next to each other.

The youngest brother was Janis Pommers, born on January 31 1914. He was a cavalry soldier and died of tuberculosis in the early 1940s. The current residents of Pomeri in Gulbene unearthed some papers and documents written by or related to Janis buried in a milk can on the property, and they were kind enough to send them to me. Though tough to read and translate, some of the letters written by Janis displayed a great depth of feeling and intelligence. The documents added insight on Latvian life from the perspective of a disabled soldier in World War II Latvia.

Finally, there was an unnamed daughter who died very early in infancy, rounding out the seven.

There is a great posed family photo of the Pommers clan taken around 1932. It is of singular importance to me and someday I hope that some members of my downstream family study this photo closely, and with the same awe that I have felt when I gaze at several generations of Pommers. Despite the world-wide depression raging at the time, and the murderous antics of Stalin next door in Russia, it was a good time in free Latvia. There was no war, no threats, a flowering Latvian culture, and plenty to eat. All six of the Pommers' surviving kids and two of the wives are in the picture. The parents, Otto and Louise, and (I believe) Otto's parents are in the picture - and if so, there are four generations of Pommers there. This is the only photo of them together, and the only photo of many of them as individuals. Also, along the right edge of the picture, towering in his military garb, is Fricis Jaunzemis, a Nogobods cousin, and below him is Alise (Bergis) Jaunzemis, his wife and a niece of Grandma Pommers. Alise is holding their first daughter, Vija, who was the only living member in the photo…until mid-2020, when she died at 91 apparently of the COVID-19 pandemic in the Hamilton/Toronto, Canada area. Vija was married and has several children and grandchildren. Her younger sister Margita also lives in the same area and their brother Jakabs lived in Hamilton until his passing, just several weeks after Vija. I have had the privilege of knowing all these people and some of their offspring, but unfortunately not in great depth. Their father Fricis died as a victim of the Gulag, and those circumstances make for an amazing story that will be recounted later.

There is a Pommers family cluster of graves in the Gulbene Cemetery, re-discovered and lovingly tended by my friends and relatives, Aina and Vilis, and their families. It is toward the center-left from the entrance. I have been there several times and while there is a quiet satisfaction in seeing the clan together in perpetuity, there is a sadness that they are unknown to me.

5.2 WORK

While young, Dad attended the local school - I don't know how far he got - but dropped out early to work on the farm and help ensure that the family could survive the after-effects of WW1. With the elder brothers having left the farm to pursue other careers, Dad was left in charge, but he didn't like farming. Seeking other opportunity, Arnolds in the 1930s started to work for the town of Gulbene as the fire insurance officer. Since there was no insurance industry in Latvia, this was a local government function of some importance due to the prevalence and severity of house and barn fires. The houses were all built of aged wood, heated by woodstoves, and were surrounded by hay and other combustibles, all creating a high–probability fire hazard. So Dad worked several miles away in downtown Gulbene, and hired others to do the farm work, managing their efforts successfully. Unfortunately, this turned out to be a two-edged sword; while running a farming enterprise well is a good thing in the normal world, it could be a death sentence for being "an exploiter of the proletariat" under the looming Communist regime, just 40 miles away at the Russian border.

5.3 LIFE DURING THE FIRST RUSSIAN OCCUPATION

The newlyweds began life together under the shadow of the new invaders. It was a scary time for every Latvian. All elements of life were taking over by Communist bureaucrats - all government functions, schools, curriculums, police, defense forces, all clubs and organizations, etc. Churches, so important to the populace both spiritually and socially, were closed and typically converted into barns or storage facilities. Ministers were hassled and often arrested - after all, they were purveyors of the "Opiate of the Masses", designed to retain the old order.

Every organization was led by political officers with dictatorial powers, reporting ultimately to the Communist Party. These local officers interpreted all actions and issued dictates based on politically correct Communist theory. The network of secret police and their informers was widened drastically, so no one could trust anyone else without tremendous risk. People would inform on others for many reasons. There were billboards exhorting the populace to inform the authorities of anti-Communist behavior by others, and informing was considered a high patriotic act. One of the Communist heroes, in fact, with his picture on billboards throughout the Communist lands, was a 15 year old boy, Pavlik Marazov. He had denounced his own father to the secret police for anti-Communist utterances at home, and for being a member of the "Kulak" or prosperous peasant class. Stalin's goal was to eliminate - yes, eliminate - all the Kulaks, by either murdering them or sending them to slave camps or exile to remote regions. Pavlik's father was shot...and this boy was hailed as a national hero, with all schools teaching children to emulate Pavlik if they were to be good Communists! Imagine the utter depravity of a State that creates heroes like this! Some citizens informed on their fellows to settle old personal grievances. Opportunists wanting to get ahead in this new order would tell - or embellish, or simply make up - tales of the politically incorrect doings of others to gain favor with the authorities. There were often denunciations made in hopes of getting the house of the soon-to-be-criminal, if it was a nicer home than your own. Others were simply terrorized by the authorities to make them inform - "So tell us, who do you know that is an anti-Communist? - really, you don't know of anyone? - we know there are "wreckers" out there trying to make our communism fail, and you claim you don't know anyone? - how can we believe that - unless you're hiding what you know - which makes us worry about your political leanings, and those of your wife and your children - but let's meet again in a few days and perhaps you'll thank up of some names". In this new, crazy world you did not have to act against the system, but merely think against the system (think about that, how is a thought proven in law??). Article 58-10 of the Soviet Penal Code (the most common charged law) specifically cites "Anti-Soviet thought" as grounds for eight years of hard labor. Mistrust was everywhere, but that severely elevated the importance of family - they were typically the only ones you could trust.

Arnolds and Anna started their life together in this insane time where hope was scarce and fear was pervasive and never ending. They kept their heads down, avoiding any limelight. They attended all the evening indoctrination meetings and nodded unfelt approval of the dictates. When questioned, they answered in politically correct terms. When the "Troika's" - three person jury/ judge/ executioner committees - came around, they avoided being trapped. Many were not so lucky. Arrests, torture, disappearances and so on were commonplace, and everybody hoped and prayed that their turn would be delayed until something miraculously changed.

My Mother described several specific incidents during this time that she and Arnolds lived through. In one of the evening indoctrination meetings, the political officers expressed that the Communist Party demanded more (for example) sugar beet production, and that they had a plan to accomplish this. Farmers should drop their usual planting schedules, and plant sugar beets immediately. Some brave soul in the audience said that the time for be planting was not right, and that the rainy weather would destroy the crop. They were told to shut up - "so you know more than the Party about farming??" - and they were viewed with suspicion from then on as having negative thoughts and doubt about the Party's absolute correctness about all things. Imagine the fear that the outspoken farmer had from then on for both himself and his family - and imagine what may have happened to them. Honest outspoken thoughts like this could mean a literal death sentence. The political officers' response to this farmer cut off all other comments by the audience, and would have led to crop failure had not the German invasion shortly thereafter made it all irrelevant anyway.

That single example Arnolds and Anna experienced first hand was highly representative of Communist Party thought then and throughout its reign. It was also a primary reason that the system didn't work and spread untold misery wherever it was tried. The problem was the Party's view of its own total infallibility. Leaders issued edicts that were politically correct but out of touch with reality, leading to total disaster. They might, for example, double quotas for potato production - or triple the salmon catch for the military needs of the motherland - or demand twice as much output from the steel plants - and expected all this to happen despite the baked-in obstacles like confiscating the seed potatoes to get quota short-term, but having nothing to plant next season; or wiping out the salmon stock; or simply not having sufficient blast furnaces to double steel production. But if there was failure to meet quota, it was blamed on the existence of "Wreckers", closet capitalists who were working quietly to destroy the Communist paradise, since the plan was perfect. It was then the duty of The People to expose these Wreckers so they could be unmercifully liquidated or imprisoned or deported to be slave labor, or to open new lands for the glory of Communism. Quotas for exposing and identifying Wreckers and other non-believers were even established, and this use of fear and slave labor did increase output of the Soviet economy for a while, until it collapsed around 1990.

On this same subject, I remember one incredible story from my readings about the USSR from decades ago, probably in the 1970s. Some details may be lost due to my memory failing over time, but the gist remains. The Party had put out a demand for more cars to be built, and a bureaucracy was created to insure this. Land was acquired in Western Russia, and a factory was to be built. In actuality, the various components needed to build the factory on time did not exist, but the bureaucrat in charge could not admit this, fearing arrest. So he signed off on the progress of the plant. Next, all the machinery necessary for car building, which did not exist, was signed off by another bureaucrat, again out of fear, and placed in the non-existent plant. Workers were hired on paper to man the plant, all signed off on by the chain of scared bureaucrats. Automobile production than began, and quotas were being met, all properly documented and attested. Finally, a lead Communist was tasked with visiting this plant to congratulate the enterprise and hand out medals for exceeding quota. He arrived...to an empty field! But the bureaucracy had saved itself for a bit, and that was their primary objective, although the ultimate price must have been steep.

A second experience Mom told me about directly involved my Dad. As the Communists took over Latvia in the summer of 1940, their first focus was to control the media, personal weapons, and the Armed Forces, with control of everything else to happen soon thereafter. With the Armed Forces, the primary means of control was by execution of the military leadership. This immediately happened at the highest levels - the Prime Minister, the Generals etc. - were all arrested and either executed immediately or tortured and then worked to death in the Gulag. My Father was old enough to not be drafted into the Russian army, but while at home, he and others heard a series of gunshots from the woods in the direction of the Pededze River, several kilometers away. Arnolds and some other locals snuck off to explore the situation, and discovered the bodies of several Latvian officers, shot execution-style. The locals hurriedly buried them and went home, knowing that this was just the beginning, and more cruelties would be expected. Mom described Arnolds walking back into the house that night, pale and shaking from the murderous evidence he had just witnessed, and soberly contemplating what it might mean for their future.

I have visited a site near the Pededze River where a year later another group of Latvian soldiers was executed. This grave site now has monuments and remembrances, and is well manicured. It is probably not far from the place where my Father witnessed the earlier murders, so I regard that general bloodstained area as a holy site, made more personal by its brief tie to Arnolds. Maybe the place was a favorite execution site for the Communists, being in a more remote spot, as two sets of executions would indicate. Also, perhaps 20 miles away, is the site of a much larger massacre of Latvian officers, which will be referenced later when recounting my stepfather Aleks' story.

Since the Pommers' farm under Arnolds' supervision hired workers to help with the farm chores, especially at harvest time, Arnolds knew that he was under suspicion by the Communists. Dad, Mom and Family Nogobods did survive until the Germans swept in from the west in late June 1941, aided by several strokes of luck: the near-miss of deportation by the Nogobods due to their farm's location, and the escape by Mom and Dad made possible by a phone connection that had miraculously survived the Russian attempt to cut the phone wires.

CHAPTER 6

ANNA AND ARNOLDS; FLEEING LATVIA

6.1 MASS DEPORTATIONS; FAMILY FEARS AND TRAGEDIES

Just prior to the German invasion, on June 13 and 14, 1941, the Communists began a mass deportation and slaughter throughout the Baltics. Mom and Dad, married almost a year, were in the middle of this along with the extended family. Some were more fortunate than others. Uncle Arturs, Aunt Elza and cousins Kitija, Inara and Olita, plus Grandma Berta, were visited by the Communist police (called Chekists, NKVD, MVD etc.) and were told to pack one bag each and be ready and waiting outside to be picked up by a truck which would take them to the Gulbene Rail Station. That station, an architectural jewel, is still there, and I have visited it to pay my respects several times. It was the collection point for a horrible ride in "cattle cars" (actually, industrial wagons), deep into Russia. They had been recommended for deportation by a member of my Grandma Berta's brother's family who I believe was also a cousin of Aunt Elza. He had collaborated with the Communists, and according to relatives, the motive was for personal gain. The Russian plans were to stuff the Latvians on the trains and transport them to Siberia to populate and work that difficult land. Typically men were separated from their families and sent to hard labor while women and children would work on communal farms in the wilds of Siberia to accelerate the growth of Communism.

My cousins remember the trucks rolling by the road in front of their house, stuffed with families and their goods - but no one came for them. Cousin Inara was very upset because she wanted to get truck ride, a rare event in those days! An official, plus the relative who had denounced them, came by to tell them they were not forgotten but it might not be till tomorrow. So they sat there - can you imagine how the parents felt, waiting to leave home and plunge into a ruthless unknown? The fears they had for their three daughters and Grandma, and the helplessness that enveloped them? After one of their longest nights ever, tomorrow arrived…and no truck showed up. Russians had stuffed the train cars to capacity with Latvians, and sent them rolling east. They had no time and no trains left to transport the remaining families who had not been picked up the day before. The trucks had started picking up people who were further from the railway station, and were working their way in. Thus a horrible fate was avoided by the Nogobods family; they were saved by their local geographic position.

Please dwell on this for a moment, on this particular working of fate. The placement of the Veckisi homestead was first influenced hundreds of years ago by where our ancestors lived and labored as serfs. When the opportunity to buy a plot of land from the local baron came up, probably around 1860, they acted. But why that exact location for Veckisi? One wonders if they could have purchased a different property, further from Gulbene, but chose the Veckisi location - or if someone else got to choose a "better" property, though further down the road, leaving our ancestors with Veckisi as the second place prize - or they had always worked that particular location, and had first choice as a form of inheritance. Either way, that exact Veckisi positioning ended up saving their future family. Had they had lived further from town and consequently been on the earlier, emptier trucks to the train station, it would have meant deportation, slave labor, hardship and a few early graves. If my dear cousins had been among the victims, their children and families simply would not exist, a branch of the family tree gone. One can only marvel at the unknowable consequences of decisions and their profound effects.

Back to the deportation history. For the next week, all the families lived in abject fear, waiting to be taken. This finally ended when the Germans attacked the Russians on June 22. As the German army was getting closer to Gulbene, the Communist armies became totally focused on pulling back into Russia. The transport terrors were finally over, replaced by the fear of the war front passing through, followed by the Nazi occupation.

Some of my Mother's cousin's family, the Jaunzemis – my maternal Grandmother's maiden name - were not so fortunate. They were picked up and taken to the Gulbene Rail Station for deportation. The father, Fricis Jaunzemis, a strapping soldier, was separated from his family and put on a different cattle car to be taken elsewhere. This splitting of men from their families was common practice. His wife Alise and younger daughter Margita were waiting on the platform to be loaded into a cattle car. The other daughter Vija had previously been placed in a hospital for a head surgery, probably in Riga, and thus wasn't taken during the roundup. Mother Alise was pregnant with our cousin Jakabs (Jack) Jaunzemis, and faked labor while on the station platform. She and her daughter Margita were removed from the platform by relatively kind guards. The Russians wanted to take her anyway, but the doctors went along with her fake birthing and in the meantime the train left and soon thereafter Jack was indeed born. This part of the family survived and eventually lived in the Hamilton, Canada area. Their aunt Rita, however, was taken, and worked in a Gulag logging camp for years; her memoir is found in a later chapter of this book. A few days after being taken, Rita encountered her brother Fricis in a segregated transit camp in Russia; she felt that he would not last long, but did not learn of his fate for years. Both siblings were victims of Communism, and their families were denied a lifetime of their loving presence.

A third story - very lucky, or I and my descendants would not exist - concerns my Mother and Father. On June 14, 1941, as the massive deportations were started, some Latvians had been selected for execution. Russians had been hastily cutting telephone lines to the outlying farms while starting the roundup of the citizens. In their haste, the lines to Pommers' house were not completely severed. A worker in the Gulbene Town Hall, who worked with my Dad, saw an execution list, with Anna and Arnolds supposedly on it. He called Arnolds and told him to leave immediately. My parents looked out the window and saw an approaching Russian patrol, and ran out of the house and down the back field past a small barn, and waded across the small creek, Kristalice Upite. I have made that walk, and took a souvenir door hinge from the barn in that field as a reminder of their flight. Fortunately, they were not spotted. But as they climbed up the far bank of the stream, they heard in the forest the clicks of gun rounds being chambered. According to Mom, there were a few moments of sheer terror that it was Russians in the woods, waiting - but it turned out to be the Forest Brothers, the guerrilla group that had been fighting the Commies the best they could. They were saved and a week later the Germans arrived. Their circumstances between this escape and the actual Russian pullout, I don't know and wish I had asked. Did they warily go back into the house? Did they stay hidden in the woods, on their own for several days? Or stay in a Forest Brothers camp, or some other safe house? Probably a bit of all that.

It is also possible that my Parents would have been deported, like so many others; but the story was told to me as being the threat of summary execution of Mom, Dad, or both, as relayed by that co-worker who made the fortunate warning call. Perhaps my Dad's job at Town Hall and his consequent increased use of hired labor for the farm qualified him for the ultimate punishment. Murder by the authorities was indeed quite a common fate for many Latvians, and maybe Mom would have been deported alone. Either way, it would have been a horror.

6.2 GERMAN TIMES BEGIN

Operation Barbarossa, the German invasion westward into Russia, began on June 22, 1941. The Russian Army was in panic mode, with retreats on all fronts. My stepfather Aleks remembers being told that the Nazis had so many Russian prisoners that they could not spare the manpower to guard them all - so many were slaughtered on the spot. Soon the Germans arrived in Latvia, taking Riga on July 1, 1941, and being in Gulbene soon thereafter. This was just 2 weeks after the mass Baltic deportations. My Mother described her experience of the German arrival that contrasts strongly with her story of the Russian arrival: a German squad rolled into Pomeri - Mom was home alone - and asked politely for food, and paid for it. There was no threatening, just polite behavior with thank you's and bowing.

The Germans viewed Latvians as racially acceptable and relations between the peoples was tolerable though there was an armed resistance. In the larger scheme of the Reich, Latvians were close enough to being Aryan that they would be the last to be disposed of in the German quest for "Liebensraum", or living space, for the rapidly growing Aryan master race after the successful conclusion of World War II. Some Latvians might even become "Germanized" and help perpetuate this master race. This racial view of Latvians kept them relatively safe during the German occupation of 1941 - 1944. Others, the "Untermenchen", were not so lucky. These lesser humans were to be worked as slaves, and ultimately exterminated to make room for the master race. Untermenchen included Jews, Gypsies and Slavs such as Polish and Russian peoples, plus any Communists or other anti-Germans. They suffered severely under German occupation. These German plans, however, were at the time largely unknown to the world, including Latvians. The Latvian view of their two conquerers was that the Russians were feared, and the Germans hated.

I asked my parents and relatives about their recollection of the German-induced Holocaust in Latvia. They viewed it from a rural perspective, far removed from the major cities of Latvia, such as Riga and Daugavpils, which had large Jewish populations and were also early centers of Bolshevism. The scale was vastly different in the countryside than in the cities, and the scale was also smaller in Latvia than in Lithuania, Poland, western Russia and The Ukraine, which composed the "Pale of Settlement". The Pale was a region which was declared by the Czar to be open to Jewish settlement between 1791 and 1917, with the rest of the Russian Empire closed; Latvia was largely outside this designated area. In Gulbene, none of my relatives remembers any roundups, and I believe that is because there were none; but sadly, I have heard reports that about 80 Jewish persons lived in the greater Gulbene area, and Germans secretively executed most of them. There were rumors and reports of Jewish roundups elsewhere, and those were believed to be the first steps of detaining and then shipping the Jewish people to Palestine. Even after the experience with the Communists, it was impossible by most Latvians to believe that men, women and children could be mass murdered by an advanced society such as Germany. Uncle Arturs recalled that he was asked by the Germans about their next door neighbor, Mrs. Siraks, who was Jewish and was a dentist in Gulbene. He told them that she was not Jewish, as did all the other neighbors, and she was left unharmed. Interestingly, I asked my stepfather Aleksandrs Siraks about his relationship with this Siraks family, since they shared the same, very unique and uncommon name; he knew of no relationship, but when I asked the same question of Aleks' relative Anita while visiting Gulbene in 2019, she said there definitely was a relationship, though unknown and probably distant. I also asked my cousin Ievina whether she witnessed any atrocities, and she did tell of a roundup of Jewish people in, as I recall, Jakobpils city when she was a young girl living there, and at the time accepted the explanation of deportation to Palestine. In fact, there was mass murder in Latvia by the Nazis that consumed most of the Jewish population, with participation by some Latvians, as addressed elsewhere in this narrative.

Several years ago I asked my cousin Ineta and husband Agris to take me to Salaspils, formerly the main Nazi concentration camp in Latvia. Located in a large field near Riga, it is now commemorated with monuments and a small museum. It was a work camp imprisoning primarily Jewish people; although relatively small compared to other such camps in Poland and Eastern Europe, 2000 souls perished there, along with countless misery and terror for the survivors. It is important to visit these places, to pay respects, to feel the outrage, to hear the wailing of the victims in the wind, and to never, ever forget.

During the 1941-1944 German occupation life returned to some normalcy for our people in Gulbene. The need to feed everybody, including the German Army passing through, made farming an important necessity so farmers were working hard and not being hassled. The front lines were far away - the German seizure of Leningrad/St. Petersburg was ongoing, and the march to Moscow was continuing through the fall of 1941. But the winter of 1941 - 1942 was brutal. The German advance stalled, and Moscow was saved. Soon, by early 1943, the Red Army started to push back as the Germans began to retreat. In October 1943 the Germans lost decisively at the 2nd Battle of Smolensk, and their retreat west, toward Latvia, began in earnest. I don't know what the news from the front was like in those days, how accurate or propagandized it was by the German captors of Latvia, but Latvians probably strongly suspected that the Nazis were losing, and badly. Our people would see and hear of wounded soldiers passing through the Country; there would be nervous mutterings by Nazi occupiers, with more frequent demands for food and equipment; and heightened rumors about drafting more Latvian men into the German Army. Our family in Gulbene must have started stressing about the arrival of a hot war, again, and how they could survive the bombings and bullets. Their joy of seeing one conquerer about to leave was overcome for most Latvians by the horror of the new conquerer, Russia, soon to be back again to continue the work that had been interrupted in June 1941…deportations, prison, torture, death camps, and execution. Imagine seeing that in your future. How can you save your family? What should you do? Wrong choices could be fatal for you and your loved ones. This was the cloud that hung over our people in Gulbene, and all Latvians.

So during the Nazi occupation, at Pomeri and the other farms, crops were planted and harvested, livestock and horses were raised, and there was relative peace. During this stretch my Mother got pregnant two times. One fetus died in utero - but sufficiently late that the sex - male - could be determined; another died about one week after birth, again male, which apparently had been expected, since there was no name given. I'm not sure of the birth order. The reason behind these tragedies was probably because Anna and Arnolds were of contrasting blood types. Anna was Rh- and Arnolds Rh+, I suspect; these little boys were probably Rh+ and could not survive in my Mother's womb. Now, there is an injection given to the mother in this situation that allows the fetus to survive. I, on the other hand, am Rh- and became the only survivor of Arnold's and Anna's children. Mom later got pregnant by her second husband, Aleksandrs, in the 1950s - but complications again happened and this fourth (half) brother also died in utero, in Buffalo New York.

Let me explain my reference to a fourth sibling, since a careful accounting only registers three up to this point. I recently learned that there was another pregnancy that was apparently terminated by Mom either in the late 1930s or early 1940, probably prior to her marriage. This was a very common practice in those days, but it must have been very difficult, as are all abortion decisions. The circumstances are and will remain unknown. Was it an abortion of convenience? Of embarrassment? Or, given her later history, was the pregnancy so compromised that Anna's health or life was in danger? Or was the fetus determined to be non-viable early on? Whatever the reasons, Mom was pregnant 5 times and had only me to show for it - so I think I was blessed by having the full measure of love that had been reserved for my siblings. Although we were not a family that expressed love verbally - I don't ever remember Mom saying "I love you" to me - I never had any doubt of her deep love for me, and mine for her. And I believe that a mother's love for her children is the primary and strongest force in the social world, and its lack is disastrous.

6.3 RUSSIANS RETURN; TIME TO FLEE

By June 1944 front lines were again approaching Gulbene. This time the Germans were being driven back by the Russians. Latvians had to make quick, existential choices - stay or leave? For some, the choice was easy. Those who escaped the 1941 deportation or execution orders, including my parents, close family members and many others, had to flee. At Veckisi, Germans were already starting to dig trenches. About 31 neighbors and relatives had arranged a meeting point to begin their escape from the Russians. Family included 6 Nogobods, my Uncle Arturs, Aunt Elza, daughters Kitija, Inara, and Olita, plus Grandma Berta Nogobods; three Pommers, Anna and Arnolds, and Arnolds' sister, my Aunt Ida; another of Arnolds' sisters, Anna and her husband Martins Purvitis, and their young son Maris, my cousin. Many Jaunzems /Jaunzemis family members were also in this group, including Konrads ("Kondis"), father of my dear cousins Andris and Vilnis; Kondis' brother Roberts and his wife Luba; Ausma, Kondis' half-sister; Alise, whose husband Fricis Jaunzems had been arrested in 1941, and Margita and Vija, her daughters, plus her son Jakabs; five of the Miezitis family, mother Milda (Jaunzems), father Teodors, children Mara, Zigurds, and Juris. Others in the convoy included neighbors Paulis and Anna Skarnelis, their daughter Nora, Anna's brother Purins, as well as Paulis' sister and her husband. The convoy consisted of horses and buggies, with milk cattle tied behind the buggies. The Nogobods had two buggies, each with one cow tied behind, for example. As the caravan departed Gulbene, the Nogobods and my Mother saw their house Veckisi go up in flames, intentionally torched by the Germans as they were creating defenses. So ended that home, in smoke and sadness, entrenched in memory as the last picture of Gulbene that most of them would ever see. What a sorrowful last visual, especially poignant because of the extreme emotional tie that these country people had to their ancestral land and homes, a sensation minimized for modern Western peoples. It was like losing a part of yourself.

In Latvian, there is a specific name given to this act of fleeing: "Baglu Gaitas", a phrase known to all of that era. "Beglu" or "Beglis" means "those who flee"; "Gaitas" means a troupe or gathering. These words express the actions well. There is also a wonderful book, "Three Small Pebbles", written by cousin Sandra Pezzino, which presents a mildly fictionalized account of this flight from Latvia to freedom by our family.

Stay or leave - just a few words, but imagine what turmoil went into that choice. While our close family really had no option but to leave, the planning had to be terrifying. It was a plunge into the unknown. The basics of life were threatened. Short term plans had to be set, with often limited communications. Where should you meet? When? If you miss by a few minutes, would you find yourself soon behind Russian lines, primed for slaughter ? What should you take? What should you bury, in hopes of recovering when you, hopefully, returned? When you fled, how would you feed the family? Shelter them? Take care of them when sick? How to avoid being caught in a hot war if the front overtook you? How do you defend the women and children from drunk Russian Army soldiers, should they overwhelm you? And those were just the immediate issues. Longer term, where would you end up? Back in Latvia, or some other country? How would you support a family as a penniless farmer who has lost all the family land, livestock and equipment? There certainly were feelings of desperation and panic to be overcome so that better decisions would be made; maybe necessity demands heroism. What a test, and how proud I am of my relatives who had the strength to survive. I want to believe that some of these attributes have seeped into their descendants, making them better able to conquer the vicissitudes of life. Perhaps that is the reward.

So our family who fled started walking through the middle of greatest, most destructive War, ever. On one side was Hitler and the Nazis, a cold-blooded murdering machine, and on the other side was Stalin and the Communists, also a cold-blooded murdering machine. Some gross numbers distinguish WWII from all other human conflicts, taken from V.D. Hansen's incredible book, "The Second World Wars". At least 60 to 65 million people were killed between 1939 and 1945, representing about 3% of humanity, compared to 100 million killed in 471 wars between 1700 and 1988. So 60 - 70% of all deaths from war in 3 centuries happened in just 6 years of WW II! Another striking data point is that this was the first war in history where the number of civilian casualties far outnumbered those of military personnel. This was what Dad, Mom and the extended family, civilians, were walking through…and they were the lucky ones, as it turned out.

Others decided to stay. All of the Pommers men, my uncles, stayed. My aunt Helena, Mom's older sibling, and her husband "Milas" - an appropriate nickname meaning "The Loved One" – and their children (my cousins Ievina, Maija and their brother, Guntis) decided to stay. According to Ievina, there was a family conference and Milas, a teacher and future school principal, kept the family in Latvia. He simply stated that Latvia was their home, and they would somehow get through whatever was coming. They did make it, sort of. Milas and Helena died of old age in Latvia; Ievina became a pulmonary physician and Maija became a teacher; but their brother Guntis was murdered under mysterious circumstances in Riga, leaving a wife and daughter behind. So they mostly all survived, but lived through the second Stalinist terror of 1944 – 1951, peaking in the year 1949. They secretively watched as their friends were tortured by the KGB, or disappeared, or were deported, while hoping to be overlooked; or best case they simply lived in constant debilitating fear and survived as second-class citizens in their own land, torn apart by the brutal Communist system that dehumanized its entire population. The family did what they had to do - joined the right Communist organizations etc. - which was required for the right to attend schools, get better jobs, and have a better shot at avoiding arrest.

But back to my family's convoy fleeing the frontlines. It basically went directly to the town of Cesis, 56 miles west of Gulbene, and camped out there for much of the summer of 1944, waiting to see the speed and direction of the front. Lodging was provided by various friendly farmers in the area. Everybody understood the situation and was helpful, because they might be next. Also, since there was a chronic manpower shortage, the refugees could provide some much needed labor on the farms. In this way our family got some provisions, plus shelter, if only in a barn. Times of stress like these also produce some interesting human interactions. Kitija tells the story of a friendly Cesis farmer suggesting a trade: that Grandma Nogobods stay with them - being too old to travel well, with a high risk of death, plus probably slowing down the Caravan when it hit the roads again - along with Olita, 18 months old, and therefore too young to travel well...in exchange for their son Ivars, who would join the Caravan and try to flee to the west. Ivars was of draft age and would be taken by the Germans during their retreat, or if avoiding that, by the Russians during their advance. This family was trying to save their son's life, but Family Nogobods refused the trade offer.

Another more light-hearted aside was that Grandma Nogobods had only ever seen the Gulbene area, and visiting the capital, Riga, was on her bucket list before she died. Well, she got to see Riga - and Berlin – and Hamburg, Germany – plus New York City – and Buffalo, New York – before her passing! So her wish was fulfilled, in spades, but under unhappy circumstances.

By mid-September 1944 the Russian offensive in Latvia was in full swing. As reports of the frontline moving toward Cesis were received, it was decided by the Caravan that they had to move on. Uncle Arturs' notes indicate that on July 30 they began to flee to Riga and then on to the port city of Liepieja. The wagons, horses and milk cows were hitched up again and the Caravan took off toward Riga, about 120 miles to the southwest. Nights were spent in barns, farmhouses or in the open. Everyone would forage for food. Every night, the families would have a discussion - mostly the men – about the next day's plans. A major risk was being bombed, which happened to our family and all the refugees. The Nogobods family had a safety routine with Arturs and Elza shielding Olita and the Inara with their bodies, while Kitija, as the eldest, was more on her own, along with Grandma Berta. My Mother also recalled the bombing raids and remembered, with horror, the dead horses and wounded civilians and soldiers. The Caravan got to Riga by mid- October 1944, which was in chaos with refugees, soldiers, the wounded, a lack of food and medicine, intrigue, and preparations for the frontline about to sweep through. Riga fell to the Russians several weeks later, on October 24.

6.4 LEAVING LATVIA

Our family Caravan then moved on toward the Latvian port of Leipaija, in western Latvia on the Baltic Sea. It arrived there probably in very late October 1944. This was at the time a major German military port with ships going to and from Germany, and frequent trips to Gotenhafen and Danzig, which are now named Gdyna and Gdansk, Poland. The wounded and dead would be shipped out of Leipaija, and supplies would be shipped in. By this time the Courland Peninsula of Latvia, where Leipaija was located, had been cut off at the base by the Russian army, fighting there while advancing around it toward Berlin. The fighting in Courland continued until the end of the war; Berlin itself had already fallen - 400 miles to the west - but the fighting in Courland kept up, the front moving back and forth, with wholesale slaughter of German and Russian troops. Latvian troops were also there, primarily fighting as draftees for the Germans (this included my stepfather Aleks), but also for the Russians. So Latvian brothers were occasionally fighting one another in this horrible stalemate. My relatives Andris and Vilnis Jaunzemis' mother grew up in this area, and Andris has visited her farm. He reported that the scars of the protracted battles are still very visible: earthen defensive ramparts, deep holes that served as protection for tanks, and hidden explosives still blowing up the unwary or unlucky explorer to this day.

Our families fled from Riga to Liepaija through Courland relatively late; at one point, our people were approaching a big river and the German soldiers were hustling them along and waited for them to cross before immediately blowing the bridge to halt a Russian advance. Here again we see the workings of fate. Had the Caravan arrived at the bridge just a little later, there would have been no bridge, and they probably would have been swept up by the Russians while trapped by the river. All of their futures would have been darkly different. Here also imagine the pressures on our family, frightened, tired, but having to move at top speed, with babies and grandparents in tow, praying that some German officer would not change his mind and blow the bridge before they escaped across. I have been driven along this route (by my dear friend Agris, cousin Ineta's husband) between Riga and Liepaija; this would have approximated the route the Caravan traveled in this scary part of the trip. It was a sobering and memorable journey, traversing that same route my family took so long ago. Most Latvians who chose to flee the Red Army had already done so much earlier, and our group really was among the last. Citizens of Riga and other places in western Latvia had a shorter journey, were typically wealthier and had taken advantage of the existing rail network to aid their escape, whereas our people were from the East and were forced to flee on foot. Some of the earlier refugees took trains all the way to Bavaria, in Southern Germany, where they ended up in the American Zone of occupation, whereas the later escapees, including my family, stayed in the north in what was the British Zone. According to people who witnessed conditions in these disparate places, the American Zone was much better. Food was plentiful.

The scene in Liepaija port was chaotic. The German army had priority on ships for its needs, and if there was any room left, Latvian refugees were crammed on board. The target was to travel to the relative safety of Gotenhafen in Germany, now Gdyna, Poland, several hundred miles to the west. Refugees got on board by hook or crook, after waiting at the port for days or weeks for the chance to escape from the tightening Russian cordon. Probably a combination of bribes and an advantageous German rule giving families with children priority over others finally got our people on board. The ship was named "Lapland", and it departed on November 2, 1944.

Imagine the final moments as Mom, Dad and the families boarded the ship, in a swirl of contrasting emotions. Everyone was giddy with joy to reach the relative safety on board the ship, but that must have been soon replaced by the sorrow of leaving Latvia and all their possessions and wealth behind. Yes, all their possessions, except for what they could carry. They were penniless, emotionally shattered, and dependent on others for survival. There had to be fear of the unknown that they were sailing into, both short term of being sunk and drowned, and long term with their futures being at best a huge question mark. Their sadness must have also been extreme towards their relatives left behind, who were to be engulfed by a merciless, murderous enemy that had already proven its depravity. As they saw with last glimpses their Motherland fading away as the ship pulled out, not knowing if they would ever be back while hoping that they would, the internal turmoil had to be at an intensity that we, living in freedom, cannot imagine.

I have visited this port and walked the old concrete pier along with my guide, Agris. It is a massive, old structure that is probably the exact location of the departure of "Lapland" and our family. Looking out to the Baltic, past the barriers demarcating the sheltered bay, I could feel the relief of our people as they started putting miles between them and their oppressors; but looking back to shore, to that last glimpse of Latvia, I could sense the tears of sadness that had been shed.

Then began the perilous sea journey to Gotenhafen. There were killer Allied-Russian subs and warships waiting in the Baltic along the route to sink German boats, plus air attacks. Evidence of the dangers of the Baltic journeys during the War is very well documented in the book "Salt To The Sea" by the Lithuanian author Ruta Sepetys; the largest single loss of life ever in a maritime sinking happened west of Gotenhafen in the Baltic on January 30 1945. Around 9400 people died on the German ship Wilhelm Gustloff when it was attacked by a Russian submarine. Some 5000 of these victims were children. The remains of this ship are still visible under the Baltic's waters off the coast of Poland. It had a capacity to transport only 1500 passengers, so imagine how crowded it must have been with 10,000 people aboard…and think of how desperate these refugees must have been to board such an obviously overcrowded ship. Several other ships were sunk during this time with major loss of life, one with 4000 deaths and another with 6500. What I'm describing did happen several months after Anna and the family were in Gotenhafen, and further to the west in the Baltic, but shipping lanes in the Baltic were always under severe threat, and having predominately civilian refugees as passengers offered no protection. Our family was lucky to board their ship, and then terrified of being underway.

On November 4, 1944 the ship Lapland with our family arrived in Gotenhafen after a 2 day crossing. This Port was also chaotic, with the military and refugees and residents all mixing together under the pressure of the war coming to soon sweep over them. Tens of thousands of people were here, having arrived in a variety of vessels. Abandoned horses and animals were already roaming the streets, trying to avoid the supply trucks hauling to and from the ships. Crates, boxes and luggage lined the quays. People in various states of fear, panic and aggression also roamed about, looking for lost family, food, and shelter. There would have been a mix of kindness, with strangers helping one another, and danger.

6.5 STARTING LIFE IN GERMANY

Our Caravan stayed in a makeshift camp, the Gotenhafen Lager, until November 13, 1944, according to Uncle Arturs' notes. Mom would have celebrated her 31st birthday there. They then moved west, primarily by truck, staying in the north of what was then Germany - now Poland

- perhaps to a town named "Posendorf", or near a place named "Tornas", from November 25 to early February 1945. (Note: the dates and places during this stage of fleeing are probably unreliable. Uncle Arturs' memoirs and cousin Mara Miezitis' recollections don't quite add up; also, the the area was transitioning from German to Polish control and place names were changed, or spellings were adjusted. Plus, of course, the family was under tremendous pressure to maintain the basics of life while fleeing a terrifying enemy without any controllable transport, so taking care to document accurately was a low priority. I located old maps of this area but my search was fruitless). Other of my readings portray this area in stark terms: no men visible at all, few other people, a civilization almost totally abandoned. Through this blighted land our Convoy just kept moving west, away from the Russians, and ended up in the Mecklenburg-Vorpommern German state.

By February 10 1945 they arrived in Moltzow, in the Waren region in the lake country north of Berlin. That date seems to be accurate. Sue and I have visited this area, and indeed it is very beautiful; we stayed in the village of Waren, on the Muritz Lake, several miles from Moltzow. It was here that cousins Kitija, Zigurds, and Mara attended school and our people lived in vacated apartments. During this time there was a slow-down of the Russian advance which allowed a few months of normalcy until April 30. But this ended, and they had to move on, going west toward the British Army, and away from the oncoming Russians. Uncle Arturs' memoir says that on May 3rd 1945 they began to flee again, and on May 6 they were overtaken by the Russian Army. This would have been near or in the tiny village of Alt Necheln, about 35 miles west of Moltzow. They were overtaken because their mode of transportation was too slow. Our relatives had been staying and working at the castle estate of a "Baron Smith"; there have been family references naming it as "Sopsogan Castle" and/or "Waren Castle", but the input is sketchy. Whether the castle location was in Moltzow or some nearby place to the west is unknown to me, and I have been unable to locate any history. The Baron was remembered as a good, caring person, and as the front line approached, Baron Smith and his family fled west with horses and wagons, and left 2 oxen and an ox cart for the Latvians. As our family left the area, some of our people wanted to take valuables from the estate, since the Russians would soon plunder it anyway. But Uncle Arturs refused to allow this, which speaks of his extreme honesty…something I also have observed among many other Latvians, like my stepfather Aleks - although they all certainly "stole" food when they could. So the Caravan fled the area, but the oxen moved slowly, and the Latvians consequently were overtaken by the Russians. Until July 1 they stayed and worked in another German castle in the Necheln area, but now behind the Russian lines.

My Mother vividly remembered when the Russian Army overtook them. The incident was seared into her memory. It was a moment of great peril, since the Russians were often drunk, used rape has an accepted spoil of war and a weapon of control, and robbed refugees whenever they could. As the Russians approached, the Latvian women dirtied their faces with dirt and soot, somehow blackened their teeth, and mussed their hair to look unkempt or sick, all to try to cut down the possibility of rape; they hid their wedding and other rings in their mouths. Arnolds and the other men dropped their weapons into nearby bushes and prepared to execute a defense, though against overwhelming odds with no chance of success.

The plan was to pretend to be fleeing from the Germans, since the Germans had a large population of non-German slave laborers. Basically, this worked. They were questioned about why they were traveling in the wrong direction, towards the Germans from whom they were supposedly fleeing; our people pretended to be confused and lost. Fortunately, all family members played their parts well during this real-life acting class. Any slip-up - like one of the children blurting out something that cast doubt on their story - could have been fatal. Oscars to all! Of course, the Russians did rob them, demanding their watches, which was the most common and prized item of theft. Uncle Arturs pretended to not understand the Russians demand for his watch, offering an old clock, and was threatened for his troubles. They took his watch and stole other meager goods. Again, just imagine the fear and loathing as armed, perhaps drunk troops threatened and robbed this small group of refugees, after they already had lost everything. Anna's heart rate must have skyrocketed, her breathing quickened, her internals quivering, as this hated enemy surrounded them. I'm sure the effects of this and like experiences had lifelong and harmful effects on my Mother and the others.

6.6 MEETING HIMMLER!

Another fascinating story was told to me by my Mother, for the first time, just several years before she passed. Some days or weeks before the Russians overtook them, Mom and the family had approached a large Manor House north of Berlin to seek work, food, and shelter for a bit. The Manor's overseer had assigned them to cut reeds - I know not why - as their work in exchange for food. Suddenly a Manor resident appeared and told them to come with him to help pull out a car that had slid into a ditch on the property. This was probably in April of 1945, with slick and muddy dirt roads. They went and rescued an official looking car, whose main occupant then thanked them, shook their hands, and gave them cigarettes – an important wartime commodity, often used as money. Who was the car's main occupant? It was none other than Heinrich Himmler! This was the number two Nazi in Germany, next to Hitler himself! Himmler was a chicken farmer who supported Hitler early on, was a total believer in the racial theory that placed Germanic "Aryans" at the top of humanity, destined to take over the world. Aryans would live off the labors of "Untermenchen" - lesser humans - such as Jews, Gypsies and Slavs, until they were no longer needed, when they would be exterminated. Strangely enough, Nazis portrayed Aryans as blond, blue-eyed, muscular, intelligent and handsome people…but photos of Himmler, Hitler, Goering and most of the other Nazi leadership reveal the opposite of this portrayal. Himmler would not be judged as handsome by anyone except his mother, and the same was true for Hitler and Goering. Himmler was evil personified, founder of the SS, and the main architect of the Holocaust, which ranks with the worst crimes in all of human history. What is so mind-blowing is that he could display an entirely different personality, depending on your racial type. To my family of Baltic peoples he was pleasant and gentlemanly. I wanted to visit this farm, but my research yielded nothing and so I could not visit it during our trip to Berlin and north Germany in 2013. It would have been so meaningful to be at the same place where my Mother had this bizarre experience.

6.7 FLEEING RUSSIANS...AGAIN

As the war ended on May 8 1945, our group was behind Russian lines in the Wismer region northwest of Berlin, from May 3 to December 1. Our Caravan started to break up now, with different people using different escape routes to get away from the Russians. The area was still fluid, sort of a frontier, with little civil authority, and no strict clamping down yet by the Communists. To add to the complications and fears, cousin Kitija came down with typhus during this period under the Russians, and was deathly ill for about 6 weeks; her Dad Arturs had to carry her around as she was too sick to stand or walk (my Mom had also had typhus, but I believe it was earlier in their escape). Kitija recalls being taken to a hospital, along with another little girl with typhus, but all beds were occupied. She ended up sleeping on straw in a hallway. Though Kitija finally recovered, the other sick child, tragically, died there.

Arnolds and Anna made their way to Berlin in early December and checked out conditions there, along with Kondis Jaunzemis, my cousins Andris' and Vilnis' dad. Being childless, these three could travel more easily, while Arturs' and Elza's family with the three kids and Grandma mostly stayed put, living in several places in the general area - but not for long. Arnolds, Anna and Kondis made several trips from Berlin back to the Nogobods family and helped plan their escape. The Nogobods were to get on the train which would take them to a central station in Berlin. Their pretext was that they were returning to Latvia, and would transfer to the Latvian-bound train at the Berlin station. Arnolds and Kondis were to obtain a truck and would be waiting outside the station, and they would escape to the British and American zones of Berlin. And on December 28, 1944, it worked!

Just imagine how it could have gone down. What if the train was late? Or if the family was bumped? Or detained, or under suspicion? Or the truck couldn't be borrowed or obtained by bribery, or it broke down? This is the pressure that these people constantly lived with. But it did work. Kitija remembers that her family Nogobods and the Purvitis family (my aunt Anna, cousin Maris and father Martins) did board the train well northwest of Berlin, and stayed together as a group. It was a crammed, chaotic train, full of Russian troops, and Russians were literally marching down the aisles and throwing every German off the train... literally throwing people off! That image has stuck with Kitija. But they allowed our group, as Latvians with children supposedly returning home to Latvia, to stay. When they arrived in the Berlin train station, they went toward the prearranged meeting point where Arnolds and Kondis had indeed procured a truck. Everyone clambered aboard – but the Russians became suspicious and were yelling that they were going in the wrong direction, that the train to Latvia was elsewhere - and finally tried to grab Grandma as she was climbing up. So Arnolds and Kondis took matters into their own hands and pulled Grandma Berta away from the Russians' grasps, threw her into the truck, and they roared off. Again, imagine the feelings when this phase of the escape ended: the pounding hearts, the raised blood pressures, and finally at least a momentary joy of salvation.

6.8 DP'S IN GERMANY

Arnolds and Kondis drove the truck with its precious cargo to the reunited family group at the Zehlendorf Camp in the American zone of Berlin. This huge camp for Displaced Persons (DP's) was run by UNRRA, the United Nations Relief and Rehabilitation Administration. It consisted of several sub-camps close together in what is now a pricey, leafy suburb of Berlin. Our people stayed there from January 1, 1945 to mid-April 1946. Again, there is some dispute on dates, and different parts of the Convoy may have moved at different times. This timing is of particular significance and importance to me because since my birthday is December 8, 1946, my conception date would have been about nine months earlier, or March 8, 1946, which means that I was conceived in Berlin! Yes, "Ich bin ein Berliner"… at least in one sense of the famous phrase uttered by President Kennedy in Berlin in 1963. On a potentially more somber note, Mom also told me that Arnolds did not want a child born into the cruel and unknown future that they could anticipate, and wanted to have me terminated - but having already lost 3 kids, having survived the thick of the war, and starting to get on the bad side of childbearing age, she won the argument. Fortunately for me and my downstream family, I was not terminated.

Mom also told an interesting story that happened in Berlin during this period. The demarcation of the city zones - Russian, British, American and French - was still loose and people would go for goods and food wherever they were available or cheaper. While pregnant with me, Mom and Aunt Elza left their American Zone and went shopping in the Russian zone, where things were less expensive. When rounding a corner, they suddenly came upon a Russian officer, almost bumping into each other, and he locked eyes with Mom, momentarily terrifying her. He was wearing the Russian Army olive/brown hat with the big red star emblem on the peak - and that moment, and that star, became burned in her memory. Strangely enough, when I was born, there was a star-shaped blemish on my forehead! Mom absolutely knew this to be the result of her shock of that terrifying

Russian star. Her visual trauma had transferred its likeness to the forehead of her newly-born son!

Most Eastern European DP's wanted to get away from the Russians as fast and as far as possible. The Baltic peoples were especially motivated because they had experienced Stalin in 1940 – 1941 and understood the existential horrors he represented. The USSR was also making demands that the people who fled be returned to them, and some were. Sweden repatriated hundreds of Latvians who had fled there across the Baltic in small boats in a grab for freedom. Upon their forced return to Communist Latvia, they were sent to the Gulag as slave labor, or exiled to the harsh conditions of Siberia, or jailed or executed immediately. Another most wrenching example of this forced repatriation involved the Crimean Tatars, a Muslim minority in Crimea and Ukraine whose story was recounted earlier. Both the Swedes who sent the Latvians back and the British who sent the Tatars back publicly expressed their enormous guilt for years.

So our people were again under pressure, living in fear that a US, British, French and Russian negotiation would lead to their repatriation to Latvia, and a cruel fate under Stalin. After surviving the hot war, there was a chance that they could be forcibly returned to the Grand Executioner. So they waited in the DP camp, prayed, hoped, planned, and moved as far from the Russians as soon as they could.

Our group got permission to move to an UNRRA Camp deeper west in Germany, in the major city of Hannover. This was of critical importance because Berlin was surrounded entirely by the Russian vassal state of East Germany. While Berlin itself had a few islands of freedom in the British, French and American Zones, the rest of Berlin was the Russian Zone, with a Russian-controlled ocean surrounding the city. It was widely assumed, and correctly so, that the Communists would soon try to squeeze the free islands of food and goods, and take them over. This would bring the refugees stuck there back into a murderous position. The Commies did try to starve free Berlin into submission, but the famous Berlin Airlift, accomplished by the Allies heavily propped up by the US, defeated this attempt.

My parents and our families boarded trucks in Berlin and were driven west through the Russian controlled country of East Germany to West Germany on April 16, 1946. Sue and I have taken that ride, probably on a road closely parallel to the one that my people drove on so many years ago, and I could again sense the tension my parents must have felt. I also wonder if the fetus in my Mom - me - would have felt the chemistry of the events. Anna and Arnolds would have crossed the border after about 100 miles of travel, and only then would they have been able to breathe a sigh of relief, and probably smile again and feel the blood pressure drop. Until that border crossing, they were still under threat to be pulled off and arrested for some imagined reason. So getting into West Germany was a really, really big deal.

Hannover, another 40 miles west of the border, was in the British Zone of occupation of West Germany. The Camp there was huge, with housing in the typical old Army barracks. It was a multi-national camp, which was a style of camp that soon was viewed as suboptimal: humans tend to cluster with their own tribe where they feel more comfortable, with fewer cultural misunderstandings and less conflict. Also, as reported by Uncle Arturs, there was a lack of food. Mom told me that this was a bad place to be stuck, and no one liked this Camp. Since DP Camps in Germany were rapidly evolving, our people were on the lookout for a better situation, and preferred to be somewhere further from the Russians. So on July 13,1946, they moved again. They learned of a Baltic Camp - a "Letten Lager" - further west in Melle, near the city of Osnabruck. Our people stayed at this Camp until probably April 1948, almost 2 years, the longest single stretch in any one Camp. This was viewed as a serious upgrade, populated by mostly Latvians and Lithuanians with a shared cultural heritage.

6.9 MOM GIVES BIRTH; A MIRACULOUS VISIT TO MY BIRTHPLACE

It was in this area that Mom gave birth to me, on December 8, 1946. Near the Melle DP camp, about 12 miles south, was a former German Army hospital named Waldkrankenhaus, or the Forest Hospital, in the village of Bad Rothenfelde. Hospitals were often located in forests so that they were harder to spot and bomb. My Mother tells how the Nuns who worked in the hospital and lived on the hospital grounds were exclaiming that I would be a lucky child because December 8 is Immaculate Conception Day. I think this anointing by the Nuns helped my Mother keep a belief that good would ultimately happen to us, despite the dark times past and more dark times to come. She was right.

There are several interesting personal stories that surround that place of my birth, with again the workings of fate and good fortune evident. As an immigrant only child of a largely unknown ethnic tribe, with farmer parents who had limited educations and limited English skills, plus an unheard of first name, Indulis, I had a realistic and fatalistic view of where I fit into America. My birthplace - Bad Rothenfelde, Germany - only increased this negative stereotype of myself. The personal translation was that I was born in a Bad Rotten Field in the war crime-perpetrating nation of Germany. When I had to fill out paperwork or verbalize my birthplace to others, it was always with a sense of embarrassment and shame. Funny how certain feelings are remembered vividly for a lifetime.

Here the story changes. I planned and executed a several day trip to Germany in 1990, following a business trip to England. There were 2 objectives - first, I wanted to find my father Arnolds' grave, and second, I wanted to see the place of my birth. The first objective was met and was joyfully recounted as the lead story early in this book - and the second objective was also more than met.

Following my day of finding Arnolds in the Wolterdingen Cemetary, I arrived by rental car in Osnabruck and spent a night there. The next morning I was off to Bad Rothenfelde to see if the Waldkrankenhaus was still there. The short drive from Osnabruck/Melle took me into the Teutoburger Wald --a beautiful range of hills and forests, and the setting of Bad Rothenfelde. The Teutoburger Wald is historically very significant as the place where the Northern Legions of Rome were defeated in a battle - for the first time - by Germanic tribes in 9 AD. After this, Rome was limited to occupying only lands south of the Rhine River, which made most of Germany free of Roman control. Interestingly, the Germans were led by a brilliant general, Arminius, who had been a slave assigned to serve as a Roman soldier, but had defected to lead his brethren. He knew Roman tactics and routed his enemy. This was an event viewed as impossible; the Romans had been absolute military masters of wherever they wanted to go. So this hilly, forested area marked the furthest northern extent of the Roman Empire and its defeat here marked the beginning of the end of that Empire some 400 years later, and thus occupies a special spot in Roman and German history.

Lost in thought, I drove into Bad Rothenfelde. It is an absolutely gorgeous village - with the remains of a beautifully preserved fortified wall in the old parklike village square - clean, a tourist magnet, and lovely in all respects. This immediately dashed my old apprehensions of having been born in a "Bad Rotten Field"! Sensing that I was on a roll, I went to the Town Hall located on the square to ask if there was still a Waldkrankenhaus and where it might be. I also mentioned to the clerk that I had been born here. The clerk lady was extremely kind and helpful, and by combining her English with my broken German, was able to understand me. She said that my birth certificate might still be in that very office, and that she would look for it. In just a few minutes she returned... she had found it! This is quite a testament to German record-keeping. She made a copy, and it was so very precious to me since after 50+ years without a birth certificate, I finally had one, just like other kids.

On to the Forest Hospital. It was easy to find and I drove up to a locked gate, unmanned, with signs in German stating that this was a military facility. The hospital was an extensive array of barracks-type one story buildings spread throughout a large site with woods within and without the wall enclosing the facility. There was a buzzer button on the gate, so I buzzed. A Voice in German asked what I wanted. I told the Voice that I was born on the premises and hoped to more closely see the area. The reply - in broken English - was "that's not possible. This is a military base." Still feeling lucky, I told the Voice that I had told my Mother that I would try to get some pictures of the hospital where she gave birth to me, and I came all the way from America to do that. Yes, I unashamedly played the Mother Card, second only to the Grandchild Card in effectiveness! The Voice said "wait there a bit". I did, and soon a Sergeant appeared at the gate, checked my proof, and let me in. He spoke English and gave me a tour. Immediately to the front right was a low building where he said the Nuns used to live. Then we wandered around, him pointing out things, while conversing about the hospital and its relationship to my personal history. As we discussed my DP origins, he said that all DP's were birthed in one particular room, but he did not know where that was. In a few minutes, however, coming from a barracks to our left, another soldier appeared - the only other person we were to see that entire tour - and my Sergeant said that this guy knew a lot about the history of the hospital. They chatted, and the new guy said that he knew exactly the room in which all displaced persons' children were birthed! This room was in the barracks he had just left, and he would take us there. So a few minutes later, I was photographing in my birth room, which my Mother later confirmed to indeed be the right room. Again, an amazing coincidence - or something more?

Later, driving back toward Hamburg, I was again lost in thought, reflecting on Mom and Dad's life in the Camps and on their joy and worry about bringing a new life into their uncertain world. Mom never had doubts about birthing me, and I was looking forward to telling her of my adventures of the day, and hoping that the room was indeed The Room. While going through Osnabruck, I reviewed the stuff Mom had told me about the DP Camps, and what I had learned from the literature.

Melle-Osnabruck was a Baltic DP camp. It was probably a former German army barracks, consisting of long low buildings with the bunk rooms off a main corridor and common bathrooms. The rooms were usually subdivided by hanging blankets for enhanced privacy - but there was really no privacy. Kitija recalls that she and other friends would peek through knotholes in walls, and lift the privacy blankets to get a taste of forbidden adult life, sort of a young DP's real-life adventure TV. There were no kitchens, and the DP's would line up 3 times daily for food distributed and cooked by UNRRA, the UN DP Camp managers. UNRRA also had quickly found it best to segregate the various camps by nationality, which caused fewer problems then by having mixed camps.

The Baltic camps became recognized by the authorities as being really good places, the best of the lot. This sounds self serving, merely praising my own tribe, but the literature firmly and enthusiastically supports this view. Our Baltic peoples quickly established and elected camp leadership, started schools, began music and arts programs, policed themselves, and attempted fair distribution of food and other resources. Camps housing other nationalities apparently had many more issues. Some sound truly horrible and dangerous, perhaps reflecting the horrible conditions of their inhabitants prior to the War's end - people who were slave laborers or concentration camp survivors. Descriptions in the literature include high incidences of theft, drunkenness, violence, and open sexual behavior. There was also a difference between camps in the various occupation zones. My readings and the personal accounts of several friends (Milda, Aaron) who were in the American zone, in the south of Germany and in Austria, indicate that goods were more plentiful there by far then goods in the British zone, where we were.

UNRRA quickly realized that having masses of unemployed men was dangerous to camp life. Therefore they found work for these men - there was plenty that need doing in war-torn Europe - and paid these DP's to keep them busy and give them a sense of providing for their families, instead of fostering a welfare attitude. Forest work, construction, and clean up of the ruins were the common jobs. Our family and friends, however, were employed primarily as guards. These were positions of high trust. Guards had uniforms and worked in different places, often gone all week, traveling by rail, and tasked with controlling what was still a lawless condition in Germany. Crime, based on need and opportunism, was rampant. There was a breakdown of moral authority, plus a need for the basics of life. Ordinary standards had been severely lowered by the impact of common sights like death, woundings, torture, rape, starvation, etc. So the guard work was very important.

Women in the Camps were also kept busy with a child rearing, camp cleanliness/hygiene, teaching the kids, plus other paid jobs. While these were critical tasks for the survival of the families and the culture, they were more a natural outgrowth of Camp life, and less an assigned one. The emphasis of Camp administrators was clearly on keeping the males busy and out of trouble. Testosterone is a powerful drug often begging for controls.

My Mom also talked of the black market as being a big part of her life. Cigarettes were a de facto currency in postwar Germany, and UNRRA gave an allotment to each DP. Arnolds smoked, but Anna did not and used her cigarettes to buy other products. Aunt Elza would trade toothpaste for food. Everyone would opportunistically "liberate" potatoes, other edibles and flowers from unguarded area fields. Mom told me that some of her roughest moments where when I would be very hungry - and there was nothing to eat. This is what motivated the black market and other such activities. Hunger overcame shame.

6.10 DAD'S FINAL HOME

On April 14,1948 our group was moved to the Wolterdingen Baltic DP Camp, near the Village of Soltau, about 50 miles south the major German city of Hamburg. This Camp had been the site of a German SS

Camp during the War, and then housed some survivors of the nearby Bergen – Belsen concentration camp after the War, among others.

As mentioned earlier, I visited this Camp's remains in 1990, guided by Gabriell and Hildegard (or possibly Vilis and Erika?) who had miraculously led me to my father's grave earlier that day. Some of the buildings and roads were still there. It was a surreal experience to stand in the middle of this now-silent Camp, imagining the hustle and bustle that happened right here on a daily basis, with again the concentrated and varied emotions that had swept through this setting. There was the joy and happiness of babies arriving and children thriving, the sense of relative safety and a food supply, along with fear of an unknown future, and sorrow towards those left behind in captivity. To imagine Mom and Dad, their siblings, nieces and nephews all wandering around these same streets, sleeping in one of these barracks, and calling this place home was very powerful. For a bit, that's what I saw in my imagination. Then it was back to reality. Now, I believe the Camp has been flattened, and the surrounding area has become Heide Park, the largest amusement park in northern Germany. In several other trips to this area, I have been unable to find any remnant of the ruins of the Wolterdingen Camp, neither in person nor on Google Earth. I feel so blessed to have seen the Camp before the inevitable decay and a new layer of progress made it disappear.

The physical conditions and organization of the Wolterdingen DP Camp seemed about the same as described for most other camps. My father Arnolds was employed as a Watchman/Security guard, along with many other Latvian man, and was gone a week at a time, working in places that had a need.

It was then that things changed drastically for our small family. Arnolds was away in Valoniel, Germany, tasked with protecting a warehouse, and stationed on the roof. The warehouse appears to be a high one story building, judging from several photos. Dad was found, dead, on the concrete below on November 6, 1948, at the age of 40. Apparently death was instantaneous, caused by massive head trauma. His body, escorted by Uncle Arturs, arrived by train at the Wolterdingen stop, with a closed casket burial soon thereafter.

For years I searched for Valoniel, cited on the Dad's gravestone, but to no avail. Then a closer examination revealed "Waldniel" listed on Dad's death certificate, and finding Waldniel was simple. It is about 240 miles south of Soltau and the Wolterdingen DP Camp where we lived, and about 24 miles west of Düsseldorf - only a few miles from the Belgian border - in the heavily industrialized part of Germany. Waldniel is now incorporated into the town of Schwalmtal. Someday I still hope to visit this place and perhaps by another miracle find the location of this final warehouse, but we'll see. I would also want to take the train from there to Soltau/Wolterdingen, the same route by which Uncle Arturs brought my Father home to his final resting place in the Cemetery across the street from the train stop.

My Cousins, Aunt Elza, Uncle Arturs, and a few others who remember Arnolds have shared their recollections of him with me. He was apparently a humorous person who loved kids, played cards, smoked, drank socially, and was liked and respected by all. He did not like farm work, and chose to work in his town of Gulbene's administration, but he managed the farm well. He also made the right decisions about leaving Latvia, navigating the perilous path through Latvia and Germany to the DP camps, protecting his clan, and helping save Family Nogobods from the Russians at the Berlin train station at the War's end. Mom's portrait of him is more negative, which I will reflect on soon. On balance, Arnolds seems to have had many great qualities well recognized by others. My cousin Kitija says that my Mom was crazy in love with him, at least during the earlier years. Kitija also said that he was an exceptionally handsome man, and in true Kitija fashion once remarked that it was too bad that I looked more like my Mother then my Father!

Having no recollection of my Father is a void in my life. There are a few photos, some where he's holding me, and I have used a magnifying glass to hone in on his expression, searching for meaning. My under-standing and belief is that he was a good man and father, loved me, was at least a fair husband, perhaps with some flaws, but generally was loved and respected by those who knew him.

I also have two physical items of Arnolds' that have survived. One is his beer stein, a porcelain piece made in Germany and given to him as a wedding present in 1940. The arrival of the stein into my hands is also an interesting story. The people living in the Pommers' house in Latvia when I first visited it in the early 1990s gave me a beer stein, a creamer, and a small vase, saying that their pigs had uprooted these items randomly sev-eral years ago near the livestock barn. When I brought these pieces back to my mother, she identified them as her and Arnolds' wedding presents!! When our family fled in 1944 they buried certain valuables on the prop-erty, planning to reclaim them when they returned home. This was a very common practice. Unfortunately they, like almost all the others, never returned home, and their valuables and mementos may remain hidden and buried to this day, despite efforts of the locals to find them.

The other piece of physical evidence I have is Arnolds' signature. I was closely examining the few old family documents we have, and read a document from the German occupation time between 1941 and 1944 regarding my stepfather Aleks. It certified that he should not be drafted as a soldier into the German army because he was the only person capable of attending his land. At that time, farming was critical to provide the neces-sary foodstuffs for both the Latvian people and the German invaders. The town official who signed this document... was A. Pommers!

So these two of Dads' items exist, both so special to me. I occasion-ally take the beer stein out of our credenza, fill it with beer and sip from it lovingly. It produces an aching awareness that Arnold's hands did the same; that his lips touched the same rim; that we are somehow close for a short while...and that a smile crosses both our faces.

Mom was given a small survivor's death benefit by UNRRA upon Dad's passing. She converted it into a gold watch and a small diamond ring, which was a common behavior employed as a hedge to rampant inflation. Recently Sue and I converted parts of this jewelry into rings and pendants for our Daughters and Granddaughters. We hope that these pieces occasionally remind our progeny of their ancestor's lives.

There is some mystery surrounding Arnolds' passing, a darker side. My Mother was sure that he was having an affair, and that the boyfriend or husband of the paramour pushed him off the warehouse roof. So there is a murder theory. This could have been simply a made-up fantasy by my Mother - she did display some jealous behavior and had some conspiracy beliefs - or she might have embellished her experiences with Arnolds to the negative when explaining the death to me, for the purpose of making my stepfather, Aleks, look better in comparison to Arnolds. Or, it could be true. Anna's brother, my uncle Arturs, was also sure that Arnold's passing was not an accident, and thought that it was a purposeful murder. There is some testimonial evidence supporting the rumor of the affair, with the name of a distant relative cited as being the partner. We'll never know. But excepting these two closest players, others in the extended family have doubts about this version.

There was, however, commonplace bad behavior among men generally during this time. Drinking, fighting, stealing and promiscuity all reportedly played larger roles than in ordinary times. My theory is that when males have been denied by circumstances from their primary roles of family protection and breadwinning, their primal biological instincts of hypersexuality/ gene dispersement and aggression may get more airtime. Women also played into this; they were the willing partners in philandering, and probably appreciated the attentions of other men when their own spouses were busy providing for necessities and being less attentive. At any rate, there was a widespread breakdown in social order in all the DP Camps, understandably, and the Baltic Camps were better than many, but not immune.

Other possibilities surrounding Arnolds' passing certainly include illness, such as a stroke, or an accident, a simple slip or a trip from an uneven roof. But our lives changed at that moment and the consequences affected both Mom and I for the rest of our lives. I was 1 year, 11 months old when I last saw Arnolds, and I have no memories of my Dad at all.

In my opening to this book I documented that bizarre set of circumstances that occurred when I tried to seek Arnolds' final resting site. Although I am not a strongly spiritual or classically religious person, I feel that Arnolds has been my Guardian Angel, and has given me "evidence" of that several times in my life. Even if that is nothing but fiction, it has been comforting to me, and the possibility that it is not fiction is certainly intriguing.

So Anna continued life as a 36 year old widow with a young son, having lost her home, her country, her wealth, her livelihood, and now her husband. The pressures must have felt enormous. She probably pulled through for her son - me - and with the help of her mother, Berta, her brother Arturs and his family, and her circle of friends. Mom told me of a conversation she had with her mother, who reminded her that she also had lost her husband at a young age, that this was the way life sometimes went, and that you had to keep going and take care of your children. You simply had to survive - there was no other choice, no time for bemoaning your circumstances, just move forward. Anna did.

6.11 GOING TO AMERICA

Our final chapter in Germany was thus lived by just me and Mom. Life continued with its ordinary pace at the Wolterdingen Camp, and Latvians started to apply for residency in other nations, especially England, Canada, Australia and America. The aim was to get as far away as possible from the looming threat of Russian Communism, and find a place where the children would have an opportunity to live decent lives. These different target nations had differing needs and regulations on who might be allowed in. Fortunately, Latvians and the Baltic peoples were highly prized as immigrants, becoming the most favored group because their DP camps were well-ordered and relatively calm. This was presumed to reflect an industrious, honest, studious culture that would be a positive addition to the new country they might be entering, and not a cost or a problem. One of the earliest, and possibly first, resettlements were of a group of young Latvian girls who were accepted by England and worked there as nurses. England rapidly learned to respect and appreciate these young ladies to such a degree that they were eager to accept more Latvians, and other nations started to follow this example. All the former Baltic DP's owe a debt of gratitude to these first pioneers who by their exemplary behaviors paved the way for all the others. I apologize again if these statements sounds self-serving and could be viewed as merely overblown rhetoric about one's own culture, since the profound effects of culture are often minimized in the political correctness of present times. You can read the literature of the times on the UNRRA and IRO Camps for yourself, and see the written desires on immigration of the receiving nations; you will see that my comments are more rational than merely emotional. Yes, culture matters.

So the process of leaving Germany began. There were documents to fill out and medical exams to take. Arturs and Elza Nogobods and their children Kitija, Inara and Olita, plus Grandma Berta, were accepted into the United States. Our families left Wolterdingen and traveled to the Bedburg-Hau Camp, near the Netherlands border of north Germany, arriving there around July 29, 1949. This is in a historic WWII area, being 25 miles from the famous Nijmegen Bridge and only 15 miles from Arnhem, where Allied troops had fought and gained a foothold in Germany by crossing the Rhine River after D-Day. Bedburg-Hau had the infrastructure to start processing DP's before their departure for their new country. It was a place of great hope, along with worry that something might change and derail the process. If any family member tested positive during the numerous checkups for any of the illnesses common in those years, immigration could be denied. The Nogobods family successfully jumped through all the hoops, and was sponsored by the Lutheran Church of Colden, New York. But while the Nogobods gained a sponsor, Mom and I were still searching for someone to speak for us.

Paperwork completed and all requirements for immigration having been met, Family Nogobods traveled to Bremerhaven (the Port of Bremen), not far from Hamburg. Here they boarded their ship, the General Hann, on August 22 1950, and sailed to the Port of New York. Uncle Arturs in his memoir recalls the thrill of seeing the Statue of Liberty on August 29,1950. They were one of the last groups to be processed through Ellis Island, where immigrants had officially entered America for years; their names are on a remembrance plaque somewhere in the building complex. They then took a train to Buffalo New York, were met by their sponsors, the Millers and others, and driven to Colden, some 30 miles south.

The Lutheran Church of Colden was Pastored by Reverend Kleindienst, and Family Nogobods got lots of special assistance from the Miller family. Clarence Miller owned a lumber yard and he and his wife "Pete" were saintly people and helped Arturs' and Elzas' family (and later, Mom and me) tremendously. They were a childless couple who loved children and humanity in general, and our family may have filled a void for them. Their relative George Miller was also a huge force for good. These were people who lived their faith and were held in the highest regard by all of us immigrants. I remember them well. Sponsors such as these gave the new immigrants an initial helping hand, and guaranteed that the new arrivals would not become wards of the state. On the grounds next to the Lutheran Church stood a small house owned by George Miller, and the upstairs apartment was given to the Nogobods to get them started. Uncle Arturs notes that they moved into this house on his birthday, August 30. The kids started attending school, a difficult task since they spoke no English; Grandma helped around the house; and the parents began to work in the area. Some normalcy appeared in their lives.

Meanwhile, my Mother continued applying to leave Germany. Nations were reluctant to accept widows with young children, feeling that they would be a drain of needed resources. Countries all over the world were hurting after the War and needed to take care of their own citizens before extending a helping hand to others. But finally Mom was approved by a sponsor, Ray Petersime of Gettysburg, Ohio, whose family had founded the Petersime (Egg) Incubator Company. She was approved for immigration as a domestic/farm worker, apparently for the Petersime household. He was a prominent Christian who also had run for governor of Ohio, and still has a Chapel in his name on the campus of Manchester University, a United Brethren Church-affiliated school in North Manchester, Indiana. My eternal thanks goes to him; this approval permitted Mom to start the emigration process. While this was happening, Arturs and Elza were trying to get the Colden Lutheran Church to also sponsor my Mother and me, which they finally did. I think that change of sponsorship actually happened while we were in transit across the Atlantic. Again, the role of fate was to play such a prominent part in our drama. This change of sponsors put us on an entirely new vector for the rest of our lives.

6.12 ATLANTIC STORMS; PEACE IN AMERICA

Anna and I sailed out of Bremerhaven on January 14 1951 and arrived in New York City on January 25. I had just turned 4, and Mom was 37. We had to be checked again to make sure that we had no communicable diseases and were who we said we were, and not concentration camp guards attempting to hide from justice. Then it was off to Buffalo by a New York Central train, and to Colden by car. This is the moment of my first clear memory. George Miller, the Postmaster of Colden and part of our sponsoring group, picked us up in a Buick, smoking a cigar. I distinctly remember the "side hood vents" that were a trademark of the Buick in the 1950s, and I remember the pungent aroma of George's cigar. He took us to Colden where Mom and I briefly stayed with Pete and Clarence Miller - I clearly remember that our bedroom had a built-in bed in a wall niche. I can only imagine what this first night in America must have felt like for my Mother. To finally be in a safe place, with a roof over her head, plenty of food, no fears of arrest, rape, torture, execution, bombings, drowning, etc., and some hope for her own future and great hope for her son. Soon we were given a room in the apartment that the Nogobods inhabited. I'm sure it further cramped their already tight quarters, but that's what you did for family. Mom got a job in the bushel factory in Orchard Park, New York, where I believe Aunt Elza was already working in exemplary fashion, Grandma Berta babysat me, and I had the love and companionship of my cousins Kitija, Inara, and Olita.

To step back a bit - our trip across the North Atlantic in January of 1951 was not so smooth. Our ship was the "General W.C. Langfitt", a transport built in 1944 and assigned to the Military Sea Transport Service in 1950. It was 522 feet long, displacing 10,000 tons empty, and could handle almost 5,000 passengers. Many such ships were built to carry troops to and from the theaters of war. The name was derived from a Civil War Union General. A friend, George, recently located the ship's passenger list, and Mom and I are listed there as "I-977584 & 5, Latvian", along with Hungarians, Polish, Lithuanians, and other Latvians. I have photos of the ship and information on its history, but I could not locate the ships log. There was some erroneous information listing the ship as being scrapped many years ago, which lead me to stop searching for it. Later, I read that after the ship was decommissioned it was floating in a ship graveyard in Newport News, Virginia, only a several hours drive from my home in Annapolis, Maryland, in the early 2000's. It was finally cut up as scrap, but much later then my initial research indicated. It would have been easy to see the ship, if not visit it, had not its demise been erroneously reported.

I so wanted to find the ship's log because we ran into a major storm in the North Atlantic. My Mother told me that the ship was in serious danger and issued an SOS. Other ships in the area were diverted towards us to help in rescue efforts if we began to sink. The passengers were all lined up top side on the main deck with lifejackets on, ready to board the lifeboats. Then conditions abated and we made it through. I may have a single memory of this incident, which was food and silverware and dishes rushing at me across a table as the ship suddenly listed to a serious angle. It had to be both ironic and terrifying to Anna to have escaped the horrors of the War, to be finally on board the safety of a ship steaming its way to a promised land…only to almost immediately face an existential peril from the sea. Mom also told me that during this storm everybody was sick and vomiting for days in the sex segregated dormitory-type berths. I was one of the very few who was okay and I was given a job to fetch water for the dehydrated unfortunates. So my first job was as a waterboy at the age of four! I have also read the accounts of other DP's who had taken this same voyage on this same ship, only earlier, and they also encountered rough weather, a rocking ship, with lots of seasickness. My impression is that this class of transport vessels featured a very rough ride when in heavy seas.

Back to Colden. Arturs and Elza in 1953 built a house in nearby Orchard Park, New York. It was a four bedroom, one bath house, surrounded by fields, and became a site of many great memories in my youth. Mom got a menial job in Buffalo at the Gerber sausage factory (all our adult Latvians, despite being smart and speaking 4 languages, had to work well below their capabilities), and she and I moved into a boarding house at 58 Edna Place. Our space was upstairs, consisting of two small rooms with a common kitchen and bathroom down the hall. The other residents were all Latvians, renting from the Latvian owners. Cousin Kitija would stay with us occasionally as she attended beautician school in Buffalo.

6.13 LINGERING EFFECTS

Mom and many other Latvians were now relatively safe in America, while leaving many more of their fellow citizens behind the Iron Curtain. The ravages of a hot war was behind all of them, but their struggle with their recent history continued, and to a much greater extent than I had realized. Let me dwell on this for a bit.

In a social setting a few years ago that included a psychiatrist, Rod, some my family history was revealed. As we were leaving, Rod came up to me and softly asked, "how did your mother deal with her post traumatic stress disorder?" It now seems an obvious question, but I had never viewed my Mother, and the other Latvians of that generation, from that perspective. So that question has permeated my thoughts regarding Mom, Aleks and other extended family...and I now better understand their reactions to the circumstances of their lives. Rod's question also opened up my eyes to all the millions of survivors of that rough Neighborhood - the traumatized Ukrainians, Russians, Poles, Balts, Germans - and especially the Jewish population, a hunted people. They all had PTSD, of course. They all dealt with it in various ways for the rest of their lives, and sometimes it won.

Mom seemed to have survived her traumas relatively well, but she must have had nightmares and other relentless fears and anxieties to conquer. Knowing what could happen in life, having lived it, presents a burden, but one must move on, especially if one is raising a child. I remember her often being tense and having a non-stop assortment of physical maladies that she would characterize as "my special system", but she shielded much of her distress from me as an act of love. Mom was also limited in some of her horizons. If no one is knocking down your door at night, if you're not a slave laborer, if you have food and shelter, be satisfied. This is a low bar taught by bitter experience, but it allows more room for contentment, if not happiness. An example of this was her telling me, while a child, to reach for the stars and have a good factory job before she died! Of course, her hopes for me grew over time.

Others in the family were not so lucky. My stepfather Aleks - he was somewhat paranoid and schizophrenic, especially in his later years. Biology? The sociology of PTSD? Some of both? My Aunt Ida, who took care of cousin Maris in Canada - she became fully paranoid and was hospitalized in her last years - same questions. Or cousin Rita, imprisoned in the Gulag and then exiled - she was paranoid in her last years, seeing plots against her everywhere. Or Mom's first cousin, Roberts (Andris' and Vilnis' Jaunzemis uncle) - depressed, and finally a victim of suicide. Or cousin Ievina's estranged husband, also a suicide.

Yet most of our family did survive, having coping skills, attitudes and biologies that worked. Those strengths get passed on to future generations; that may be the sunlight through the clouds.

At this point Aleksandrs Siraks entered our lives, eventually becoming my Mother's second husband and my stepfather. I will detour from this narrative focused on Mom and Dad and the flight from Latvia to next cover the early life of Aleks, who had a different Latvian odyssey that also ended in America. Following that will be some chapters about the lives and challenges for those Latvians who stayed in Latvia, a most difficult and muted history that calls for more exposure. Finally, we'll finish with our family history in America.

CHAPTER 7

STEPFATHER ALEKS' STORY

7.1 FAMILY AND HOMESTEAD

Aleks Siraks, my stepfather, was probably born on December 18, 1916 according to the old Julian calendar. Around that time this old Russian calendar was switching to the modern western calendar which we currently use, so a bit after his birth his birth date was recorded as December 8, 1916 - and December 8 is also my birthday! To add to the confusion, his first name at different times was listed as Aleksandris, instead of the original Aleksandrs, and it is Aleksandris which appears on all his American records.

The Siraks family farm was named Jaun Usni (which roughly translates into "New Nettles"). It was located on a side road off the main highway, the P36, in a tiny area/hamlet named Stradi; this is the same highway where the Nogobods' and Pommers' homesteads were located. It was also the standard 60 hectares/150 acres in size, and it had been acquired later in time then the Pommers' and Nogobods' properties. This is what the "Jaun" (New) signifies. Since they were essentially neighbors, with only a few years of age difference, Aleks knew my Mother Anna and my Dad Arnolds plus their families for their entire lives, and vice versa.

I had very little information about Aleks' family, since I had not questioned him much about it, and he rarely began any conversations on the subject. During my September 2019 visit to Gulbene, hosted again by my dear friends and distant relatives, Aina and Vilis, I met with Anita, a grand-niece of Aleks (daughter of the daughter of Aleks' brother). Together with other relatives we visited the remnants of the Siraks farm, and Anita doubled my knowledge of Family Siraks. Aleks' paternal grandparents were Simanis and Anna Siraks - coincidently my Mothers' name after marrying Aleks - but the maternal roots are unknown to me. Aleks' father was named Otto. He had been first married to a neighboring lady who died young, whereupon he and his first wife's sister, Helena (nee Baskers), married, and raised a family. Their first born was Ida; next came Minna; then Janis, Aleks' only brother and grandfather of family historian Anita; next was Milda; and finally Aleks as the youngest. Mother Helena died in December of 1943, six months after father Otto had passed in June.

The two older sisters became fervent Communists early on, probably in the 1920s. Aleks viewed their actions as being traitorous and quasi-criminal, and he never forgave them. Any mention of their names and deeds were reacted to by Aleks with an amazing vehemence that never diminished. These two sisters had both married radical Bolshevik Communists, and then moved to Russia to support the cause. As Lenin died and Stalin filled the leadership vacuum over Trotsky, Stalin began to murder the vanguard Communists under the cold calculation that his rivals for power would come from this early pool of fervent believers. Somewhere during this time, the sisters' husbands were killed, and the sisters became enemies of the people in Russia - a horrible designation.

Ida, the eldest sister, had lived somewhere in Russia with her husband and 2 children, Karlis and Edvins, both now deceased. After her husband's murder, Ida and her sons eventually moved back to Riga. Ida was a physician, and apparently remained a devoted Communist and had a significant political role in Riga. She has been long deceased. I am always amazed at the attitudes of people like Ida who suffered greatly under Communism and its henchmen, but remained unabashedly loyal to the dictates. Literature of the era reveals a substantial minority of victims that felt this way. My guess is that if one was to abandon such deeply held beliefs despite such horrible consequences, the believer's life would be empty and embarrassingly stupid, and the ego would not permit this death of the soul.

Minna, the next oldest sibling, had a similar tale. Same as Ida, she married a Latvian Bolshevik, went to Russia - where her husband was murdered - and then settled in the Ukraine. She also had 2 sons, Karlis and Alfreds, whose fates are unknown. Karlis was apparently an avant garde artist and every summer, for years, would visit the Siraks homestead and paint the barn that Aleks had built, along with the remains of other buildings on the farm, in wild patterns. Had Aleks known what Minna's son had done to his barn, he probably would have lost it! Aleks did view that barn, still mostly standing during his visit in 1993, but there was no crazy art work on it, thank God. Minna also has been long gone.

The early support shown for Communism by Latvians such as Aleks' older sisters was very common. Latvia had been ruled by German Barons and Russians Czars forever, with the Latvians being mere serfs. The advent of Communism in Russia in 1917 seemed a wondrous philosophy, promising heaven on earth and plenty for all. It consequently attracted many followers among the downtrodden Latvians - along with many enemies, as reports started arriving of the cruelty of the Communists as they began their murderous rule in Russia. So Aleks' family was a microcosm of the political turmoil of the times, with hatreds that lasted a lifetime.

Aleks' lone brother was named Janis. He died quite young, probably in the 1930s, and left 3 children behind, Biruta (1927-1991), Velta (1929-2015) and Gunars (1931-1994). Biruta, married to Grigori Saveljevs, was the mother of my Siraks' family historian, Anita, and her brother Janis.

Alek's other sister, Milda, survived until old age and the siblings were able to meet again in 1993. I had taken Aleks to Latvia after its independence from Russia and witnessed the reunification of a brother and sister after nearly 50 years of virtually no contact. It was a most touching moment. As much as Aleks hated his two older sisters, he absolutely loved and revered Milda. Interestingly, my Mom had refused to go back to Latvia with us on this trip, saying there were too many bad memories for her to handle.

Milda's story is a sad one, and so typical in many ways of the fate of numerous Latvians while under Russian domination. She and her husband had two daughters, Ieva and Astra, whom I got to know a bit. The husband was a telephone worker. During one of the Russian inroads, either in 1941 or 1944, he was arrested and executed, with no particular reason ever cited. When that type of tragedy happened, the family would be declared as "Enemies of the People". This was a very serious charge that drastically altered all aspects of life, and all for the worse. They were often shunned by others, with friends, coworkers, strangers and even family being fearful of guilt by association. Jobs, income, housing, and social life all were relegated to second class status. Well into the 1950s there was a constant, grinding fear of arrest, execution, exile or the Gulag for families so designated; they could be easy targets for denunciation to the KGB by others seeking to curry favors with the authorities, a common practice. This environment changed people well after the harshest threats had actually lessened, starting with the reign of Nikita Khrushchev. Milda's family survived all this, but sadly, the daughters seemed deeply wounded, victims of this evil.

Aleks grew up on the family farm, doing all the wide range of typical chores that the agricultural life required. He also attended school - I visited the site, a beautiful old building - but only to about the sixth grade, when he had to quit to help on the farm.

Aleks was a natural born engineer, one of those people who could see how parts fit together to make machines, or anything else, work to their desired function. He was quite brilliant in this phase of life, and with a better background would have been very successful in any engineering profession. As an example of this, he built a radio out of various parts, probably in the early 1930s, and without the help of guidebooks or the Internet. He also architected and then built a large barn which survived at least until 1993, when he and I visited the area. According to Grandniece

Anita, Aleks was widely known and respected as a very progressive farmer. New, best practices were adopted, and results bore out his wisdom in doing so. For example, his cows were known to produce the best milk in quantity and quality, and other area farmers went to Aleks for advice. He also was a beekeeper, and I remember him reminiscing about the complexities of honeybee behavior.

In his first trip back to Latvia, Aleks and I walked across his former family's fields, and entered the barn he had built. It was still proudly standing, though getting rundown from lack of attention. This was all that was left of the Siraks' homestead. As was apparently common practice, a huge hole had been dug by bulldozer, with the house and other buildings shoveled into the hole, covered by dirt, and turned into a farmed field when the Communists incorporated this farm into a larger collective farm in the late 1940s. Seeing this structure at a distance, then crossing the field on foot toward the looming barn, and finally entering it with Aleks, was a very emotional experience for both of us. Aleks seemed to be in an altered state, with his mind flooded by memories of the familiar fields, the life his family had lived there, the people to whom this was home, all triggered by the single stark reminder of all that - his barn.

When I returned just a few years later, the barn already gone. Perhaps it waited for Aleks to return before finally collapsing, at the behest of a Guardian Angel? In Sue's and my visit in 2019, some of the stone side walls and entryways still remained standing, impervious to the hazards of time, as if to serve as a gravestone to the Siraks' family. This silent empty field and its single monument marked the work, joy, births, deaths, drama and sadness of a family.

Aleks recalled the 1930s as good times, despite the worldwide recession. Their farm was sufficiently successful to feed them all; there was a roof over their heads; Latvia was free; and the governance of the Karlis Ulmanis administration - a benign dictatorship - worked well for country-folk. So the remaining family - Aleks, his mother and father, sister Milda, and brother Janis - farmed in relative peace and comfort. Aleks sang in the Gulbene choir (we have an old photo), hunted for deer, boar, rabbits and such, and started a lifetime passion for fishing, specifically mentioning the lovely Pededze River which flowed a few miles away. The catch would include pike, yellow perch, and "foreles", a trout. He was an accomplished outdoorsman both by training and instinct. Although they had horses, he did not mention his own horse to me. Instead, he talked about riding his bicycle a lot, including 35 mile trips to places like Madona where I believe his sister Milda lived after her marriage. The sad note was that his only brother died during this time, and Aleks was always very emotional about this loss.

7.2 LIFE AS CANNON FODDER

In the late 1930s Aleks was drafted into the Latvian Armed Forces. This began a fascinating military odyssey. He is one of the relatively few people who was a member of three separate armies in the same war. Two of them, the Russian and German Armies, were in severe opposition throughout Word War II, characterized by extreme homicidal hatred, while the third was the Latvian Army, a tiny neutral force between these two major combatants. It must have been mind-warping to hear vicious propaganda spewed by Army A about B…and soon be marinating in horrible propaganda delivered by B against A, which you had just left. Words must lose their meaning when used as weapons from such contrasting perspectives; it was an absurd insanity.

Aleks' military assignment was as a "Sapper", or military construction engineer. Besides designing and building fortifications, pillboxes, tank traps and so on, sappers also were the demolitions experts who blew bridges, laid and disarmed minefields, and then would became frontline troops to fill in for casualties among the infantry. This was very dangerous work, and apparently Aleks was quite good at it, resulting in the Latvian Army promoting him.

The Molotov– Ribbentrop Pact between Germany and Russia in 1939 delivered Latvia to the Russians. As World War II broke out, the Russian Communists entered the country (June 15-17, 1940) and Latvia had no choice but to surrender. The Latvian President, Karlis Ulmanis, was summoned to Moscow, forced to sign an invitation for the Russian troops to enter and "save" Latvia, whereupon he was arrested, imprisoned and tortured, shipped to the Siberian Gulag, and soon killed. The Russian military then took over the Latvian Army. Their first move was to murder much of the local officer corps, and replace them with Russian Army officers and Communist political operatives (variously named KGB, NKVD, "Chekists", etc.). These psychopathic groups conducted continuous indoctrination sessions and did a search and weeding out of potentially unreliable Latvian soldiers. Aleks recounted an interview session with the political officers where they asked about his class background, occupation, whether he hired other workers for the farm - hunting for "exploiters of the proletariat" - and felt his hands to see if they were "soft", indicating a bourgeois background, or "hard" (calloused), indicating a working class background. Aleks passed, having "hard" hands. The stress of such a grilling had to be extreme, and added to the other horrors of Aleks' life. One does not get past this without scars.

7.3 A LUCKY BREAK

Aleks began the years 1940 - 1941 as a newly drafted member of the Russian Army. Around June 25 1941 the German blitzkrieg reached Latvia and the Russians were in full retreat. Aleks' Russian unit headed east to the Russian border marked by a river - my Gulbene guides Vilis and Aina think it's called Ritupe - and crossed a bridge into Russia. The commanding officer sent two men back to the bridge to blow it up. Aleks was one of the chosen. This became a key moment which radically altered every downstream event of the rest of his life. The two sappers went back, prepared the bridge with explosives, and then made the fatal decision to cross the bridge back into Latvia, and only then demolish it. This made them deserters from the Red Army, a crime punishable by summary execution. It also put them in severe danger as Red Army-uniformed men advancing toward the German Army. The remainder of Aleks' Red Army unit was never heard from again. Was Aleks chosen because he was an outstanding explosives expert? Did he have some special connection with the decision-making officer, who knew that whomever was picked would use the opportunity to desert? Or was it merely random luck? Whatever the cause, it serves again as a stark reminder of the role of fate and fortune in life.

I unfortunately don't know the details immediately following the blowing of the bridge, or how close the front was at that time. I wish I had asked questions of Aleks more persistently. The two deserters must have ditched their Soviet uniforms, acquired other clothes, and stealthily made it back to their homes. Did locals help them? Did they "borrow" civilian clothing? Did they walk or hitch rides, or "borrow" bikes? What was the first contact with the Germans like? Did it happen somewhere on the road, or when Aleks reached Gulbene, among neighbors who would vouch for him to the German authorities? Again, the stresses were immense, and lasting.

Grandniece Anita didn't know the details of Aleks' trek home - remarking that people didn't talk much in those times - but knew that Aleks suddenly appeared at the Siraks family farm. He found his brother Janis' widow and her 3 children living there (one of the children being Anita's mother), plus his Mom and Dad. The date was probably in late June or early July of 1941. He began his farming activities again, and was largely left alone since the growing of food was important both for the citizens of Latvia and their German occupiers.

Two years later his Dad died. Aleks never told me of the circum- stances of his father's passing and unfortunately I didn't ask. Supposedly the two got along well, and Otto was a decent, hardworking man, and a good father and husband. Six months after that, in December 1943, his Mom died, and there is a heartbreaking tale associated with that sad event.

Aleks had just been taken into the German army and requested leave as Helena was near death. He was denied. This broke his heart, illustrative of his very deep affection for her. Later in life, the sad sentiment of that event would occasionally break through to the surface of this ordinarily stoical man. A great mother is always greatly missed.

7.4 RUSSIANS, REDUX

The Germans began losing the War due to a combination of a horrible Russian winter in 1943-1944 and the continual Allied assaults on both the Eastern and Western fronts. Their supply lines were severely overextended, and they had foolishly anticipated a quick takeover of Moscow. When the Russian resistance stiffened at the gates of Moscow, Hitler's plans for a quick victory went awry, the brutal winter set in, and the Germans were left totally unprepared. As the Germans retreated back from Russia and through Latvia, they took all the Latvian man they could and drafted them into the German Army. Two SS "Volunteer" units were formed, the 15th and the 19th, filled with Latvian conscripts. Aleks was drafted into the 19th unit. Some Latvians were eager to join, having found via bitter experience that for Latvians, Russians were vastly more murderous than the Germans. Most, like Aleks, simply wanted to survive but had no choice - all were take forcefully by the Germans since Germany was running out of men. Having deserted the Red Army, Aleks faced certain death if captured by the Russians, so his only chance at life was through the Germans. Thus Aleks found himself in the third Army of his World War II experience, this time retreating through Latvia.

In popular understanding, SS units have been presented only as radical Nazi volunteers, the leading military fist of the German Army. That certainly was true at the beginning of the Nazi period, but it started to change as Germany swarmed over its neighbors. Some men in the German-conquered lands of Western Europe joined the SS of their own free will, often as true believers, including volunteers from Finland, Sweden,

Norway, Denmark, Holland, Belgium, Spain, France and Switzerland. But as the War progressed with growing Nazi losses, Germany started drafting men from these nations, including Latvia. The "Latvian Legion" began in January 1943 with the forming of the 15th SS Division, with some volunteers initially but most being drafted; it fought only on the Russian front. In January 1944 the second Latvian unit, the 19th, was formed. Just prior to this is when Aleks was taken. His unit also fought only the Russians, and was instrumental in the stalemate on Latvia's Courland peninsula that lasted until the War's end, after the main front was hundreds of miles to the west in Berlin. This unit had a remarkable record, fueled by the existential fear of losing to Russia. It was so distinguished that SS leader Himmler called for Latvia to remain an independent country after Germany had won the war, as repayment - but this was rejected by Hitler.

It appears that the only factor for the Latvian SS units was the fear of Soviet Bolshevism, fueled by first-hand experience. Soldiers were fighting to give their Country the only chance, however negligible, of freedom. Fighters were willing to die on the battlefield with honor rather than live in Communist paradise. Following an earlier UN edict, the US Displaced Persons Commission finished its research into the actions of the 15th and 19th units and concluded in 1950 that these Latvian regiments were conscripted against their will, were entirely different than the German SS units, and played no role in the war crimes of the Holocaust. In fact, members of the 15th and 19th played very prominent roles as guards at the Nuremberg war crime trials. This was the backdrop that freed Aleks to later leave Germany and live in America.

Let's return to Aleks' individual story, picking up from the retreat of his unit from Courland. To my surprise, Aleks describes this retreat as relatively benign - but I would not be surprised if he understated the situation either out of modesty or a desire to stop the conversation. It seems that his specific unit was minimally engaged in the horrible front-line action that dragged on in the Courland Peninsula, that western part of Latvia in which Aleks' unit fought. This conflict is famous in military history since it was fought over and never won by either side until the War ended. The Russian advance to the West actually went around this peninsula, through Poland and on to Berlin, leaving Courland isolated, surrounded by Russians on one side, the Baltic Sea on the other side, with no resolution. Aleks' unit retreated to the port of Leipaija, that same city from which Anna, Arnolds and the others had departed earlier to reach Gdansk, Poland. Somewhere near Leipaija he was wounded by shrapnel from Russian artillery, being hit in the knee, leaving a scar but without any major damage. Next, Aleks probably arrived in Danzig, Germany (now Gdansk or Gdyna, Poland) by German troopship, but that arrival point is a guess on my part. That late in the War, the ship may have steamed further west to a port in Germany. This being right at the end of active conflict, the German army was literally falling apart. Aleks described that his small group - perhaps 10 or 12 Latvians - split off on their own, hugging the Baltic coast in Poland and Germany, trying to avoid hotspots, and with a single objective - finding non-Russian Allied troops and surrendering to them. They had to avoid capture by the Russians at all cost, since that would be a death sentence. Unfortunately, Aleks' commanding officer was killed in action during this retreat, so it was not without peril.

7.5 POW; DP; AMERICA

So as World War II ended in early May 1945, Aleks' small unit finally encountered British troops in northern Germany. They surrendered without incident. Then the next travail began. Initially, the British Army did not know how to deal with them. They were officially German SS troops, who as a category had earned the reputation of being the most strident Nazis, the executors of atrocities throughout Europe. Thus Alex and his unit, along with all the other Latvians under the German flag, were taken as prisoners of war and sent to a POW camp in Belgium. At first conditions there were rough. It was a crowded and unsanitary facility, with insufficient food. Latvian officers were beaten. But soon the world responded appropriately, and a UN declaration acknowledged that these Latvian SS troops were draftees with no choice in the matter, and were not German war criminals. They were then released and treated as Displaced Persons, joining the other Latvians who had fled as civilians - such as my Mother and Father.

Thus ended Aleks' military life, the final chapter of having served in three armies. He got no pension, no special military health care, no embraces from a grateful nation…no nothing. How sad. Although Aleks never complained, it must have been so hurtful to have his war odyssey simply overlooked by all, as if it had no meaning. There wasn't even a Country to go back to. Like his service, it too just disappeared.

After release from the POW camp, there is a picture of Aleks, very slim and scrawny, looking somewhat starved. Through some old documents, I could trace some of his "employment" in post-war Germany, which was much like that of the other DP's: guarding various sites, working on forestry, farms and as factory labor, and so on. Soon he found where the Latvian DP camps were and where his old Latvian neighbors now lived. This brought him to the Wolterdingen camp where our extended family and former neighbors all lived - and near which Dad was eventually buried.

Going back a bit - when I first found Arnolds' grave site, the Latvian gentleman (probably Gabriell) who miraculously helped me also brought me to the Wolterdingen Camp remains, some of which still existed as ramshackle barracks and overgrown roads. I was led to the foundation of what had been a hothouse, and Gabriell told me that he remembered the night that the former Latvian POWs arrived at the Camp. This included Aleks. Gabriell said that they arrived very late, and spent their first night in the Camp sleeping in the hothouse, before they were assigned ordinary quarters the next day. Fascinating, again, how my Latvian guide knew both the location of Arnolds' gravesite and the circumstances of Aleks' first night in Wolterdingen, insights into the hidden lives of the two most important men of my life.

Aleks then merged into the traditional Latvian DP's life in Germany, working as a guard and applying to other countries to take him as a refugee. Eventually he was approved to enter the US, and took the ship into the Port of New York in 1952. Work had been arranged for him at the Gaylord Sanitarium in Meriden, Connecticut, and that organization may also have been his sponsor. The Sanitarium was a health facility, probably for TB, as well as a working farm. Aleks was employed as a farmhand; an old picture shows him working with the dairy herd. To get to this point, Aleks again had to provide proof of his noncriminal past and good character. There are documents and testimonials that certify that he was not a war criminal, did not have a drinking problem, was generally of good character and a hard worker.

Upon arrival at the Port of New York - where Aleks snapped a classic immigrant's photo of the Statue of Liberty rising out of the sea fog - he was given some donated used clothing. One of the items, a sport coat, had a dollar bill folded in a pocket. That was his financial starting point in America, and Aleks was very appreciative of the stranger that had donated both the coat and the dollar.

Due to the suspension of mealtimes while entering the Port, docking, disembarking the ship and registering, Aleks had not eaten for a day. He then got on a prearranged train and arrived at the Sanitarium late in the day, past the mealtime. The next morning, he was invited to breakfast and the servers could see that he was extremely hungry, and gave him several breakfasts. He fondly recalled these as the best breakfasts ever, and always remembered the kindness of these servers. I have driven past Gaylord Sanitarium several times, and it still exists in Meriden, Connecticut as of several years ago. Simply seeing the place, the barns, the driveways, the fields, helped to bring Aleks' stories to life.

Housing there was in a dormitory. He received a room and board plus a small salary, as did all the other DP's who worked there. Since Alex had little English and limited transportation means, he basically had no place to go. Consequently, he saved all his money. It helped that he was not a smoker or drinker - in fact, he actively despised both of these activities, having too often witnessed the downsides of drunken behavior through-out the tumult that was his life. His frugality allowed him to live a decent life, and I have no doubt that he was an outstanding employee, thorough, reliable, and trustworthy. He started to save money for a car, which was of extreme importance to him and reflective of his lifetime love of cars and driving. Soon he had enough saved to buy a 1952 green Studebaker Coupe - a "Commander" model. Studebakers at the time were very advanced in their styling and were a leading-edge sort of car, even though they went out of business within a decade or so. This brand had also been shipped to Europe both during and after the end of World War II to fill gaps caused by bombed car factories and disruption of the local automotive supply chain, and the Studebaker had achieved cult status in Europe for styling and reli-ability. Specifically, the Russian Army received many Studebaker trucks through the generosity of America, and perhaps that is where Aleks got his familiarity. So Aleks quickly achieved an objective, a car that made him feel good and could transport him mentally and physically away from the struggles of his recent past. In a life full of difficulty and disappointment, that moment of driving off in his own car must have felt so good - I can visualize Alek's broad grin, reflecting the joy in his heart.

7.6 COURTING; MARRIAGE

During his vacation times, Aleks started to drive. He visited other Latvians in eastern Canada and the US, since lines of communication had by now been established by the countrymen. He became a photography nut, developing his pictures in darkrooms he would create wherever he lived. Consequently, there were many pictures of the people and places he visited, including some pictures of ladies that he may have dated during these trips. Men were still in somewhat scarce supply with so many casu-alties during the War, resulting in increased competition for single males.

But these hundreds of photos did not survive. Sadly for me, my Mother Anna destroyed them all years after she married Aleks, telling me upon my questioning that she did not need reminders of Aleks' life as a single male! Yes, Mom had some jealousies.

It was on one of these travels that Aleks visited upstate New York - specifically, 58 Edna Place in Buffalo, New York - where my Mother and I rented two rooms with a shared kitchen and bathroom. Here the courtship of Aleks and Anna began. After numerous visits to Anna, Aleks and Mom decided to go to the next step. Aleks moved from Connecticut to Buffalo, and got a job as a helper machinist for the New York Central Railroad. This move involved some sacrifice of potential on his part. A non-DP friend he had made at the Gaylord Sanitarium, called "Dore", a young hard-working French Canadian, wanted to start a construction company with Aleks as his partner. It may have been a great team, with both partners apparently being thorough, conscientious and honest workers with engineering minds. But Aleks wanted to be with Anna, and they moved in together (plus me!) to larger quarters several blocks away, at 134 Best Street, Buffalo. This was a two bedroom apartment, and I actually had a bedroom from 1954 - 1956 - incidentally, my last private bedroom until I went to college. On February 27 1955 they got married, and I now had a stepfather. The excitement of having a father, like other kids, is still very vivid to me after all these years; and the other strong memory I retain is the color of my Mother's wedding dress - forest green.

CHAPTER 8

THOSE WHO STAYED:

LATVIAN LIFE UNDER COMMUNISM

The preceding chapters presented a narrative about my close families' lives, travails, and escape from Latvia, serving to illustrate conditions of their 200,000 countrymen who fled. Next, I present some insight about the circumstances for the Latvians who remained in Latvia under Russian rule from 1940 - 1941, and again 1944 - 1991. This would also have been the story of my immediate family in Gulbene had they stayed in Latvia.

Here is some information about the Communist activities during the early part of their reign, based on research by a consortium of Latvian historians. During the first occupation from June 1940 to June 1941, called the "Baigas Gads" (Year of Terror), officially some 21,000 Latvians were repressed, although this is a fuzzy number that does not include summary executions. Over 5000 were arrested, and of these 700 were shot, and more than 3400 of them died in the Gulag - an 80% fatality rate. Andrei Vyshinsky, the infamous Soviet prosecutor of the chilling show trials in Russia during the 1930s, was the main representative for the Soviets in Latvia, and he appointed the Latvian Augusts Kirkensteins as the official leader. By May of 1941 there was an official measure passed in Moscow to remove from the three Baltic nations all "Anti-Soviet, Criminal and Socially Dangerous Elements". In practice, this included disfavored political parties and anti-Soviet organizations; the Home Guards, local police, and former officers; landowners with more than 30 hectares and other successful farmers; business owners and former bureaucrats; as well as actual criminals. This was the basis of the June 14 -15 1941 deportations and arrests.

To review, the entire Nogobods' family had been visited by the Chekists/KGB on June 14 1941 and told to prepare one suitcase each and wait to be picked up by a truck that would take them to the train station in Gulbene...but no one stopped for them. Thus Arturs, Elza, Kitija, Inara, Olita and Grandma Berta never made it to the train station, yet had unknowingly started their long trip to America. My parents Arnolds and Anna escaped into the woods upon receiving miraculous notice that they were targeted for deportation, or worse, and thus also ultimately escaped.

Many escaped, but some of the relatives were taken. Fricis Jaunzemis was sent to the Gulag while his pregnant wife Alise and daughters fortunately were spared. Our cousin Rita Jaunzemis slaved in the Gulag and then exiled for a total of 16 years. Cousin Kitija's future brother-in-law, Uldis, was taken in 1941 and survived 8 years in the Gulag plus 8 more in exile in Russia. My Stepdad Aleks' nephew was executed. Other luckier members of our family who stayed simply rode it out.

Thus our extended family suffered all of the three outcomes for those who would or could not flee from Latvia. Some, typically women and children, were deported or exiled to inhospitable places in Russia to work as slaves on state farms or industries. Others, more often men, were tried and executed or sent to the Gulag camps to slave in the brutal conditions in mining, forestry, RR construction, road building and so on. The third group remained in Latvia and tried to survive the threats leading to the other two fates. Here's a closer look at these three conditions, with added details and quantification to add substance to the stories.

The tales of the deported and arrested Latvians were not told for many years. Survivors spoke only guardedly about their experiences until the 1990s. This was a silence of 40+ years, broken only after the Communist regime wilted away. The victims who were eventually released, often after 10 to 25 years in exile or the Gulag, had to sign documents stating that they would not talk about these experiences; plus, they were simply terrified. But in the 1990s, the first-hand experiences began to be told by many, not just by the few heroic earlier souls like Solzhenitsyn, Ginsburg, and Shalamov, and so the silence was finally broken.

8.1 THOSE DEPORTED: STORIES OF WOMEN AND CHILDREN

A Latvian lady, Melanija Vanaga, who survived the 16 years of deportation horrors, wrote a memoir entitled "Suddenly a Criminal: 16 Years in Siberia". Recently this has also been made into a movie entitled the "Chronicles of Melanie". What makes this is especially interesting to me is that Melanija was arrested in Cesis, a beautiful town some 50 miles west of Gulbene, and she was on the June 14 1941 train that went from Cesis to Gulbene, stopping there to pick up our relatives and neighbors. This train then continued into Russia, and deep into Siberia. Had our family been snared in this net, as the Communists had planned, this would probably have been their exact story. So, to illustrate the typical life of deported Latvians, I have summarized some of Melanija's experiences, buttressed by information from the many other books, discussions with different family members, documentation in museums, internet information, and YouTube videos.

"Get Ready To Leave"

On June 14 1941 the Nogobods family home, like thousands of others, was entered by armed Chekists and told to pack some bags and wait for a truck to take them to the train. This was the very typical way that the journey began. No questions were answered, no advice given on what to pack, with standard platitudes offered to keep people compliant and non-resisting ("don't worry, everything will be fine"). Fortunately, the Nogobods never were picked up and my Mom and Dad escaped to the woods, but most were not that fortunate. A truck would arrive, the people and their bags would be hustled aboard to join the other unfortunates, and this process would be repeated until the truck was full. It then disgorged its passengers at the train station, at all times under armed guard. Immediately the men - with few exceptions - would be separated, and for most, this would be the last time they would see one another. Some would be in stunned silence while others would be sobbing and wailing in terror; children would pick up on the extreme emotions and react by clutching their mothers and siblings, screaming and crying. All would be quickly hustled aboard the waiting cattle cars until each was crammed full, and then bolted in.

Train Trip To Hell

This train at Gulbene station had about 90 barred cattle cars, outfitted with two levels of wide planks along the interior walls. Being the second stop, there were already many prisoners enclosed by the time it reached our families' area. According to Melanija Vanaga, who had been put on the train with her husband and son in Cesis, the train had stopped in a pine forest en route to Gulbene and there was machine gun fire for about a half hour. Murdering of unarmed citizens thus began early. Apparently some male prisoners in different cars had loosened their bars and tried to escape - but their fate is unknown. The odds of survival would be poor.

The train left the second stop at Gulbene on June 15 and traveled to Daugavpils, in the extreme south east part of Latvia, right next to the Russian border. The inmates were hungry, thirsty and terrified. More people were pushed into the cars. At 4 AM a.m. on June 18 the convoy left, to the sound of gunshots as executions of men continued. The route then took them to Indra, the first town inside Russia, and on to other railroad stations such as Devosa, Drisa, and Velikije Luki, all on the way to a larger station, Mga. This was the standard route for deportation transport from Latvia, as has been described by Ms. Vanaga and many others.

For the inmates, exhaustion, hunger, thirst, and fear grow exponentially. They were being reduced to animal status. Some started to panic, while some went literally crazy - but there was nowhere to escape. One mother aboard Melanija's wagon killed her three children with a razor; these poor victims were buried next to the track. Let the sheer horror of that sink in. The other women and children in the wagon witnessed this, and were changed forever. I wonder how Mom and Aunt Elza could have survived these circumstances - how does one respond to witnessing moms killing their kids? Or the ripping away of their husbands, while hearing gunfire along the tracks? How could Aunt Elza have comforted and cared for her three daughters in these insane circumstances? How do you swallow the sheer terror of every moment, and still function? Would Grandma Berta have had any chance of surviving?

Soon an epidemic of dysentery began among the inmates. This was very common on all prisoner transports, and is continually mentioned in the literature. Since the toilet was merely a small hole in the floor, and there are 30 people stuffed into each car, sanitary conditions were nightmarish. More people started to die - a total of 12 out of 30 in Melanija's car. Of the 5 Nogobods that were to be on this train, plus perhaps my Mom, how many would have survived? Who of our family would have been lost?

The inmates were fed every 2-3 days. For this Cesis - Gulbene train, the "food" was mashed corn with some oil on top. People started to use up the food they had brought from home, and a wide variety of human behaviors under stress started to manifest; some shared food, some stole it - but it got harder and harder to remain "normal". On most transport trains, the typical meal was heavily salted herring fish. This was a form of exquisite torture, as is reflected in all the writings of the prisoners who survived. Salted herring causes overpowering thirst, and drinking water was often withheld because it was hard and possibly dangerous for the guards to distribute it - as well as it being an unpleasant task to open the cattle car doors and observe the inhumane conditions inside. Since this would all grow progressively worse further into the trip at an accelerating pace, the guards often simply did not provide water. Also, as was told by guards in the literature, if prisoners were given water, they would then be urinating more frequently, causing an unhealthy, unsanitary mess - so the solution was to let them be thirsty. My, how the Communists cared for the masses! Such love!

Dear reader, please try to visualize the scene, painful as it might be. Imagine the wails and moans of thirst-crazed people; the screams of those out of their minds; the sounds of retching and diarrhea; the visions of fellow humans falling apart before your eyes; the dead and dying all around you, especially the old and very young; the smells of humans becoming animals. This was the environment of the trains. But the guards were also in a tricky situation, in effect also prisoners of the system. The Communist creed, which judged people on their class backgrounds, had declared all these inmates to be class enemies, incorrigible by natural law, and a threat to the "heaven on earth" that socialism would provide. No mercy was to be shown to these unfortunates. Public proclamations and rules actually declared that mercy to class enemies was in itself a crime, and sometimes humane guards soon became the guarded. Again, I personalize these conditions to my Mom, dear Aunt, Cousins and Grandma - how can this be? How can a political system allow this to be done to humans? It is truly beyond comprehension, and causes a blinding rage towards the people who managed this, and those who created a political system that sanctioned and rewarded this outcome. Why have the perpetrators escaped with little outcry from the civilized world? Where are the commissions from the World Courts at least citing these atrocities? Just silence.

And this is just the journey to Hell, not yet Hell itself…

The train then passed through the outskirts of Moscow, and then on to the Ural Mountains. Passage through the Urals - really a set of hills marking Asia from Europe - was a distance of about 90 miles and this leg of the trip happened at night. This marked the boundary of Siberia, which became home to the victims in the train, and for many, their final home.

Ms. Vanaga relates that in the city of Sverdlovsk the Cesis-Gulbene train was shunted off to a remote track for several days. Other trains with other unfortunates, including many Lithuanians and Estonians, were also there. Conditions became worse - the toilet holes became blocked with dried excrement and stunk horribly. The water was bad, the air stagnant, and many people were fainting. At the stop it was learned by the inmates that the war back home had really begun, with the Germans invading Russia and the Baltic states on June 22 1941. Trains filled with Russian conscripts for the war effort were heading west - opposite from the prisoner trains, heading east - and this is what caused the delay of the prisoner trains.

By Midsummer Night - the festive "Janu Diena" to the Latvians - the train had traveled 600 miles, going straight across the taiga, the swampy forest that characterizes so much of Russia and Siberia. This had been done in 10 days of travel for Melanija, from Cesis, and would have been the 9th day of travel for Mom and family Nogobods starting from Gulbene. It was here that the inmates were for the first time allowed to exit the train, unguarded. The taiga, a trackless marshy forest prominent in Siberia, was the guard. There was nowhere to run.

Next the train want to Novosibirsk, a major Siberian city and train depot, called Station Taiga. Here the Estonian population was removed and shipped on a the rail line heading north, toward Tomsk, another large Siberian collection point. The suffering continued for all, with dysentery ravaging the prisoners.

Finally the Latvian's train reached the small city of Achinsk, in the Krasnoyarsk district of Siberia. Achinsk is about 3000 miles from Latvia, and an equal distance from Vladivostok on the Pacific Ocean… thus being at the center of the Eurasian landmass, as remote as it gets. This was the end of the line for Melanija Vanaga, her son, and the other surviving Latvians. The date was July 4, 1941. This also would have been where Mom, Aunt Elza, Grandma Berta, and Cousins Kitija, Inara and Olita would have found themselves, had they survived the hellish trip. They would also be wondering, with great agony and fear, about the unknown status of their men, Arturs and Arnolds.

Camping; Sentencing; The Slave Market

The inmates, all women and children, were discharged into a large, barbed wire-enclosed field already crammed with slumping, sleeping beings resembling humans. They were expecting to be reunited with their men, as told to them by the guards, but it had all been a lie, meant to keep them quiet and not panicking. There were three barns at the end of the field, but they were full and there was no room for the Latvians. Being a very small tribe, Latvians were usually guaranteed to get the worst of any conditions. So they lay in the field, through rain and sun, day and night, weeping, moaning, depressed, and fatigued from the three week hellish journey, seeing their lives entirely upended and despairing over the fate of their beloved men. Some remained in this field for two weeks, with no food or sanitary facilities. Dysentery was rampant; many died because of it and other conditions, and were buried nearby. Again, this was probably the exact place where my closest family would have been had fate not intervened and left them behind in Latvia. My Father, Uncle and other men would have been sent to the work camps where a much worse outcome would have typically awaited them. Cousin Fricis Jaunzemis did die during the mens' transport or soon thereafter in a work camp, as detailed elsewhere.

Back in the outdoor prison, soon the Chekists arrived. They set up a table, two chairs, and a stack of printed forms. Their ruse was that they were simply registering the people and having them sign the necessary registration form - but really it was a form making the signer a "voluntary transferee" for penal servitude for 20 years, for the use of the state as it saw fit; i.e., 20 years of slavery!

After this charade was completed, horse-drawn wagons from the local collective farms ("kolkhozes") appeared. The inmates were selected by the collective farm bosses for assignment to the different farms and other such nearby workplaces. Many of the younger, healthier women without children went to the forests as loggers, and this would have probably been my Mother's fate. Some went to different factories, such as a turpentine works, but most ended up on the collective farms. Author Melanija was the least desirable of the convicts because she had a child, and being one of the last of her group to be selected, was assured of ending up in the worst collectives. Aunt Elza, being in circumstances similar to Melanija, would probably have ended up the same.

The "free" population of the area, who were usually the offspring of previous exiles (Siberia was a dumping ground for unwanted people throughout Russian history), were the workers and managers of the local industries and collective farms. According to a trove of literature, they hated the new arrivals. Besides being a brutish, uneducated frontier culture, the natives had been taught by their Communist overlords that the new exiles were the exploiters of the working class, wealthy peasants who had been tyrants, servant-beaters and abusers of others. If they were not, would the all-knowing State have sent them here as prisoners? These enemies of the people should be shown no mercy and their suffering should be dramatic because it would accelerate their reeducation and progress to becoming the Soviet people that would be the foundation of the Communist state. Seriously abusing these new inmates was thus considered a moral act in this new socialist world.

Melanija and her son Alnis thus were assigned to work to the Tyukhtet region, northwest of Achinsk and literally at the end of the road. Tyukhtet was a village of tiny, sunken houses, many underground. Filthy children in rags were wandering about, with their mothers standing hollow-eyed nearby. The new arrivals were housed temporarily in the former church. Everyone was ill; some prisoners were losing their minds. The "hospital" had no medicine, no food, and everyone taken there died. Everyone. Then the local slave market began - 300 women and children were assigned to different jobs by the collective farm leaders. Melanija was sent to the livestock station located 4 miles away. One wonders where our family would have ended up.

Other deported persons ended up in even tougher circumstances than those of Melanija. Especially in the later deportations, some families, with a subset having their males along, were dropped off by themselves in the Siberian wilds or along rivers, with basically no goods or provisions. They were to establish exile villages and provide new centers for lumber extraction, mining, state farms and fisheries. If they survived the first year, they might get seed and some tools or boats and nets from visiting Gulag bosses the following year. Building immediate shelter and scraping for food became existential tasks - if you failed, you would die. Many did.

Work

All the literature of those times and places recounted that whatever the assignment, the work was horrible, hard, and essentially unpaid. The managers were often ruthless. Sexual exploitation was common. "Norms", or work objectives, were sent down from the leadership and had to be fulfilled, even if one had to work day and night to fulfill them. Often norms were out of touch with the reality and impossible to fulfill, leading to cheating, stealing, and so on. Meeting the norm by any means necessary became an existential struggle, since the punishment, usually the denial of food, could be lethal. This was what all survivors called it: slavery.

Melanija was assigned to an "animal collection point" as her job. Housing for 30 people was an old bedbug-infested wooden barracks with rows of stacked planks for beds. She was a shepherdess, driving sheep and cattle assembled at this collection point back to the city of Achinsk, 50-60 miles away, to meet established meat norms. Under all weather conditions, from mosquito infested summer heat to Siberian winter blizzards, the herding want on. The norms had to be met. During the 5 day drive, there was no food or shelter, and inadequate clothing and footwear. There might be delays at the collection point at Achinsk, so the suffering would be prolonged. Scavenging in the woods for berries and mushrooms was the the primary food source, while sleeping in the open under all types of weather conditions. In the meantime, the children remained at home, on their own.

Upon arrival at Achinsk, a crooked system with serious consequences would be encountered. The herd animals were counted and weighed, and bribes, favors, and trading would take place to make up for the animals' loss of weight while being herded, and the actual loss of animals who often died during winter herding. A lost animal would be deducted from the herders "pay", which could mean starvation later. Norms simply had to be met, often by hook and crook. Upon completion of delivery of the animals, the herders would walk back home, to continue with their chores there, like hay-gathering and tending the herds, all while taking care of their needy children. This exhausting process would just keep repeating.

The Early War Years; Survival

Just staying alive was the singular focus of the deported slaves, especially during the War years between 1941 - 1943, when all Russians were hurting. Slaves would be shuffled off to wherever the State needed them, but always to remote, freezing places with insufficient food and shelter where no one would freely go. Overcoming the universal depression this caused became a major, daily chore. The search for sufficient food to survive became paramount, as is reflected in all Gulag literature. Anything and everything was eaten. Inmates were consumed by the thought of food; it occupied every waking moment and lived on in their tortured dreams. Interestingly, as expressed by Varlam Shalamov and many other victim-authors, it was bread that was longed for, not meat or fruits and vegetables, but real bread. So I wonder, with horror, whether Mom, Aunt Elza, Grandma Berta and the three daughters would all have survived. I fear that the answer is a resounding no. Some would have been lost.

Many prisoners had their term of confinement extended during this period, up to life terms, with continuation of the worst work and the worst pay. Extension of the sentence was a very common practice, cited by numerous authors. The all-knowing and all-powerful State insured that there be a large slave labor force to fulfill the State's economic wishes, however unreasonable those might be. Quotas mattered; people and their suffering did not. The path to paradise on earth for all mankind would not be deterred by some deaths, perhaps unfortunate but necessary. Human progress demanded this sacrifice, and if a family was in the way, so be it. As Stalin once stated, "one death is a tragedy; a million deaths is a statistic".

During these lean war years the typical food allotment for non-working deportees such as the young, sick, and old was roughly 4 - 6 slices of bread per day, translated to bread quantities as we would understand them in the United States. For laborers, the allotment was about 2 - 3 times that amount. These were starvation diets. A few slices of bread per day would not sustain a working person - or any person, under any conditions, even if it was real bread, made of grain. But the slave's bread was adulterated with sawdust and grasses, so its nutritional value was insignificant. There was no other food provision - no meat, fish, fats, oil, dairy etc. - just this "bread". To survive, you would seek food by stealing, trading, taking from the weak, or doing whatever was necessary. Eating grass and weeds was a very common response. The reports of widespread poisoning caused by slaves eating jimsonweed is common in Gulag literature. These deportees were also paid a tiny salary minus a mandatory loan back to the State, plus other deductions, and in the end one might have enough to buy a pound or two of flour, per month - if the bosses didn't steal it.

Besides these horrible physical conditions, the deported women and child slaves were in agony by not knowing what had happened to their men, and not knowing what conditions were like for their families left behind in Latvia. The literature of the Camps often spoke of the hope by many of the unfortunates that Stalin would soon recognize his error and set them all free. Many prisoners, both deportees and Gulag camp laborers, actually believed that Stalin knew nothing of the prison state, and had been betrayed by bureaucrats below him. This thought gave them some comfort that this monstrous nightmare would soon be righted by the fearless leader in whom so many had fervently believed; perhaps it kept some victims from going insane, but ultimately everyone found out that that it was but a false dream.

1944 - 1947: Some Changes

During the spring of 1944, with World War II still raging, many Latvian deportees and other slaves in the various departments of the Gulag were displaying the final signs of starvation. The earlier harvest's yield had been used up, so it became common throughout Siberia to see stomachs swollen and distended; faces turning yellow; various illnesses flourishing; and people becoming dull witted, evil, and constantly nervous. Raw, leaking sores from previously frozen appendages were common, and there was continued bloating and poisoning from eating grass and wild greens. There were no drugs at all. The death rate was high.

But by the fall of 1944 the situation throughout Russia was starting to improve. The D-Day invasion of France by the Allies started to take the pressure off the Soviet Union, which was advancing towards Germany. The exiles had more food available, since there had been a good potato and cabbage crop. The specter of outright starvation began to lift. Barriers to information and news were somewhat eased; deported women could technically write to discover their husbands' whereabouts. Most heard nothing, but some started to get answers - too often, this was an affirmation of their death.

For the exiled women and children, the summer of 1946, a year after the end of the War, brought some profound changes and rays of hope. For example, the Communists decreed that orphans were to be allowed to travel back to Latvia, and travel restrictions generally were loosened. Documents to permit travel from the camps for the exiles were occasionally permitted.

This might happen by luck, or by bribery with whatever one could provide, via goods, other services, or money. If money, the bribe price was very steep - with some reports citing around a year's total income of an exile's salary. As was the case for all products and services in the Soviet Union, there was a black market in transportation tickets, typically on trains, but this was very dangerous. You could get turned in easily by someone in the know who might get benefit by squealing. Again, some got out that way, but others were caught and rearrested.

This loosening of the State's grip unfortunately ended in the summer of 1947. Arrests began again throughout the Soviet Union. Exile communities with the semi-slave inhabitants were not exempted. Stalin had set quotas for more slaves to work on new projects designed to hasten the advance of Communism in Russia, and then throughout the world.

Melanija Vanaga in her book described the experience during this July 1947 crackdown in her exile community of Tyukhut, summarized here to make this latest terror come alive. All the adults were required to assemble on the main street. The First Secretary of the Region mounted a red platform and started screaming at the crowd of unfortunates. The Cheka /Secret Police had set up signs to "justify" their activities - such as "Sweep the Lazy from the Village" and "Away with the Parasites". Those first targeted were both the defenseless and the hated groups. These were the unemployed or under employed, poor workers, the war injured, old women, pensioners, "wealthy" homeowners, and so on. They were called out by name, one by one, by the Secretary, to stand before the crowd and be bullied and insulted. The crowd, loaded with informers, was asked to "vote" on them, and after "unanimous" consent, the unfortunates were taken by the Chekists to a temporary jail. This went on all day, and as darkness fell, the crowd was ordered to come back next Sunday to continue the evil show. The fear was such that the crowd applauded; to show insufficient glee would increase the chances for the reserved players to themselves be subject to arrest. This description reminds one of the Cultural Revolution in Mao's China later in history - sadly, all these depraved systems soaked up evil from one another.

Those newly rearrested were sent further east in Siberia as slave labor to construct a railroad. The families of the arrested were quietly taken throughout the next week and dispersed. All week the Village inhabitants worried and prepared for the next round of arrests, scheduled for that next Sunday. That meeting never happen, but the larger purpose was served - the populace was controlled and cowed, and the Communists had total control to do as they wished, without fear of repercussions.

Imagine how crushing this must have felt. After some liberalizations by the authorities for a year, with many victims allowing themselves to feel the first stirrings of hope for a better future for them and the children... suddenly the boot came down on their necks again. Just as you could see a little sunlight, the darkness enveloped you again. Those actually caught in the new net had to give up their homes, familiarities and routines to be shoved into a new unknown, where just basic survival again became paramount. Those who stayed behind were merely plunged back into depression and terror.

1948 - 1952: Some Light

A major change around this time was that more news about those previously arrested was whispered by newly released prisoners. The exiled Latvian women and children started to hear new details of what had happened to their arrested men, and where they might be. Edge-of-life stories abounded, and end-of-life stories were unfortunately common. Though released prisoners had to take an oath of silence, details of the Gulag and the exile experience leaked out. Stories circulated about Latvians that had been sentenced to logging camps in the Urals, with fellow inmates dying daily from the strict regimen of dawn to dusk work, starvation rations, beatings, and inadequate tools composed of only of ropes, saws, and axes. Tales were told of the high death rates in the horrible nickel mines in Norilsk, above the Arctic Circle; in construction of the Vorkuta railroad; in the potassium mines in Solikamsk, with deep shafts, narrow passages, and no safety considerations; in the freezing gold mines of the Kolyma region where if you were an actual miner, and not "support" staff, you would probably die within a month. The stories told of Kolyma/Magadan were especially chilling. Kolyma was called the Auschwitz of the Gulag, and there is detailed history available of this horrid region as written by former inmate-authors such as Ginzburg and Shalimov. As an ironic sidebar, Kolyma was founded and managed by Eduards Berzins, a Latvian Communist, until his execution in 1937. Sometimes there is justice…

As conditions eased a bit, both the free and exiled women whose men - husbands, fathers and sons - had been arrested, accelerated their search for information in hopes that their whereabouts or status could be established. Melanija Vanaga's testament in this arena sounds fairly typical, so here are some of her actions. She sent 214 letters over a five-year period seeking any news, but unbeknownst to her, the local boss had stopped all the mail from being sent and would not answer her pleas for information. Her last "update", years ago, was that he had been sentenced to 10 years hard labor in special corrective camps without the right of correspondence. At the time, Melanija did not know that the phrase "without right of correspondence" was a customary code indicating that the prisoner had been executed. From another exiled prisoner, Melanija heard that her husband had been in the Sverdlovsk Camp in the fall of 1941, and then sent away with many others, to parts unknown. Since his prison term was set to expire on June 14, 1951, Melanija accelerated her search, but to no avail. The odds of good news were grim, however; of all the men with 10 year terms, Melanija knew of only one who returned, and a total of only 2 husbands of all her exiled friends survived the Gulag. She learned the bitter truth about his death later.

This general betterment of conditions was again interrupted in 1949, when on March 25 about 43,000 Latvians were deported under "Operation Priboi". These victims were farm families banished to Siberia to labor in state farms or carve out new settlements under harsh conditions. Estimates are that more than 10% died in faraway cities of exile such as Omsk and Tomsk, and in the Amur River region of Siberia, bordering China.

1953 - 1957: The Devil Dies; Serious Changes

Joseph Stalin died of a stroke in March 5th 1953. Almost immediately conditions for deportees and other prisoners eased. Some political prisoners were released, the rate of arrests lessened, but real criminals were also released in great numbers and formed roving gangs that preyed on the populace. Exiles now had to register with their Commandant less frequently, and travel restrictions were generally loosened. The female slaves and their children could finally take a deep breath, cautiously look around, and have the beginnings of hope.

News of the fate of the men accelerated and became more open. The first story of the Gulag experience - Aleksandr Solzhenitsyn's "One Day in the life of Ivan Denisovich" appeared, and for a while was published in Russia by order of the new Soviet dictator, Nikita Khrushchev, although soon printing was halted. Details of daily life while toiling in the Gulag were first revealed during this so-called "Khrushchev Thaw". Many survivors told their tales while they could, but remained fearful of a clampdown of these truths, and possible future punishment for having exposed them.

In 1956 and 1957 releases of both deportees and Gulag survivors significantly accelerated. Sometimes these were by group, such as Jewish peoples, the Kalmyk tribes, and Germans. Many of these newly released simply stayed where they were - their homes back in their native lands were gone, as were many of their relatives. So there was no "home" to return to.

Latvians were released on an individual basis, by the granting of an application. Some also stayed in the Siberian localities which had become home; others made the journey back to Latvia by truck and train. There are many reports of how the returnees were immediately shocked by the devastated and ruined Latvian countryside. Homesteads had been abandoned and lay in ruins as part of collectivization; there was a general untidiness, in sharp contrast to the past; there were Russian names on streets, and so on. The country had radically changed, and it remained a somewhat foreign place for decades. For example, when my stepfather Aleks first re-visited Latvia in 1993, he was surprised and depressed how this once tidy country had fallen - and this was almost 50 years later.

The population and culture had also changed for the worse. The returning prisoners found that the group that had imprisoned them - mostly Russians - were now the ruling tribe, though a minority of the population. Their former homes might be inhabited by Russians, with no legal recourse. Latvians were clearly second class citizens in their own land. The old work ethics had been replaced by a communal view of work, which unfortunately spawned laziness since everybody received the same whatever their work habits - so why kill yourself to produce more? Paranoia was normal and well justified; suspicion and mistrust were standard behaviors to guard against informers; religion had been shoved underground; the arts were infused with politics; poverty and hunger was the norm; and that fundamental human desire, freedom, was lacking.

Many of the returning prisoners and exiles with country roots ended up working in the communal kolkhoz farms, where they were the lowest of the low. This was a serf-like existence, more reminiscent of life under the Czars prior to 1861 than the state of the modern world. Others did whatever work they could to survive. Those with family or connections had it a bit easier, while the others with fewer personal resources had a tough go. Old friends would be typically fearful of embracing the returnees, while strangers would often fully shun these unfortunates, all in preparation for the next crackdown, should it occur.

Had my Parents, Aunt, Uncle, Grandma and Cousins been taken, as was the plan - and survived - this would have been their world. It is doubtful that all of them would have made it. Most deported Latvian men either died in the Gulag or soon afterwards, unless they had a special skill or connection that kept them out of hard labor. The women had a better chance but the labor contribution of the elderly females or mothers with children was minimal, so they were of less value to the State and would be treated more poorly, which would have lowered their survival rate. I believe my surviving people would have returned to Latvia, since they had family there, but to a bitter existence.

8.2 LATVIAN MEN: TO THE GULAG

What had happened to the Latvian men separated from their families as deportations began in June 1941? What might have been my Father's and Uncle Arturs' fate if the deportation truck had picked them up and deposited them at the Gulbene train station? With the arrival of the Russians in Latvia on June 16, 1940, a year before the mass deportation, the atrocities had begun. Mass arrests, primarily of men, had begun on the next day, June 17. According to government statistics, 20 new prisons were created by September, and the Central Jail in Riga was expanded since all existing prisons had been filled to capacity. By April 1941, 980 people (the US equivalent is 160,000) had been executed in Riga's prisons. On April 25 1941, 900 (US 150,000) Latvian prisoners were moved from Riga to Russia in 40 railcars. They were all charged under the infamous Article 58, the all-encompassing rule to arrest anybody for "anti-Soviet thoughts or actions". Of this group, 70 prisoners (US 11,000) were machine gunned during transit through the Ural Mountains. The survivors ended laboring in the Gulag Camps. They were the harbingers of the brutal life for Latvian men who were taken later throughout the Communist reign.

Cold, Dark Places; Deadly Work

Of the Latvian man deported throughout 1941, many were sent to Gulag camps in Kamchatka, a huge peninsula in the far eastern, Northern Pacific part of Russia. Almost all starved to death in a few months. The

Camps had several rings of electrified fences, "death zones" between them, with watchtowers, machine guns, and vicious guard dogs. 8/10 of a cubic meter of space was allowed per inmate for bunking, which didn't even allow the wretches to sit up. This was pure slave labor, with no wages, starvation rations, and a high probability of death and consequent replacement by the next wave of unfortunates.

Another distant place that consumed many Latvians was Novaya Zemlya. This is a group of large islands in the extreme north of Russia and Europe, with the Barents Sea on one side and the Kara Sea on the other. Its southernmost point is about 250 miles north of the Arctic Circle, so the landscape is barren, and the weather is cruel. Winter temperature average well below zero Fahrenheit on most places on the islands; summers might get readings of 40 F; and there is a constant wind. The Gulag camps here were little-known, secretive places that had a huge mortality rate. Typically there were only a few thousand non-camp residents, but already during the early Gulag years in the 1920s there were reports by former inmates of a population exceeding 150,000. Conditions were horrible. The barracks housing the inmates had a mud floor, rows of stacked planks for sleeping, and an open fire for drying shoes and clothing rags. Work hours were from 5:30 in the morning until late in the evening, with the small break at noon. As was typical, food was granted based on fulfillment of quota. There was a "Red Corner" to re-educate the slow learners and to have any Latvian nationalistic delusions knocked out of their heads. Work here was mostly in the mines. There were no safety considerations, so death was common, for many reasons. True criminals - robbers, rapists, murderers etc. - had their own barracks, and they were used by the prison system to suppress the political prisoners, who were viewed as the lowest form of life that deserved any and all mistreatment. These true criminals ganged up and tortured, stole, and raped the politicals - who occasionally organized and returned the favors. Just imagine if you worked hard all day in a dangerous mine, fulfilled your outrageous production norm and thus earn just enough food to keep you alive for one more day - only to have a barely working gang of thieves steal your work, and thereby possibly your life. There was no appeal - it was simply jungle law. Later, these islands were the major nuclear test sites for the Soviet Union.

Here's what survivors reported. Mining was probably the most common work in the Gulag, with details being prominent in the works of Solzhenitsyn, Shalimov, Vanaga, and hundreds of others. Mining by both prisoners and exiles was horrendously difficult and dangerous. Every miner got lung silicosis and died relatively early (which often did not make it into the official death statistics). Some mining required new shafts to be constantly created to reach new ore veins, and prisoners might have to walk extensively to reach these new mines. This may sound simple, but for starved and exhausted prisoners, this extra strain could easily be fatal. Stonecutters would cut a narrow slit to start a new shaft; a rickety ladder would be placed; drillers would ascend and drill holes for explosives - dirty, dangerous and heavy work, with frequent rockfalls and accidents; exploders would follow, then ventilators, then workers to pick out ore, prop the ceilings, and transport the ore up and out to the enriching center. In other geographies, as documented by Varlam Shalamov and others, the mines were open faced pits, typically on slopes, and a quota of the rock face would be measured out by the guards as the norm. The inmate would hack out this rock with a pickaxe and shovel, load into a wheelbarrow, transport the heavy, unsteady load along wood planks to a dumping center, and repeat. In Kolyma, where Shalamov served several terms, the combination of exhausting work, starvation rations, severe illness, horrible weather and so on meant that a miner would only survive several weeks unless he got a staff job in medicine, accounting, or food services.

As cited elsewhere, Gulag camps were all over the Soviet Union, with most scholars pegging the number as being around 30,000. Besides the Kamchatka and Novaya Zemlya camps mentioned above, there were large contingents of Latvian men in Pechora, Kotlas, Norilsk, Magadan, Vyatlag, Sevurallag, and Usollag. In Norilsk, at a museum and monument park called "Golgofa", there are striking memorial monuments in the native languages of the prisoners who were enslaved there - many were Latvians, including more than 560 army officers, of whom only several dozen ever returned. So the majority died, and mostly were buried where they fell - whether in forests, along road or railroad embankments, or next to mines. 18 hour work days, starvation rations, and lack of adequate clothing, shelter and medical facilities devastated the prisoners. There were also mass executions, such as at Kotlas, where a prisoner train was stopped by snow and nervous guards executed 2000 prisoners. For those prisoners who survived their 5 - 20 year terms, a new term of imprisonment would typically be added. By 1945, nearing the end of World War II, most of the male Latvian prisoners from the arrests of 1941 were dead. As an interesting and unpleasant aside, the famous and heroic prisoner and chronicler Varlam Shalamov notes in his works that it was a common and readily observable fact that Latvians died faster in the Gulag than other nationalities, but his analysis is unique: they were taller than other groups! Shalamov had observed from his multiple tours in the Gulag that tall men died earlier. The common explanation had been that Latvian prisoners had led better lives than most, and consequently suffered and died earlier than those used to a more brutish life. I suspect Shalamov's well-informed theory is the correct one.

My focus has been mostly on the incidents of 1941, which directly affected my family. The Gulag, however, had to be fed slaves over a much greater time span. During the years between 1944 and 1953 many more Latvian men were taken to toil in the vast Camp network, still under conditions much like those chronicled earlier. Repressions peaked particularly in 1944, 1947, and 1949.

The Latvian men's experience in the Gulag seems quite typical of the Gulag experience. Smaller nationalities like the Latvians probably had a tougher time, but the entire system was hellish and brutish and otherworldly, barely imaginable from the comforts of our life in the West. It is greatly disturbing that the story, so well documented, has been basically underreported and there have been no trials or massive world outrage to speak for the millions upon millions of dead. So it seems important to write a few lines about this stain on humanity, in hopes that the political system that spawned it is more exposed, and systems like it get buried early.

Resisting, Hiding, But Nowhere To Hide

By 1945, Latvia was under total Soviet Russian control. In all three Baltic Nations the "home guards", men of combat age not signed up as Russian soldiers, were all hunted and mostly killed, whether by execution or by being worked to death in the Gulag camps. The latter were typically listed as dying a natural death. In February 1945 there was a massive hunt for the Latvian "Forest Brothers" and their ilk - men who went into hiding and grouped together as guerrilla forces to fight, the best they could, against the Communists. It was hopeless, but there was little choice.

The Forest Brothers built bunkers and shelters in the woods, hunted and scavenged for food, stole, and crept into relative's houses and barns at night for warmth and food. Most were eventually found and murdered. Often their bodies were hung from trees as a warning to others. Wives and relatives would be mistreated and often raped. These warriors had a life expectancy of 5 - 6 months, but felt that they had no options.

Some men resisted as individuals. Melanija Vanaga's brother, Arnolds, was wanted by the Russians when they returned in 1944. He escaped to the forest by himself, was hunted by Communist police and dogs, and escaped initially by tying himself to the top of a fir tree. During snow storms he would sneak into his farm and get some food and warmth from his mother, who was constantly on the watch for him and his hunters. Imagine her stress levels! Storms were favorite times, since snow would wipe out his tracks. Within three months, he was captured, imprisoned, and tortured, with his jaw broken by the torturer's tongs. The soles of his feet were beaten with leather swatters. He was locked in a cell, naked, and alternately roasted and ice-frozen. This lasted for one year, until he - like everyone else - confessed to his fabricated "crimes", and was sentenced under the infamous Article 58 to 15 years in labor camps. Arnolds was shipped to Riga, and from there by train to the northern Russian port of Archangel where he and the others were loaded on a ship, into wooden cages. The water route went from the White Sea to the Arctic Ocean, then up the Yenisey River, past the town of Ust-Port, to the collection point for prisoners at Dudinka. From there, a train took them to Norilsk, a city entirely composed of labor camps for nickel and other metal mining, located north of the Arctic Circle. Arnolds was barely able to eat because of the broken jaw, and ended up lame with deformed feet from the previous torture plus the horrible "shoes" that were totally inadequate for the environment, but immediately went to work. Unfortunately, Arnolds' tale was fairly common among the Latvian men who went into hiding, and he may be considered among the lucky. Of all of Melanija's female deportee acquaintances, only two of their males had survived. Again, this story might have been the fate of my Dad, Uncle Arturs and the other family men had they been unable to fortunately escape to the West.

Interestingly, Google Earth can be used to take a look at Ust-Port, Dudinka, Norilsk, and other such towns cited as destinations for taken Latvians. I have spent many hours looking at these locations of hell on earth, and view them as places made holy by the unjust suffering of so many innocent Latvians and others. All the settlements around there began as labor camps. Various other books and YouTube documentaries show old photos of these places, as well as what remains of these sites. Again, this is my gesture to pay some tribute to those who so unjustly suffered and perished silently in the clutches of a horrible, evil system.

Melanija's Husband - A Common Male Story

Let me return again to Ms. Vanaga's recollections. Here is her husband Aleksandrs' story. This is chilling because it likely mirrors the probable fate of Dad and Uncle Arturs, had they been picked up the the Communists, as planned, and placed on that Gulbene train with Aleksandrs.

The first stop was in the city of Daugavpils. On the night of June 16, 1941, the men's train convoy left that station, before the women's and children's train departed, and then stopped at the Balbino station in Russia (now Belarus). They then walked 30 km/18 miles to the Juhnova estate, near the Moscow-Smolensk Highway. This had formerly been a concentration camp for Germans and Latvians during the Latvian struggle for independence in 1917. 10,000 male prisoners were in this camp, split into groups of 100. They were imprisoned by a low electrified fence, enclosed within a high electric fence, then surrounded by a sand "neutral zone" - the kill zone - and finally a third electric fence, along with the dog patrols and heavily armed guards with the right to beat, wound, or execute any prisoner at will. "Food" was provided once per day, and water and sanitary facilities were at best primitive. Being summertime, it was hot and very uncomfortable. Some prisoners lost their minds; others committed suicide, often by throwing themselves on the electric fences. The convoy was imprisoned at this site for several weeks, and on July 28 1941 they began the next phase.

Goaded by guards on horses and dogs, the weakened and sick prisoners walked back the 18 miles to the railhead. Their baggage was returned, although often ruined by mold and vermin. 60 prisoners were herded into each livestock car, and the train departed on the Kazan-Sverdlovsk-Turinsk line. At Turinsk, all were unloaded and robbed of all their valuable possessions, like rings. They were then force-marched for a full day to a camp, spent a night, and then continued marching camp to camp. At their final forest camp they were put to work the next day - no rest from the grueling tortuous journey was allowed.

Prisoners in these logging camps had to hand cut trees, strip, stack, and transport them. If quotas were met, they would be fed. Rations were "tomato leaf" soup, two times per day, and 300 grams of bread per day (10.5 ounces), which varied with the work that had been completed.

Everyone was sick, almost all the time. Infected cysts and diarrhea were universal, and dysentery, pellagra, scurvy and other such illnesses were common. There was no doctor, medicine or any medical facility available. Mosquitoes and flies plagued the prisoners by day, and bedbugs and lice by night. Many prisoners died, and were buried by their fellow prisoners in shallow graves or under stumps and forest litter - the prisoners were too exhausted to properly bury their friends. Those few who tried to dig deeper graves often could not make it out of them, and themselves died there and were buried along with the body they had intended to bury. It was common for the dead to be envied by the remaining prisoners.

Aleks' job was dragging logs out of the forest. He strained himself, probably had a rupture or hernia, both quite common, and got very sick and fought for his life the best he could, catching lizards for food, etc. But by winter he was too sick to move logs and was sent to distant meadows to haul hay. Having only the summer clothes he had been arrested in, his hands and feet froze, with ulcerations and severe loss of flesh. The barracks provided little relief for prisoners as sick as Aleks; everyone slept on frozen ground, and snow on the roof and the ceiling frost melted during the day, keeping the barracks wet and alternately frozen. Aleks became totally unable to work, and was simply left to die in the barracks. Soon he was called for transport to a new camp. At the transport camp in Sverdlovsk he was re-sentenced to a life term in correctional labor camps.

The fellow inmate who relayed all these details to Melanija about her husband Aleks thought that he died in 1942. The officials kept lying to Melanija about her husband, which was a common practice, but finally said that he had died of a heart attack on October 22 1945. They had lied to Melanija for 10 years! It is also of note that Aleks may not, like millions of others, go into the statistics as a Gulag death; instead, he died of "natural causes". The true toll will never be known, but assuredly the number of victims is vastly higher than any admitted or published number.

I have highlighted the stories of Melanija's brother and husband as detailed examples of the plight of Latvian men taken during this time, and the probable fate of the men in my immediate family, had they not escaped.

There are now many Gulag tales published by people of all nationalities; the obvious similarities of the stories indicate an evil, well-oiled system at work. It methodically working humans to death for decades in support of a philosophy that promised enhanced life but delivered horrible death.

8.3 A VISIT TO THE "CORNER HOUSE", RIGA

The final form of repression was the vast prison system that existed throughout Russia, and later, the Soviet Union. In Latvia, this system started in 1940, shrank a bit starting with the death of Stalin in 1953, but only disappeared when Latvia freed itself in 1991. For many, prisons were the final stop, with execution following the passing of sentence; for others, prison was but a step towards the other 2 options outlined above, exile or the Gulag. I visited one such prison - here are some observations.

In August of 2014 I visited my relatives in Riga and Gulbene, Latvia. Ineta Skudra, my cousin Maija's daughter, arranged for me to attend a guided tour of the "Stura Maja" ("Corner House"), the main KGB prison in Riga. This prison was a duplicate of literally thousands of KGB prisons throughout the Soviet Union and its Captive Nations, with size being the basic differentiator. So seeing the Corner House was like a mini-visit to the famous prisons such as the Lubyanka and Lefortovo in Moscow, where many celebrity prisoners such as Aleksandrs Solzhenitsyn had been imprisoned. Primarily innocent people who had been arrested were sent to these places. Here they were interrogated, usually forced to sign confessions to their imagined crimes, sentenced and either executed by "lead poisoning" (a shot to the head) or transported to the Gulag. The typical infractions were "anti-Soviet behavior" in violation of Article 58 of the Soviet Penal Code, a code so broad that anyone could be prosecuted under its terms. No action or behavior was necessary - thought crimes with the no outward manifestation could be successfully presented with near 100% conviction. You could break a piece of farm equipment and be imprisoned; or be turned in by a neighbor who wanted more space in the crowded communal apartment; or have a grudge or jealousy settled; or be a member of a class of people who are being rounded up, such as successful peasants - often called "exploiters of the labor of others"; or simply to meet quota for slave labor to hasten the modernization of the Soviet Union. Though many prisoners were simply sent to the Gulag without a stay in prison, and groups with women and children were exiled without trial, there was a sizable minority that went to prison before their final destiny.

Corner House is on the corner of Stabu ("Post") and Brievibas ("Freedom") Streets in downtown Riga. It was known to all, with dread. No one wanted to even walk near it. Typically anyone who entered this place as a free person would not leave in that category. The tour I joined began in a gated courtyard surrounded on all sides by the prison walls, and this was where the secret police vehicles - known as Black Marias - would bring their newly seized unfortunates. A small door let the prisoner to the small reception hall, just a room with a counter, where the prisoner was identified, registered, and lied to about what was to happen, to keep him or her quiet ("don't worry, if you're innocent, you'll be out soon, because the State does not make mistakes"). Than the unfortunate was stripped, probed and issued used prison garb, all designed to dehumanize the victim and have him or her lose hope or any thoughts of resistance. Next was a march accompanied by guards through the silent corridors, lined by cells of various types, all with a massive bolted door and a shuttered peephole. The prisoner was usually put in a tiny solitary cell at first, called a "dog kennel", to add to the fear and make him or her feel alone; lights were left on at all times and daytime naps were prohibited, all enforced by jailers making rounds and checking peepholes of their 5 assigned cells.

Corner House was heated excessively all year, to add to the discomfort of prisoners, and allow thirst to be an additional weapon of the authorities. After the initial few hours or days, typically alone, with minimal bad food and water, the new prisoner - already degrading toward becoming an animal - went to interrogation. The path to the interrogation rooms was through red-carpeted hallways, to deaden sounds and hide blood, and signal lights indicated the presence of other prisoners being led through the halls; the jailers did not want any contact between prisoners. Wire fences were strung between floors to prevent suicide. Interrogation rooms were small, with a single desk behind which sat the KGB interrogator, plus a single hard chair for the unfortunate, with a solitary bulb providing light. Articles of torture would be on display, such as clubs, etc. The interrogators had quotas and needed to get confessions and referrals of others as criminals. First approaches to the prisoner were usually soft - "just sign this confession and we will go easy on you, we already have proof from others' confessions about your guilt", or "we have strong implications from others who have already testified against you", or "we have hard evidence about your crimes…and there is no escape". If the prisoner claimed innocence, beatings or other tortures like being hung by the arms etc. would be started. Usually the prisoner would be housed in a group cell between interrogations, heavily crowded, with strict rules of no talking and no daytime sleep, with lights on all the time. Even the bulbs were encased in metal to deter prisoners from breaking the glass and committing suicide with the shards. Communists were very concerned about their victims not committing suicide! That irony has no bounds.

Corner House had 5 floors, 44 group cells with 175 beds, but a cell with 6 beds, for example, might house 36 unfortunates. Typically the prisoners would be sitting on the floor between each others legs, wedged together. The stench was horrible, oxygen was in short supply, and often an air of mistrust hung over the cell because there were informers among the prisoners. Interrogations were typically done at night, so night sleep was deprived, and with no sleep allowed during the day, sleep deprivation became a very effective form of torture. One would also hear recently tortured prisoners moaning and crying as they were led back to their cells after an interrogation, thus adding to the fear and crumpling any thoughts of resistance. All hope disappeared - the State crushed all its victims.

One of my most memorable stories of Corner House was recorded by a victim who was sent to the Gulag but recorded some of his memories.

After the initial isolation cell interrogation, he was put in a group cell. It was heated to 90+ degrees, and crowded with men sitting silently on the floor, stripped naked because of the heat. He noticed that the prisoners would periodically lean forward quickly, then straighten back up, and soon repeat. He was puzzled by the behavior, and thought it to be some kind of ritual. Soon after finding his space on the floor, he understood. Sweat would pool in the hollows between their gaunt shoulders and their neck, and the prisoners would drain these hollows with the motion! Soon, he was doing the same deadly dance with the others. What a visual…

There was a small elevated courtyard - maybe a 30 by 30 foot square - used for "exercise". It was surrounded by screen mesh above and below, so that a prisoner could not commit suicide by jumping off, and nothing could be tossed to them from the outside. Every 10 days a prisoner would be allowed to walk around this square, for 15 minutes, under armed guard. In memoirs, several unfortunates recounted the importance of this exercise yard: they could see the sky, and know that the old familiar world had not disappeared; and there was a nearby church that would rang its bell on occasion, which was cited as a glorious sound by many.

At Corner House I also toured briefly an execution room, one of three, which all prisons had. This is a chilling place. It was small - perhaps 20 x 20 ft. - with a heavily padded door for entry, and opposite, one for exit. It was dimly lit, and somewhat soundproofed with robust wood walls covered by layers of thick, black rubberized fabric. There was a built-in drain for blood around the perimeter of the tiled floor, which was connected by a hose to a water supply. Typically the prisoner would be stripped and given a final interrogation in a nearby room; if this session proved unsatisfactory to the authorities, the victim would be led to the entrance door by two guards, one on each elbow, and then through the door. Behind it was the executioner with his pistol; as the victim and escorts entered the door, the executioner would step out behind the victim, and fire a single small-caliber shot to the back of the head. The executed soul would be wrapped in a cloth, dragged through the "out" double door into the courtyard, and finally into the belly of a truck…thus ending back in that same courtyard where the whole macabre dance had begun. The floor was then hosed down, and the room was ready for the next victim. When the free Latvian government finally took control of Corner House, there remained spent-bullet and bullet-mark evidence of some 300 executions, but the true grisly count is unknown. Spent cartridges would have been cleaned up; walls would have been repaired; and many victims carried the small-caliber evidence with them to their graves. But executions were the minority sentence, with most victims being sent to work camps. Literature of the times cites that in some more heavily populated areas, the executioner's hands and arms would get too tired to function, not to mention the psychological load of killing thousands of innocents. It's not always easy being an executioner.

So prisons like this were scattered throughout the Soviet Union and its Captive Nations. There has been an interesting debate going on about what to do with them. Should they be preserved as museums, or converted and rebuilt into something of present-day use, thus moving on from the past? Russia strongly endorses the latter approach, wanting to bury its bloody past and hope for a brighter future, while many others want to keep the memories of the innocent victims alive as a way to hopefully minimize any reoccurrence. My vote is for the museum option. Specifically regarding the Corner House, there is an interesting national split about the path to take: Latvia's strong 25% Russian minority, though shrinking, is a powerful lobby - backed by the threatening Russian State presence on the eastern border - to bury the remnants of the brutality that the Soviets subjected on the Latvians. Some Latvians would also want to forget this past, both because some were complicit in these horrors, while others just want to look ahead to a brighter future and not be reminded of this past. I don't know how this debate will end, but I was privileged to have toured the Corner House and paid silent homage and recognition to its thousands of innocent victims.

8.4 LATVIAN LIFE FOR THOSE NOT TAKEN

About a week after the June 14 1941 mass deportation in the Gulbene area, Russians started to leave in response to German air attacks. Locals took over governance with some resulting chaos and conflict. The Red Army fled in haste to the northeast, abandoning their heavy equipment but looting farms and shops. The Cheka/Secret Police attempted to murder accused and arrested Latvians, but were too busy preparing for their own evacuation to have much success. They simply ran out of time. By July 4 the Soviets had evacuated from all of Latvia.

For this week, neither Russians nor Germans were in the Gulbene area. Former soldiers maintained order and limited looting. Surprisingly, there were few retributions against Latvians who had collaborated with the Russians; they were viewed as pitiful and pathetic creatures. When the German Army arrived, it was with small groups of soldiers and there was little conflict since the Soviets were gone.

Life under the German Nazi occupation from 1941 through 1944 was difficult - unless you were Jewish, Gypsy, or a Communist, and then you were dead - but there was food to eat and a somewhat normal life. In 1944 the Russians again entered, and the reinvigorated terror again began.

This second coming of Communist new order in Latvia had an unbending and overarching world view. It rejected ownership of private property; saw danger in personal initiative; hated religion and viewed it as the "opiate of the masses", an escape hatch from the dictums of the new rulers; deplored spiritual values as anathema to their scientific determinism; and fully rejected the traditions and mores of Western culture. These were some of the bedrock principles of Latvia for hundreds of years, despite the dark efforts of previous conquerers, and the impact on Latvians was devastating. Let's take a look at some elements of Latvian life for those who stayed in Latvia.

Indulis Pommers

Soviet Military Presence

Starting in 1944, Latvians were immediately subjected to overwhelming military occupation by the Soviets. The Red Army was a visible presence, with bases throughout, all strictly off limits to the locals. The Secret Police had a more hidden presence, recruiting spies and making arrests to terrify and thus control the people. Borders were sealed by the Border Guards, so escape from this Socialist paradise was virtually impossible. A powerful counter-intelligence group ("Smersh") suppressed access to information from outside influences. In the immediate post-war phase, violence in both the towns and the countryside was extremely high. Rape, theft, beatings and murder were common, usually perpetrated by the occupying Russians and police groups with free rein to seek out partisans. To survive, Latvians had to keep their heads down, earnestly utter the politically correct phrases, too often help their oppressors as a survival mechanism, and quietly hope and pray for deliverance. This especially large military occupation remained until Latvia became free in 1991, and many Soviet military personnel settled in the Country permanently. Already by the end of 1946 over 44,000 Russian military people had established residency there, moving into the homes of the Jewish people who had been murdered or fled, and the Latvian victims no longer there.

Several years ago my Cousin-in-law Agris gave me an eye-popping tour of an underground city, Ligatne, built by the Soviets as a command center in case of major conflict with the West. Designed to be safe from even nuclear attack, this was where the Soviet leadership was to meet and live while carrying out their war plans. There were meeting halls, bedrooms, kitchens and so on with power, communications, air ducts, sanitary facilities and everything else needed for long term confinement. What made this so fascinating was that this city was built under a Latvian village - and no one in the village, or anywhere else in Latvia, knew of its existence! This speaks to the power of the Russian military to do whatever they wanted, with silence guaranteed by the universal application of fear. That is raw, naked power in practice.

Another event I personally witnessed in Latvia during a visit around 2013 demonstrated the lasting effect of the previous Russian military's chokehold on the people. My Gulbene relatives, Aina and Vilis, took a day off from their demanding farming schedule to give a day long driving tour of Latvia. Cousin Ievina, MD, joined us, along with Cousin Maija, as I recall. Vilis took us all the way to Daugavpils, in south Latvia near the Russian border. On the long drive home, I asked if we could drive up to the Russian border because I wanted to see what that line dividing social and political systems felt like. Everyone agreed. Driving north and then turning east, we began our approach towards a boundary river with a bridge and the customs officials and border guards. The approach was chilling. The road had some fields and large pine forests alongside, but virtually no houses. Signs placed every kilometer starting 5 km out gave warnings, "you are approaching the border, 5, 4, 3, 2, 1 km away". A few hundred yards from the actual bridge and border station, invisible to me because of the road's curve and slope, we stopped at a tiny border hamlet for a moment. I was excited…but Dr. Ievina was terrified - "I cannot go any closer, I'm scared, let me out, now". Honoring her wish and being unwilling to just leave her, we took a left turn and headed home to Gulbene. That moment brought home to me the the fearful conditions that Latvians experienced while in the clutches of the Russian Bear, and how deeply ingrained those terrors were, long after the immediate threat was gone.

Social Sovietization

Most Latvians, like people throughout history, simply wanted to survive these dramatic upheavals and find some normalcy and joy in their lives. But severe change in their daily existence was forced upon them immediately when the Russians returned on the rising tide of their war efforts in October 1944.

Russian was immediately declared as the official language. Books, newspapers, film, music and art were "Sovietized", with themes reflecting the Communist Party line, such as "Proletarian Internationalism", "Scientific Communism", the horrors of life in the Western Democracies, the love of Soviet leaders for their people and so on. Everything was censored and had to be approved by the Party. Religious subjects disappeared, unless to be mocked. Teaching was Sovietized in these same ways, and all curriculums reflected the Party line. Several of our relatives were in the education field - specifically my cousin Maija and her Dad, who was a Principal - and they survived by performing as required, as relayed to me by cousin Ievina. Latvian history was falsified, with teachers having to teach how the Latvians and Russians had always has a historic closeness and mutual fondness.

Social and economic stratification in Latvia was also immediately reordered in 1944. High-status Latvians had been in parallel with the greater world's typical stratification categories: doctors, scientists, teachers, the educated, high achievers, great parents, great providers, great farmers, military leaders etc. were at the top of the heap. But with Russification, this all changed. The extremely privileged were the police state operatives, such as the Communist leadership and the secret police; they got the best food and goods, access to cars, superior apartments, vacations and travel. Next were Communist party members, followed by others who looked like true believers, such as members of the Young Communist League. If you had no tie to the Communist organs, you became a second class citizen and life was poorer and riskier for you and your family. Cousin Ievina recounted that almost everyone tried to join an official Communist organization, whether they believed or not, since this was the only path forward toward a better life. It also helped to be Russian. For example, 80% of administrators in Riga were newcomers to Latvia, mostly Russians, and they also got the management jobs and preferred assignments. So Latvians were immediately second class citizens in their own country. Cousin Ievina, a physician, described how during her studies she was literally at the end of the line of any group if it was composed of Russians.

Political Sovietization

As the Russian troops swarmed into Latvia in late 1944 to enforce their domination that lasted through 1991, Soviet-trained "organizers" were shipped in from Russia. A high proportion of these cadres were Latvian Nationals who had left for Russia earlier, either by choice or against their will, but had become Communist believers. Key was that they spoke Latvian and often had existing contacts in Latvia. These cadres spearheaded the takeover of all Latvian political functions, with the force of military threat behind them. So local parish councils were filled with these newcomers, as were all administrative positions upstream to the national level. These new Bolshevik rulers had absolute power, and were financed by and reported to Moscow. There was no recourse for locals disputing the new rules, however harmful they might be for local issues.

This last occupation beginning in 1944, on top of the first Russian occupation of 1940 - 1941 and the German occupation of 1941 - 1944, devastated Latvia. Local political leaders were often arrested and killed; those who remained lived lives of terror and went quiet to protect themselves and their families. The infamous Article 58, used to convict Russians of anti-Soviet behavior or thoughts since 1926, was typically the legal cudgel that resulted in deportation of Latvia's political class to the wilds of Siberia, or punishment labor in the Gulag Camps, or execution. All proceedings were extra-judicial, had no defense or appeal, and were over in a few minutes - just enough time to pronounce the sentence. After all, the "Courts" were very busy doing the hard People's Work to rid the new progressive society of undesirable elements. One's heart goes out to those members of the NKVD, the special military tribunals, and the KGB/Cheka who worked tirelessly to filter out the evil dregs within the society.

National leadership, both Latvians and Russians, was hand-picked by the Soviets, and reported directly to Moscow. There were some figurehead Latvians in various positions of apparent authority, but the rules were made elsewhere and passed down. Any Latvian harboring nationalistic thoughts had to stay silent, or better yet, enthusiastically and loudly lie as a condition of keeping their job. Everybody knew this, and it created a deep rot in the system which ultimately toppled it.

Through all three occupations Resistance continued via the organized Forest Brothers and by individuals acting bravely. The hope was that somehow conditions would change, and more importantly, that the Western democracies would recognize that this growing monster would soon be on knocking on their own door. The Democracies would help as an act of self preservation - but it was but a dream. The West was war-weary after the huge losses of blood and treasure; disinclined to enter a new conflict against forces that had just been their allies; and popular sentiment and left-leaning media did not really believe how evil the Communists were. So, left alone, the Resistance was gradually butchered away. Partisans had an average life expectancy of only 6 months. Weep for them with me.

The final triumph of political Sovietization coincided with the death blow to the Resistance on March 25 1949. On that date, 43,000 Latvians were deported to Siberia; another 100,000+ were punished politically but remained in Latvia; and 600,000 others (30% of the population) were severely repressed by being discharged from their work, dismissed from school and prohibited from further education. All citizens suspected of nationalistic leanings were thus neutered. Most of the remaining population naturally felt terrorized and were harassed and suppressed in less obvious ways. Thus was formed a sub-class of the poor that had no means to better themselves: all doors were closed. Freedom, already on life support, totally died on this date, as did the classic Latvian society. Some Latvian prisoners who had been taken in 1941 and survived to return home in the 1950s found these same hopeless conditions - they had essentially no rights, no path to better themselves, and were resigned to a life of bitter hopelessness with basic daily survival being the highest goal.

Economic Sovietization - Farming

The collectivization of farming began soon after the 1944 Communist takeover of Latvia. Beginning in 1945, right after the War, the Soviets decreed the all private land of more than 50 acres was be to forfeited to the State by the owners. While this was slowly being enforced, some farmers hung on and tried to make a go of it, but they were subjected to crippling taxes and social and political pressures. Consequently, most countryside farmers who had not been deported became employees - "of their own free will" - of collective farms ("kolkhozes") or State owned farm ("sovkhozes"). These entities sold their yield to the State at a fixed price, while any remaining private farm got less for their yield, along with the tax burden. Those better-off, more successful farmers who tried to survive independently were then labelled as "kulaks", and as was the case in Russia and The Ukraine in the 1920s and 30s, this group was severely repressed. During 1948 farmers were made to "voluntarily" join the collective kolkhozes. They became state workers, subject to the whims of bosses often ignorant of agriculture, yet responsible for the output resulting from flawed central planning. Their wages were subject to partial "borrowing" by the State. People unsuitable for kolkhoz work - members of politically undesirable classes not yet arrested, or with weakness or experience that did not translate well to difficult farm labor - were not allowed to join the kolkhozes, and then were defined as the new "bourgeois class", to be hated by the "working proletariat". These "bourgeois people" were then individually attacked in the press, openly robbed, and taxed to impossible levels. When the taxes could not be paid, they would be arrested, and their property simply taken and appended to the kolkhozes. Consequently, every person was continually scared and paranoid, with no means of escape.

In March 1949, the final mass deportation of Latvian "kulaks" - independent successful peasants - occurred, which further helped eliminate the Resistance. The kulaks were arrested and sent by the old train routes to Siberia. Included among them were many of the mothers and children who had made it back to Latvia during the aforementioned thaw. As usual, arrests were made at night, quietly, with the typical lies to make the unfortunates go without resistance. The authorities over the years had become experts at this. Homes of the arrested people were typically given to recent Russian immigrants to Latvia. The new prisoners were again often separated by gender and family situation, but there were many more full-family deportations than before. The men and childless females typically were sent to some established camp in the Gulag structure. In this 1949 crackdown, most Latvian men were reportedly sent to Camps in the Tomsk area of Siberia. Mothers, children and sometimes full families were, as before, exiled to state-run farms and industries as slave labor. At best, conditions remained horrible for the new arrestees, with weather, shelter, food and health again being existential challenges.

So by 1948 the free farmers had been largely taxed and squeezed out of existence; the remainder were killed or deported in the March 1949 repression. This ended free Latvian farming, and the Latvian social structure of independent farmsteads was replaced by the "Russia Village" model with communal fields. Consequent crops and livestock failures, due to the bureaucratic bungles, made food scarce. Secret Police and informers were everywhere, so the entire culture was paranoid. By mid-1949, over 70% of Latvian farms were collectivized, and what remained independent were tiny and struggling. The collectivization had won, to the detriment of all.

Several years ago I visited what had been a prominent kolkhoz in Gulbene, now converted to a large farm managed by the former leadership. It was huge, with an industrial look about it, and some of my relatives had worked there. My brief discussion with the boss was cordial and very interesting, since he expressed a viewpoint of current events that was foreign to me. A Russian missile (as proven conclusively later) had recently downed a passenger aircraft over the Ukraine, with major loss of life; the boss felt that the tragedy was caused by Western forces trying to shoot down an airplane somewhere in the area that had Putin as its passenger, and hitting the wrong airplane by mistake. He seemed quite convinced...

Economic Sovietization - Industry, Housing

Soon after the Russian arrival in 1944, a re-industrialization of Latvia began. The emphasis was on building huge factories, reflective of the Communist fascination with mega-projects, as happened throughout Russia. Latvia had a better infrastructure than much of Russia, and consequently attracted attention. This was a command economy, dictated by Russia, not Latvia, to supply the needs of Russia. These new factories were predominantly supplying the needs of the Soviet military, with particular emphasis on electronics and textiles. Since the Latvian population had been reduced substantially by the Soviet repressions and population dispersal, Russians were imported to man the new factories. By 1989, in the twilight of Communist rule in Latvia, 34% of the population - nearly 1 million people - were Russians. To house this influx, huge apartment complexes were built, often with multiple 5 story buildings clustered around a central area that might have a children's playground or small park.

I have stayed many nights with our Latvian relatives in these apartments. They were built as basic concrete units for shelter, with a kitchen, bathroom, living room and perhaps 1 or 2 bedrooms, all very small by US standards, with no elevators (by law, elevators were required only in buildings higher than 5 floors) or garages. People made them as comfortable and individualistic as their incomes permitted, and I found them to posses a sense of home. But living in these complexes was a crowded and communal affair, by design, and this amplified both the cooperative and hateful nature of humans when crowded together. This was a far cry from the traditional Latvian dwellings of farmsteads, single homes, and small apartment buildings.

Several other personal stories will illustrate the effects of Soviet power across all spheres of life on the Latvians who stayed. My dear first cousins Ievina and Maija, my Mom's nieces, visited the US in September 1991, just as Latvia was becoming free again and travel was permitted. They had flown into New York City and were picked up there by cousin Olita and husband Neal, and taken to Olita's Connecticut home. I picked them up there to drive them to Mom's home on Conesus Lake in upstate New York. As we drove, I asked the Latvians what they had for dinner the prior night. They answered, "Meat". Me: "What kind"? They: "Meat"! The implication was that meat was a good and special meal, and the type was irrelevant - indicative of a general lack of it in their recent cuisine. An hour later a second illustrative event happened. Dr. Ievina was photographing scenery along the Mass Pike when she violently lowered the camera and her entire torso, uttering a loud "Eh" of surprise. Her response to my question was that she had unwittingly photographed a highway overpass, and hoped that no one had noticed! In Communist Latvia, photographing bridges and other such transportation structures was illegal, and her instincts had taken over.

Yet another revealing incident happened during the first night after arrival at my parents. After the joys of being reunited after 47 years, everyone went to bed. During the night, the sisters had awakened and tiptoed into the kitchen while dealing with their jet lag and excitement. On the kitchen table was a bowl of fruit, primarily bananas, and they ate them all! The next morning they ashamedly confessed that they could not stop themselves, that the lure of so much exotic fresh fruit simply overwhelmed their manners. Later, they went to a supermarket with my folks and later told me that they at first had thought that it was all staged, that such an abundance of goods was not real.

I also recall their nervousness at flying back to Latvia, but having to connect in Moscow. My cousins had stocked up on American goods and were wearing and carrying lots of stuff, and were tense about getting all this safely through customs and other potential impediments. Yet their tensions seemed very mature, indicative of being well accustomed to such worries and prepared to handle whatever hand was dealt.

Perhaps a good summary of this trip by Maija and Ievina that reflected the vast gulf between the socialist paradise of Latvia and the capitalist hellhole of America was their response to my question about what difference they had most noticed. The answer was "Smiles. In Latvia, no one smiles; in America, everyone smiles". And that, dear reader, says a lot.

CHAPTER 9

"MY YEARS OF PRISON AND SUFFERING"

MEMOIR BY RITA JAUNZEMS

A NEW ADDITION TO GULAG LITERATURE

[INTRODUCTORY NOTE: *Rita is my Mother's first cousin, and one of the many unfortunates swept up in the June 1941 deportations of Latvians by the Soviets. Her father, Julijs, was my maternal grandmother Berta's sibling. Rita's mother, Minna, gave birth to six children: Milda, Fricis, Rita, Roberts, Konrads ("Kondis"), and Ida, who died young. Fricis, already mentioned earlier, was the Army officer who was taken and met a bitter end soon thereafter, leaving his widow and three children behind. They, and Milda, eventually made it to Canada. Roberts and Kondis fled Latvia along with other members of our family in the Caravan in 1944; they made it to America. Kondis Jaunzemis and his wife Ritma had two US-born sons, my second cousins Andris and Vilnis, who remain close friends of mine.*

Rita (1906 - 2000) survived 16 years as a working slave in Siberia, displaying mental, physical and spiritual strength plus strong genetics and fortune to live to the age of 93. After her time in Russia and Latvia, which forms the bulk of her memoir, she completed her life in the freedom of the West. In 1970 she got a short-term visa from Latvia to visit her sister Milda in Canada.

Upon visa expiration, her brother Kondis arranged a complex political asylum and snuck her into the US to live with his family in Niagara Falls, NY.

Kondis and others, notably cousin Kitija, took care of her financially, and the rest of the family - wife Ritma and sons Andris and Vilnis - provided a sense of family and home. Rita began working locally as a housekeeper, and later moved to continue her work for a Latvian Church in Minneapolis, MN. Later again she moved back to her family in Niagara Falls, and spent more time with her Canadian relatives. During this stretch she entered into a loving relationship with a Latvian man until his death in the early 1980s, following which she moved back into the Jaunzemis home. Since her brother Kondis had died in 1978, this was still a difficult time for the extended family, made more so by Rita having unfortunately become paranoid and distrustful of others. By 1989 Rita was in an assisted living facility, where she became a danger to herself, followed by her final move to a geriatric center that could handle her severe Alzheimer needs. Discussions with cousin Kitija and especially cousin Andris revealed some aspects of Rita's condition: she had hidden money throughout her apartment, thought others were stealing from her, and hurtfully turned on her closest caretaker, cousin Vilnis. This marked the sad end of a sad life.

I recount these actions not to tarnish Rita's heroic life, but to illustrate the depth of damage caused to just one victim of a hellish system of governance. Consequences to the survivors last a lifetime in one form or another, and amplify the crimes. Just doing body counts is not enough. Rita's tortured behaviors at the end are common reactions among Gulag survivors; memoirs and taped interviews I have seen with surviving victims often reveal people who maniacally hoard food, have trust issues, or exhibit other psychotic behaviors.

Rita's hand-written memoir in Latvian was retained by Andris and Vilnis, and then passed on to me and cousin Kitija. The memoir had been the basis of verbal presentations delivered several times by Rita to Latvians in Canada. Kitija did the initial translation; I then expanded the translation and added notes from other sources to add context and further some descriptions. The results are published here, for the first time - and it's past time for her story to be heard, as she lived and felt it. Her story must be added to that of others so that lessons can be learned, suffering and victims are not forgotten, and monsters exposed - all in the hope of minimizing future such horrors. Here we begin with Rita's own words...]

9.1 RITA'S PREFACE

I think that most of you by now have heard stories and read books and memoirs about the Soviet Union's practices of torture and brutality on its subjects, the squeezing of its peoples, and the exterminations that were planned and executed by the State. I also spent 16 years in Siberia and was victim to that agony. So here I will tell you my unique story, since each person with similar experiences will have an individual perception and understanding. Thus, my telling might vary a bit from that commonly told by others.

9.2 FREE LIFE

O Latvia, our lovely, beautiful homeland, with your forests and streams, fields and flowers! How easily my memories return: my Father, with a seedbag flung over his shoulder, walking in our fields in the spring, sowing seeds for the next harvest; Mother would be milking cows and bringing full buckets of fresh-smelling milk into our home. Yes, the milk was truly fragrant! Latvian milk was special that way. As a young girl, my job was to attend to the herding of the cows, with the capable assistance of our dog Arnitis.

Detailed memories come back to me. Often when our herd of brown cows would be grazing, Arnitis and I would sit down together in the field. One morning the sun warmed me so pleasantly that my head dropped down and I dozed off. Suddenly there was a loud yell in an angry tone that made both Arnitis and me to jump to our feet. The cows that I was responsible for had broken through the fence and got into the newly planted wheat field! This made my Dad very upset, since all jobs on the farm were important and I had failed my task. On the farm, everyone, including all the children, had duties and were expected to do them well. So I got some pink stripes on my bottom, and some tears fell, but Father wasn't angry for long. I of course blamed Arnitis - he should have warned me about the herd wandering off! - and the next morning I punished him by refusing to share my breakfast.

So went our summers, helping on the farm, and in winter we attended school. Our parents, like most Latvian parents, tried to teach us to love our work and do it well, and to study hard and do well in school. All children, boys and girls alike, were expected to grow up to be a credit to the Nation.

There came a time when we had to get really serious about our school studies. For me, this was when I attended the dairy business school in Smiltene. After graduation from the school I began work at the local milk distribution center. The dairy industry was very important to Latvia. Dairy products such as butter and milk were a prime source of export, especially to Britain, and brought in much needed foreign revenue during Latvia's years of independence. In those days of my youth, I was pretty, full of energy, and enjoyed my work and life in general. Those are the memories I remember about life in my Homeland. The horrible years to come couldn't extinguish these memories; some of the light remained. But our Homeland was taken by a foreign force and it was painful, filled with blood and tears.

9.3 ARREST AND TRANSPORT

Then came the year - 1941 - that changed everything, and we couldn't know how it would all end. The Soviet occupation of Latvia in 1940 continued into 1941, with the climax reached on June 14. On that day I too was affected by the developments. I was working as a manager in a dairy distribution plant in the upper Zemgale State, the Jakobpils area, in the town of Saukas. This is an area southeast of Riga, south of the Daugava River. It was the morning of June 14. Our company management and many of the workers were already there, starting work. I was standing near the scales, weighing the milk. I felt a hand tap me on my shoulder, and turned around to see in front of me our newly appointed Communist town elder, or mayor. He told me to go to the cafeteria hall of the milk plant, and pointed to the door. I said that now was not a good time because work had begun, as he could see. He again motioned with his arm to the door leading out, where I was escorted by a Russian officer and two Chekists - the Communist political police enforcers, at different times known as the NKVD, MGB and later KGB - who were armed with rifles carried on their shoulders.

I was marched to the workplace office and then told to lead the Chekists to my apartment, which was on another floor of the building. In the apartment, the Russian pulled out a piece of paper and handed it to me. It was written in Russian, and I gave it to the village elder to translate it for me. He read that I was under arrest. I asked, what is this about? Why? The answer was, I don't know. The Russian officer then ordered the two soldiers to start to go through all my belongings, looking for gold or anything valuable, or anything that could be construed to be anti-State. Of course, everything was opened, removed, inspected, and ruined. Since the soldiers couldn't find anything of note, they asked where I had hidden my gold. I replied that I had none, except for some small trinkets that the soldiers could readily see. Then they totally tore up my couch, looking for hidden gold. Next they went to my writing table and searched all my documents, photos, papers, and letters, and all were all taken. They told me to prepare for a journey. I removed my white work dress and hat and put on my summer dress. The village elder told me to take some food along, because my situation might not be resolved until the evening. So I left my apartment with only a light coat, a pair of shoes, and two sandwiches. As we exited, the door was locked by the elder/mayor, and he kept the key.

Outside there was already waiting a heavy truck, full of people that I knew. They included the Saukas Town secretary, Janis Kanepajs, the local police Commissioner Bruners and his wife, and Stradins, a militia member and local farmer. All had bags with them. I asked Bruners why, and they were all surprised that I came only with what was on my back - but I had been told that my belongings would be examined and that I should pack only for the day. He replied that they were told to pack for an extended trip. I had no clue that this "examination of my belongings" would be turned into16 years of torture and hell.

> [**NOTE** — *this was the common way that arrest occurred. They caught you by surprise, with no warning, gave no reasons, and hustled you along so you head no time to plan even a minor resistance. Lying about your near future was also standard, the point being to have you compliant - after all, you knew you were innocent of any charges, and you would only be gone for a few hours or a day for questioning, and then your innocence would be established and you would go home. Also common was the theft of all your valuables by the authorities as they were looking for evidence of your crimes.*]

The truck then proceeded to the Daudzevas train station (which still exists off road P 86, Southeast of Riga). Having been last on the truck, I was the first to be pushed into the cattle wagon, alone, and then they locked the door. What I then felt, alone in that cattle car, and began to understand, was that my hopes about my future and my Fatherland itself was being taken away. It became clear that I was being treated as a criminal, and was on my way to Siberia. With this, a stripe had been drawn across my young dreams about my future, my Homeland, and the rest of my family. I was only 34 years old.

I stayed awake and listened all night to truck noises, the sounds of moaning, the crying of women and children, and arguments in Russian and Latvian. The next morning the locked cattle car doors were opened and women and children were stuffed in until there was standing room only. Throughout the night the moans and cries of the imprisoned innocents continued. The train then started and we begin to go on our journey on the Gulag road. Railway stations at Plavinas and Krustpils were the next stops. At each of these, prisoners who would been assembled at the stations were herded on board. From these new arrivals we learned where we were. The next stop was the train station at Daugavpils, in the south east of Latvia near the Russian border. Here we stopped for a day and the night. While at Daugavpils, most of us tried to write tiny notes identifying ourselves and threw them on to the rails. The hope was that some kind person would find them and notify our relatives. We did this even though at all times armed guards were patrolling along the entire train. More unfortunates were stuffed into my cattle car, which was finally crammed with 78 people. We could only sit or lay down in shifts, being stacked together like sardines in a can. For personal needs, there was only a hole in the floor. The wagon stank badly, and everyone felt dehumanized.

While the train was in Latvia, we received nothing to eat or drink. The prisoners had only what they had brought with them from home. Since the children felt the hunger more acutely, the parents gave their food to the kids. Once, soon after crossing the border into Russia, the railroad track took a sweeping turn, and we could see the extent of the train cars behind us. We counted 38 wagons, but we knew there were more. Once we entered Russia (now Belarus), a daily food ration was begun. It was a meager ration consisting of one slice of dark hard bread and a small, very salty dried fish, per day. Though hungry, we could hardly eat this food because the bread was very salty and the fish was even saltier. I survived this part of the journey by eating the sandwiches I had taken with me from home. Already, this was a starvation diet but most prisoners still had some food left from home.

The next stop was that a major transit camp east of Minsk in what is now Belarus. The station was named Bobruisk, in the Tveras region, and everyone was ordered off the train. We, except for women with children and old people, exited. The prisoners jumped out of the cattle cars and were called out by name, and were herded by guards and dogs to form lines of four people abreast, and then were force-marched on foot 40 km (28 miles) to the Juhovas transit camp. *[Note: This had formerly been a large estate, now converted into a huge temporary prison. This is the same place mentioned by Melanija Vanaga's brother in her book while describing his arrest and transit, and was probably a place that all Latvian prisoners during this time had in common].* There we met more Latvians who had been previously deported, all imprisoned behind barbed wire fences. Barracks buildings had been constructed within the barbed wire on the estate's park lands, and we were driven into them. Since it was summer, we were able to spend our days outside, but at night we were locked in the barracks, sleeping on the bare floor behind locked doors. We covered ourselves with whatever we had brought.

On the other side of the fence was a group of men. Tragically, this was the last place I was ever to see my brother Fricis. We all ran to the gate separating our groups, calling out the names of our loved ones. I spotted Fricis, and we both ran to the fence line. My brother asked "sister, do you have some meat or bread?" I gathered what I had, and my friend Emilia Benjamina gave me 3 pieces of her bread (saying that she was too full eat it!). I sewed up the bread in a small kerchief. The men had been lined up for their rare bath in the sauna, and when they returned I gave him the bit of bread I had collected. A guard noticed and yelled to stop or he would shoot. Fricis was able to blurt out that his whole family was taken prisoner in Gulbene, but he did not know what had happened with them. *[Note: In fact, as mentioned earlier in the story, they had all made it out alive by faking that a birth was occurring while at the departure platform of the Gulbene train station].* My brother never returned from those Gulag places of torture. After being myself imprisoned in several different Gulag camps, I finally got an answer to my inquiries about Fricis from the Gulag authorities in Moscow. They said he died in October 1942, 16 months after I last saw him. The cause of death is technically unknown.

I would like to add, as I learned years later, that my sister-in-law Alise (Fricis' wife) was 8+ months pregnant with her son Jakabs as she was being loaded into the cattle car at the Gulbene train station. Fricis had already been separated into a different wagon, a separation very typical of the Communist prison transport plan. She also had with her their younger daughter (Margita, about 10), with the other daughter (Vija, about 12) being in a hospital in Riga for head surgery at this time. So Alisa pretended that she was in labor, started screaming in pain, and started pounding on the walls of the cattle car along with other prisoners. The door was unlocked and the guards attempted to take her off, leaving her daughter behind. Alise simply refused to leave without her daughter, and was fortunate to have guards with some human feelings left. Finally they were all taken to the local hospital. The Chekists returned to the hospital several times to see if she had the baby, so that they all could be stuffed back into the cattle car, but the doctor refused to discharge her, and got away with it. So that is how she and the girls, Vija and Gita, escaped deportation, and the circumstances of the birth of her son Jakabs (Jack), who was born about a month later. *[**NOTE:** As referenced earlier, eventually they all escaped Latvia and emigrated to Canada and freedom. Jack has traveled back to that train station on the anniversary of the deportation, and witnessed both Latvians in mourning, and some Russians acting in an indifferent or mocking manner. According to cousin Maris, traveling with him, Jack was openly enraged. Also, sadly, Vija and Jakabs have both passed away in 2020, very close to the June 14 date].* Rita continues: So my brother Fricis never knew that he had a son, or what happened to his family. Imagine carrying that weight while being unjustly persecuted, tortured, starved, and worked to death. I also did not know my family story until I returned back to Latvia after having spent

16 years in Siberia. But after all this time, I did get to meet my nieces and nephews in Canada.

Now let me try to tell you of the rest of my hard road, the difficult, suffering years spent in Siberia. While imprisoned at the Juhovas transit camp for 2 weeks, the news broke out that World War II had started. The Germans had entered Latvia and taken Riga back from the Russians. To us, this was a very joyful event that gave some hope that our Soviet tormentors might be defeated. We inmates celebrated by clapping hands, dancing and singing, although not enough to suffer an immediate retribution from the guards. There was hope that we might be saved. Instead, the doors were suddenly unlocked and we were roused from our sleep at night in the barracks. Guards were yelling at us to be ready in 10 minutes to go back on foot to the Bobrovsky train station, 28 miles away. Here we were forced again into cattle wagons, which had become even more crowded. The bathroom was simply a filthy hole in the floor, which added to our dehumanization. We took off the same day. This time, our cattle car only had the young and strong.

So our trip eastward into Siberia continued. It was midsummer, the air was still and the smells were foul, and there was nowhere even to sit. As usual, we were only fed once a day. The diet remained a salty slice of bread, and a saltier piece of dried fish. Water was not provided, and the thirst of the inmates flooded their minds and was a constant, grinding torture. If the train stopped in a railroad station, we would all starts screaming for water and creating a ruckus that would be heard by anyone at the station. Then the guards might bring one pail of water for the 80 people in the cattle car to share. This was only enough to wet each parched mouth, but not enough to drink and mitigate the thirst torture.

9.4 IN THE GULAG; CAMP LIFE

After 3 days of traveling like this, we stopped at a narrow-gauge railroad platform. Another selection was made, with the younger and stronger prisoners separated from the rest. I was one of that younger group. After less than a day's travel, the train stopped in the middle of a dense forest. There were a few houses visible. We were assembled in rows, and were then force marched, prodded by guards, to one of the houses that had been visible from the train. As we approached, we could see several Chekists in their uniforms around an outdoor table, and 2 other people that turned out to be Latvian translators, since most in our convoy spoke little Russian. As we women passed the table in front of the translators, we could hear them tell the Chekists that we were members of anti-Soviet Latvian guerrillas, politically fascists, and prostitutes. These were all lies, as we, you, and everyone knew.

The next day our group was directed to enter deeper in the woods. We stopped in an area where there were some round canvas tents already set up. These tents were empty except for bare wood planks which would serve as our beds, and two barrels. One barrel served is a makeshift stove, and the other was our toilet. At night they locked the doors. Although it was only August, we were far enough into the Siberian heartland that winter had begun. The ground was frozen and it started to snow. Everyone was suffering from the cold, and I remember our hair being frozen to the fabric that lined the tent. After a fairly short stay in this tent compound we left, and the tents became occupied by POW's, Germans and others captured in the Volga Campaign. We were transported to our new Gulag slave camp, Vyatlag 232, by the Gulag administration to replace the dead prisoners in that Camp.

[**NOTE:** *Vyatlag, founded in 1938, was located in central Russia. The village of Lesnoy in the Kirov area of Russia is the center of this Gulag operation, about 600 miles northeast of Moscow. It is a heavily forested area, and much of the ground is marshy and spongy, making any kind of transport activity very difficult. The weather is unpleasant, with extreme cold, massive storms, frequent rain, and so on. It was a forestry camp with*

*some other side activities such as brickmaking, wood process-
ing, furniture building etc. This was one of the largest Gulag
concentrations in the Soviet Union, with about 100,000 prisoners having been there during the peak years of 1938 through
about 1955. About 20,000 of the prisoners died there. During
the war years, through 1945, the death rate was calculated at
24%; interestingly, at Buchenwald, the infamous Nazi camp, the
mortality rate during the same period was about 14%. This is
not to minimize Buchenwald. All data of this kind is notoriously
tricky, and the Communists especially hid and manipulated it,
but the numbers are nonetheless striking. The prison population
at Vyatlag was maintained at about 30,000 prisoners at any one
time. During the World War II years, 1941 through 1945, conditions were exceptionally harsh. Prisoners were expected to work
16 hours per day: it was horrible work, hand sawing, limbing,
stacking and dragging logs to meet impossible quotas to get meager food which was tied to quota achievement, and was at best
case a starvation ration; winter freezing, and summer attacks
by mosquitoes; waiting, exhausted, in lines for the these meager
rations, or to be counted before and after work; competing to
dry out inadequate wet clothing on the barracks stove; catching
some sleep while under attack from lice and bedbugs; and dealing with numerous endemic illnesses like scurvy, pellagra, dysentery, typhus, frostbite and the effects of starvation, where the
body eats itself. The food ration during this time was also totally
inadequate, just flour and grain often mixed with inedibles to
form a sort of bread. There was no fat, meat, fish, potatoes or
other vegetables or fruits which were required to sustain life in
those harsh conditions. Many Latvians and Baltic people were
imprisoned at Vyatlag, and there are memorials erected in different spots in remembrance of those stuffed into the common
burial pits scattered throughout the area.*

*Crimes against the prisoners were also being constantly commit-
ted by the guards and the camp management. Sometimes guards
would provoke prisoners to escape, and then kill them for sport.
Food theft was rampant, since food meant both an extended
life and power to barter, trade, or otherwise enrich or even save
your life. Theft could be in small ways, such as the bread slicer
shorting each inmates ration just a little, and thereby increasing
his/her own intake and having barter potential. Or, theft could
be huge. In Vyatlag, a gang of 12 people stole 170,000 rubles
worth of food - denying the starving prisoners of that amount.
General stealing was common, with the true criminals mixed in
among the political prisoner population able to take extra food
and all other goods by force. Rape was very common, both as
a forced event, or in exchange for food or favors. By January
1943, it became policy in this camp that weaker prisoners were
to be denied food which was to go to stronger prisoners, as a
way to fulfill the norms that the state demanded. The criminals,
who often formed organized gangs inside the camps to prey on
the other political prisoners for their own enhanced survival
chances, were also a primary tool encouraged and used by Camp
administrators to maintain order over the larger political group
of prisoners. For example, in Vyatlag, thieves demanded a 25
ruble bribe from every political prisoner, and in fact murdered
nine who would not or could not pay. Some of this take would
typically go to administrators. In the 1930s and 1940s, these
criminal gangs had great power within the camps because the
political prisoners arrived in the camps as normal people, though
typically half starved, beaten, terrified, ill, and not organized.
The criminal gangs saw them as easy pickings. But after World
War II ended, in 1945, things changed a bit. The camps began
to fill with a new breed of political prisoners who were former
soldiers, partisans, and so on. They put up a fight individually,*

and occasionally even organized into groups that intimidated both the criminals and even the camp leadership. When Joseph Stalin died on March 5, 1953, this news filtered into the Camps, to a mixed reaction. Some Camps remained silent, wondering if the news was true, wondering whether it was planted news to watch the prisoners reactions; but in some camps, including Vyatlag, the news of the monster's death was openly celebrated. Conditions in most camps improved a bit immediately after Stalin's death. Prisoners started feeling bolder and Camp commanders got more nervous. Revolts in various forms broke out. While there had been major revolts in the Gulag before, always brutally crushed buy Red Army troops invading the unarmed protesters and executing them by the thousands, in 1953 it started to change. In Vyatlag in November 1953, 530 prisoners refused to work, demanding pay, clothing, and better living conditions. Many of these demands were granted by the weakened authorities - and then the prisoners struck for amnesty, with some success. Unfortunately, after these minimal successes, the organizers were imprisoned.]

Now, back to Rita's story. Her reflections chronicled here were made during the 16th week of her imprisonment at Vyatlag 232: There was a zone of 2 barbed wire fences, with the inside row being composed of 5 runs of wire, and the outside fence composed of 15 barbed wire rows. Every corner had high guard towers complete with armed guards and bright floodlights. Men and women were separated in this camp, the usual arrangement. In each barracks there lived 100-120 prisoners. Sleep facilities consisted of two levels of platforms, made of boards, covered by dirty cloths of various colors that acted as mattresses and blankets. The lower level had 4 small windows. In the winter, in the middle, there was a single small 60 watt bulb. Also in the middle was a makeshift tin metal stove that was supposed to heat the barracks, but it was insufficient. The air was stagnant. Generally, the barracks unit was very dirty, dank and low. This was depressing to inmates who had suddenly been yanked from their clean homes. If you wanted to sit up on the lower platform, your head would hit the bottom of the top bunk. If you sat up on the top platform, your head would hit the ceiling. Also, the barracks were infested with vermin - lice and bedbugs. *[Note: this occurred everywhere in the Gulag and is remarked upon in all prison literature].* Rita continues: in no time we were overcome by lice and bedbugs. We covered our heads and faces with any available rags the best that we could, so that they would not crawl into our ears and noses. I was assigned to a top upper bunk. On both sides of me slept Russians. Russian women in the Camps were almost always thieves and criminals in their former lives. They immediately set upon me and the other newcomers and stole from us whatever we had left over from our transport. They would of course also try to steal the little bit of bread which most prisoners tried to save for the next morning's breakfast. Our bread ration was given to us once per day, in the evening. We would hide this bread under our clothes and shirts, on our chests, to try to stop it from being stolen, which the Russians would try to do during the night. The hope was to have enough bread to survive the following day.

In the entrance area of each barracks was a water barrel. This is where we could wash our hands and faces of some of the filth accumulated during a day's work outside in the forest in the mud. In winter, the water would freeze. We would then melt snow in our hands so we could wash, but doing that increased the cold that we were already suffering from. Twice a month we were allowed to go to a sauna and were given half a pail of warm water and a sliver of green soap. With that, we could wash a bit. While we were washing, our clothing was put in a hot chamber, to kill the lice. Upon exiting the sauna, there was a pile of clothing left for us, and we took whatever was left at the time we got there. There was a great immediate relief from having lice-free clothes, but this only lasted for a few days. Sometimes this change of clothing improved your clothing situation, but sometimes not.

Either way, in no time we would be infested by lice again, and we would look forward to the next washing.

Camp toilets were located outside, about 150 feet away. Earlier inmates had simply dug a hole in the ground covered by two planks, hammered together with some boards. One simply squatted on these planks and did their business; it was degrading and disgusting, by design to make us feel more subhuman. In winter nights, lighting was by the moon and everything was frozen, dangerous, and slippery; but in warmer weather the smell was horrible and the area was filthy and infested with flies. Winter conditions were preferred, but there were extra problems for the skinny and starving inmates who had to go. Everyone would have to get dressed to protect a bit from the freezing cold, and you would try to do your business all at one time. Often by the time you would get your clothes off enough to go, it would be too late. Then for 2 weeks you would get no different clothes. You had to go to work every day in the clothes in which you had the accident. Conditions were made more hellish by the stomach problems experienced by so many unfortunates. Dysentery and diarrhea were common, debilitating to the victim and disgusting and unhealthy for the other prisoners.

Clothing was poor and inadequate. I was not the only one who had non-fitting clothes; it was a common problem, resulting in getting frozen and getting sick a lot. I had left Latvia with only a light summer dress, so I was early on often chilled and caught colds easily. When it started to snow, we were given cold weather winter clothes. These consisted of padded pants and coats, "valenkas" boots, and a winter hat with ear flaps. All these articles of clothing were old and worn out and roughly sewn together. The valenki were a combination of boots and footclothes, with 99 patches, and they were so heavy that only the dead could comfortably wear them. So we had no real shoes or boots; instead, we had these rags that we would wrap around our feet. They would of course soak through easily, and in the winter frostbite was a common and debilitating problem. We were sure that this clothing had been salvaged from the war front, because blood was often still visible.

In summer we were given pants, without the padding, and something resembling tights or gym clothes. The women were also given a small scarf. Footcloths were on our feet both summer and winter, but in summer we also were given slippers. These were made of the rubber scavenged from old tires or rubber belts. They were heavy and extremely filthy.

My work was entirely in the forest: sawing down trees; hacking off all the side branches; and splitting the logs for firewood. We each worked alone, using a flexible hand saw to cut down the trees, and then split the logs on wood blocks using an ax. Quotas were assigned.

[NOTE: the authorities established these quotas and would change them over time depending on their orders from the state. For the slave, making quota meant literally life or death because it was tied to a food ration. Consequently, all kinds of cheating, threatening, bribing and so on occurred. In a typical camp, the inmates worked as part of a small group that had a prisoner boss, the brigade leader. This boss, his behaviors, and his relationships in the camp became prime determiners of the fate of his team. A rough boss might simply steal a weaker team's quota. They would eat, the weaker team would die. Or the boss might provide favors for the Camp cook - scarce goods, sex, other services - and thus obtain more food for his team. Sometimes the weaker, sicker members, the "goners" who were expected to die soon, were hastened toward that end by stealing their rations to better feed contributors to the norm. This was an absolutely brutal survival game.]

Back to Rita's journal. Our brigade leader would every day record each worker's output. Depending on the output, we would get different food rations. The quotas or norms were so large that the women could not deliver them. For missing a norm, the prisoner might be punished not just by decreased food ration, but also by being placed overnight in a detention cell. I was in such a cell one night; I had broken 2 saws in one day. This of course had interrupted my work and output, but the administration saw it as a punishable offense.

The wood norm was set at 10 cubic meters per day (about 353 cubic feet). That is, you had to cut the trees down, remove the branches and burn them, then saw the log into 1 meter (3+ feet) lengths, split the larger-diameter logs, and stack the results into a pile 1 meter (3+ feet) high and 3 meters (10+ feet) long. That is the dimension of the daily norm or quota. There would be questions about the amount of wood each slave produced, but we wouldn't know each worker's exact output; that reading depended on the reasoned judgement of the brigade leader, who knew all and oversaw everyone's work. Sometimes numbers were adjusted for individuals to make it better overall for the group. So the brigade leader was a very powerful position, although a slave him or her self.

We also had to transport the logs to the Railroad center for loading. This work was so heavy, unfamiliar, with no training or guidance, and in such cold weather. In winter, temperatures of -25 or even -40 degrees C (-13 to -40 F) were common. Clothing was meager, and you fought to stay alive all day, every day. The diet was so lacking that there was little energy left to actually do the work, much less march for miles to and from work. Our strength was quickly sapped by the extent and excess of our labor. We Latvian prisoners were treated especially harshly by the administration, who were Russians. We were called fascists, and the Russians had been trained to treat us as subhuman beasts whose only value was the labor that could be squeezed out of us. Cruelty toward us was a positive and laudable action, according to the creed of the Communist Russian overseers. When I first arrived, there were many Latvians in the work brigades, and we would pray together on holy days, gathering together under a pine tree in the forest, praying to the Almighty God to keep us strong, to keep our faith in Him. The Russians didn't like this, since the Communists were officially atheists and had actively purged churches, priests and believers up to and including elimination. Consequently, the Latvians later were split apart and sent to different brigades and camps to minimize the tribal fraternization and potential problems. This made our hard life even harder.

Twice per day rations were issued, morning and night. All prisoners received the standard ration, which was 400 grams (about 14 oz.) of black "bread", always adulterated with sawdust, ground acorns and so on, with flour being a minor component. A bit of something called "soup" was also part of the ration for meeting the norm. It consisted of water, greens, rotten tomatoes and other random spoiled goods. In summer, the soup was made with green lupins and field grasses. It was a thick grass soup over which was poured a teaspoon of oil. If the norm was met by a slave, an extra 100 to 200 grams of bread were allotted, along with a small piece of salted, dried fish.

I later calculated that the caloric value of this daily norm was 800 to 1000 calories, but that the work was so heavy that more than 4000 calories were used up to achieve the norm! But that was precisely the goal of the Communists: to gradually starve to death the undesirable persons while extracting the maximum work from them. What horrors we went through! But more slaves could easily be had.

9.5 THE WAR YEARS; DEATH STALKS

The early war years of 1941 - 1943 were the times of the peak horror. In our Camp, and throughout the Gulag, many slaves died. Of those arrested and transported with me in June 1941, I state with confidence that 98% did not survive. Each morning our barracks were full of dead people, and they would be collected and thrown, naked, into a large wooden box. Entire barracks were also filled with prisoners who could no longer walk due to starvation. These sights became so common that we got used to it and it seemed normal. We took it without emotion, feeling neither pain or pity for the victims. We were all on the borderline of death. One would acknowledge that tomorrow, or some other day, we would be carried out in the box. That appeared to be the only escape. *[**Note:** I only remember meeting Rita once, already at an advanced age and sick; when I haltingly asked her about her experiences, she kept repeating "lici, lici", meaning "dead, dead", and with a shudder spoke to me of the sight of stacked bodies, seared in her memory].*

Rita: What we witnessed in the camp was a continual growth of malnutrition, and lack of vitamins and minerals. We were sick with scurvy, pellagra, dysentery and typhus from the lice. Prisoners' teeth would start falling out from their bleeding gums. Hair would start falling out in clumps. People became more skeleton-like with sharp faces and hollow eyes, with bones protruding through the thin flash. One was constantly hungry, dreamed incessantly of eating, but at times the available "food" could not be digested.

Everyone was constantly tortured by incessant hunger, and inmates responded to this in very individual ways, using different strategies to get food. Many would wander around near garbage pits and hope to find anything edible that might have slipped out. It was common to take grasses and nettles and cook them with the bread ration to extend the meal. Many foraged and ate various plants they found in the forest, and especially prized were mushrooms. Sometimes the mushrooms were poisonous, and many people died. I did not do things like that and somehow fortunately escaped the starvation. Also, as mentioned elsewhere, there was constant trading of any available goods or favors or sex to try to get enough calories to survive another day.

We did not hear much about the fate of the men who had been arrested with us. For many of my fellow female prisoners, this was extremely difficult, with the circumstances of husbands, fathers, and brothers unknown. I saved myself from the all-engulfing pessimism by giving thanks for whatever small events that had any glimmer of good, and maintaining hope that this torture would someday end.

In general, women were stronger and fared better than man in several ways. They handled starvation better. *[**NOTE:** this was a common Gulag observation. Women typically have a greater fat reserves than men, and the men were typically assigned to harder tasks requiring greater caloric output, and were typically heavier, all of which required more food then most women needed. The ration amounts, though, were typically the same for both genders. General work conditions, the type of work, and the brutality of the guards and criminal gangs, was also much harsher for males, who were also viewed as being more dangerous prisoners, more likely to fight back or organize to make guarding them more dangerous].* To continue Rita's story - so the men died earlier of starvation, and also lost any hope of overcoming the suffering earlier and thus died more quickly. Women also seems spiritually stronger in that they did not lose hope as easily, somehow taking strength from the starving person's constant dream of eating dark bread until they were full.

One of my roommates, the Russian woman who slept next to me, worked in the kitchen. Naturally, she was well fed and would bring back to the barracks bread that would dry out. She would wrap this extra bread in a kerchief and hang it near her face, between our beds. That created such a temptation for me to take it; a temptation that was exceedingly hard for me to overcome. I would grope this bread bag at night, and the knowledge of it being so close to me would keep me up at night. Yet the need to take this bread was so big that it almost overcame my strength to resist improper behavior. I rationalized in my mind that taking and eating this dried bread would be different from taking and eating non-dried bread. I told an older Latvian prisoner of my tortured thoughts, and asked her how to deal with it. She disagreed with my thoughts of stealing the bread. When I came back to the barracks the next day after work, the bread bag was gone. The Latvian prisoner had spoken to the Russian and asked her to remove the temptation. That was good - thank God, it kept me from stealing it. Had I done that, I would have been beaten senseless by the Russian woman and her gang, as happened to so many others. It was very likely that the bag of dried bread was hung next to me intentionally, to provoke me into theft and serve as an excuse for the Russians to beat me.

When my prison term finally ended, I was in relatively good health, especially when compared to so many others. But during my slave work stretch at Vyatlag 232 the hard work, poor rations, scarce health care and generally horrible living conditions had reduced me to extreme thinness. Once, I was so weak from hunger that I could not make the trip back to the barracks from our forest work site. The guards started to hit me with the rifle butts and kick me with their boots, which left me so injured that I couldn't get up and walk. The guards then ordered 2 Russians from my brigade to drag me, one on each arm, back to the barracks. This they did, and when we arrived at the barracks I revived a bit. It had been snowing, and I was freezing and my arms and legs were aching terribly, since those appendages had been twisted while dragging me through the snow. While this was going on, I did not shed a single tear, since this would have been noticed by my torturers and give them satisfaction. But later, in the dark of night, I cried out of fear, hurt, and desperation. But part of me was also relieved and felt fortunate. That particular day the guard dogs, which typically help corral us while marching to and from work, had not been present. The dogs were well-trained by the guards and on command would bite or tear you apart. They could be vicious when ordered to attack prisoners. I saw prisoners who had been attacked by these dogs, bitten on the face and hands, with ears torn off and clothing shredded.

During this time of extreme hunger, I also became sick with typhus. I nearly died. We all lived crowded together, infested by ticks and fleas, and the lice carry the bacteria that causes typhus, which resulted in many cases. Once during this time I lost my vision. Another time, still while sick with typhus, at night while I was sleeping, a nurse could not feel my pulse and, thinking I had died, pushed my eyelids together. In the morning she came by to check my corpse and was shocked to find that I was alive! But as prisoners, our lives were expendable. We were like cattle waiting in the slaughterhouse. The guards cared more for the well-being of the horses and dogs than of us slaves. For example, if a horse broke a leg while working with a brigade in the forest, there would be a full inquiry by camp management. Every prisoner working with the horse would get some form of punishment for their presumed negligence or culpability leading to the loss of a valuable asset...a horse. But if in the forest a prisoner died, under any circumstance, no questions were asked of anyone, since it was just a prisoner.

I also survived being hit by a falling tree, which was a common occurrence. I was thought to be dead. Again, I was fortunate because the falling tree was slowed down by the branches of standing trees, and only the thinner top part of the tree crashed down on my head. The brigade leader had been working next to me and was aware that the tree would crash down, but said nothing to me, and was never questioned about the lack of warning. I was unconscious. Several hours later I woke up, to find that the doctor had already stitched up my head wound. I was too malnourished to even protest the incident to the medical staff. The camp doctors and nurses were also prisoners like us, and could work in their medical specialties in the camp hospitals. They did the best they could given the harsh rules they had to live by, and the lack of medical equipment and medicines.

I also got very sick with yellow fever, and again was not expected to survive. This incident revealed more details of prisoners' behavior. Another Latvian lady from the camp came to visit with me and said "Rita, you are going to die soon...can I have your dress?" She was talking about that summer dress I had been wearing when I was arrested, and which I had managed to keep. It was like a talisman to me, an object of much greater importance than just cloth and design, but a link to the time when I was a real human, caring for more than mere survival. I wore it only in the evening after work, on my birthday, Christmas, and on November 18, Latvia's Independence Day. I wanted to tell someone to bury me in that dress. But God's grace was again with me, and I survived the yellow fever. Unfortunately, one time that I wasn't wearing the dress, the Russian women stole it. I think the larger wisdom taught to me by this entire incident was that humans always desire and need some kind of shiny bauble to be near them.

9.6 THE LAW; WAR ENDS; LIFE IMPROVES

Crime and punishment in the Soviet Union during this time was bizarre. The persons deported along with me on June 14 1941 did not know what our crimes were. Five months after the transport, at the work camp, I and my group were called in front of a troika, a 3 person legal tribunal commissioned in Moscow. We were simply told what are crime was and what our sentence was to be. There were no discussions, no proof or evidence, simply cold declarations that shattered lives, and then on to the next victim. The shortest sentence was 5 years, and the longest was 25 years. All of my group was charged with violations of the infamous Article 58. I was sentenced under article 58.4 to a term of 8 years. [*NOTE: As mentioned elsewhere, Article 58 was the all-inclusive, widespread and often nebulous section of the Soviet penal code. It applied to anything deemed anti-Soviet, whether by deed or thought, with no proof necessary. 8 to 10 year sentences, followed by an approximately equivalent exile, with the place chosen by the authorities, was very typical*]. Back to Rita's story - I was sentenced under article 58.4 for being politically unreliable. Members of my group who previously had real or perceived contact with partisans, the active resisters to the Communist takeover, or perhaps were related to partisans, were sentenced to 25 years and initially jailed. I on the other hand did not suffer the torture of jail and was taken directly to the slave camps, along with the other June 14 victims. Our fate to the War's end was set. Besides the time to be served as slave labor, there were other elements to our punishment. Written communication was forbidden. No newspapers or any other information was available. There was no news published about us.

Then, in the second half of 1944, there began a sudden glut of news, day and night over the Camp loudspeakers, about the favorable progress of the War. We heard that we were winning the War, and in the middle of the next year we were told that the War was won! At this point our circumstances improved, but just by a little. We could now write two letters a year, but only send them within the Soviet Union. During this time I started letters to my relatives in Latvia but never received an answer. This was so hurtful, and dashed hopes I had of finally hearing from my people. The reason was quite simple - my relatives had fled Latvia. But I did not know this. Finally, from Vecgulbene, the District of my birth, after many written requests, I did receive a reply from some postal authority in Vecgulbene that the persons I was writing to were not at these addresses. Wondering about what had happened to my relatives was very difficult - were they in slave camps? Being tortured in prisons? Already dead? Or did they escape? Finally, there was one lady in the Vecgulbene facility that handled and cleared mail and information requests who remembered me from the past, having lived near my father's house. She looked up my prison address and wrote to me saying that my family had left, and provided me with some information about their whereabouts.

Later, I wrote to Ernest Lica in the town of Saukas in Latvia. We had worked together in the dairy at the time of my arrest. We corresponded a bit. Soon, his family sent me 2 care packages - which contained bacon, butter, wool socks, and mittens. In 1963, after I had been freed and went back to Latvia, I went to visit this family. I got to personally thank them for these packages, which were critical to my survival. Earlier, in 1953, after the death of Stalin and the ensuing easing of conditions, I had also started to correspond with my relatives in North America, who also started sending help packages. My address at the time was very simple: Vjatlag 232 - 12, indicating the 232nd camp designation within Vjatlag (Vyatlag), and the 12th section within that site.

At the War's end in 1945, conditions did start to improve. The food got a bit better. We were told that our meals now included ham from the United States. But since all were fed from a common pot, and we slaves ate last, by the time the ham got to us slaves, we couldn't even taste it.

The highly prized ham was buried in the other camp food, and was always pilfered by the camp administrators. In the barracks, the lice and bedbugs were under better control, with extended heat treatments. We could still go to the sauna once a week, and at that time got some clean clothes. The outer clothing also improved, along with some newer general clothing that showed up occasionally. There was still no pay for our work - food, clothing and shelter was all we got. Slavery was very valuable to the state. There was also a noticeable increase in civility to the prisoners from the guards and administrators. This did depend on conditions and what was needed from you, but things did improve. The country had been devastated by the War, and so many working hands had been lost that workers were more needed than before, and there was a greater attempt to keep us alive.

9.7 CAMP ENDS; EXILE BEGINS

In 1949 (at age 43) my sentence was over. I had served the 8 years as a prisoner, and now my time as an exile began. As is strangely typical for Communists, at 1 AM I was awaking from my sleep, and told I was free and to be ready to leave in an hours' time. What was there to gather? In a few minutes, I put on my work pants that I had earlier worn at work, and packaged the rest of my meager belongings. The guard took me to the same narrow-gauge railroad station where I had initially arrived, and sat me in a cage in the back of a rail wagon. That's how horses are transported. Without being told where I was going, the train departed and travelled for almost a day and a night. The train finally stopped next to a large concrete house in what looked like a large city. I was released from my cage and we were escorted into that large concrete building. This turned out to be the transit prison in the Siberian city of Krasnoyarsk. I stayed there about two weeks until enough prisoners arrived to justify the continuation of the journey to the next post. A major surprise occurred here for me - at night we slept in a bed with white sheets and pillows with pillowcases!

From there we traveled to the city of Kansk (about 250 km or 150 miles further, but still in the Krasnoyarsk region). At this point I was taken into a separate room and the authorities showed me a document that explained why I had been sentenced for the eight years of slavery. Those to blame were Latvians. This document had been written by a coworker in the dairy where I was working in 1941, claiming that I had told an anecdote which mocked the Red Army. An official stamp was in a corner of the document - "for arrest". I remembered that in that Russian-dominated dairy workplace back in 1941 I was given a warning to improve my work, and if I wouldn't or was unable to do so, I would be fired. This was a common Russian tactic in these times - everybody was encouraged to be hateful and suspicious of those around them, and any behavior could be slanted to make someone else look bad, or criminal. *[NOTE: this really was a common practice throughout Communist lands during these times. Those who turned others in were designated as heroes. One particular such event was a boy, Pavlik M. - referenced earlier, but its horror bears repeating - who turned in his own father, who was ultimately executed! Pavlik was on posters throughout the land as a hero to be emulated by every good young Communist. Some people denounced others openly to settle scores; some to curry favor with authorities; and some upon being squeezed by the Cheka to accuse others, or they or their families would be arrested. This both kept the number of slaves up, and controlled the population by terror].*

Rita continues: The person that gave me the document that explained my arrest was a Latvian, since the document was written in Latvian but he read it to me in Russian. As a fellow countryman, he told me what was probably going to happen next. A transport of 120 people was being formed at Kansk station, and I was to be part of it.

This turned out to be the case. We 120 prisoners were loaded into heavy trucks which took us to Taseevo (or Taseyevo), about 180 km (110 miles) northwest of Kansk. Upon arrival we were divided up to work in different endeavors such as forestry, salt mines, and collective farms. I wound up doing forestry work again about 10 miles from the bank of the Taseevo (or Taseen) River. I was taken to the forestry site by a car - a rare experience for me. This was where I was to live. There were 31 people in our forestry work group at that time, and more workers joined us later. Initially we all shared a large room in a barracks. Later this room had a small area sectioned off with a plank wall in which we 3 women, out of the initial 31 people, could live. After about a year, some prisoners who had been exiled here built small houses with real walls, rudimentary cottages. A small exile settlement began to take root.

The lumbering work continued, but there was one huge difference: we were being paid in money on a quota and piece work basis. Food and clothing were no longer provided as in the prison work camps. Fulfilling the norm set by the authorities was tough, because it was set so high, and our income went to buying food and clothing. We walked to work unguarded, but every night had to report to the Commandant after returning from work. There was no right to travel outside of our area without specific approval. In our little settlement there was a small store, and soon a restaurant opened where we could buy a hot supper after a day's labor. On Sundays and holidays we did not have to work. Otherwise, we could only miss work with the leader's approval. Payday was 2 times per month, on the15th and 30th. Since the pay was small, you had to manage your money carefully so that you would not run out of food between pay periods. Locals would sell us potatoes and milk. Bread, usually in small loaves, was also baked in a local bakery. I remember so clearly that after I got my first pay, I bought a loaf of bread and 200 grams of sugar. I crumbled some bread into a bowl, sprinkled it with sugar - which I hadn't tasted in years - poured cold water on it, and ate as much as I wanted. This was in fulfillment of a pledge I had made to myself 8 years ago! It was so good.

In the restaurant, the meat served was often that of the brown bear. The locals would hunt bear and provide the meat. It sounds odd, I must say, since different wild game often is thought of as being unpleasant to taste, but it tasted much like beef. The exception was if it was an old bear - then it tasted of pine needles. In truth, the brown bear eats clean foods: in summer, berries, nuts, and grasses; in bad years, in the winter, they would feed on the new shoots of pine trees. If you found where a bear had raided a wild honey spot, you couldn't pass it by. The contents were a welcome addition to the diet. Being around these bears sounds dangerous, but a bear typically does not attack other forest creatures or humans. It can get dangerous when the bear is protecting its young, or when in winter the opening to its cave is disturbed, awakening the bear from a sound sleep in its warm den. Hunters would look for bears and other forest animals, plus fish, all of which provided sustenance for our little community.

Now that we were no longer starving, we just had to make sure that we lived within our budget boundaries. We went to work the same way as always, working the logs, always bent over and feeling weak. In winter we wore padded clothes to shield us somewhat from the cold. In summer, we wore ordinary pants, which offered some protection against the hordes of mosquitos, flies, and other pests. "Maksa" plagued us greatly - they are tiny tiny flies, the size of a small seed. In summer there were also hordes of black flies, which loved to bite and feast on our blood. You could not even think of going about without a full face covering, or bare hands and arms or legs. We got to purchase special items to stop the biting. Thick nets made of horsehair were used to cover our heads and faces. Our pants and shirt sleeves had to be tied off at the ends to stop the bugs from crawling up into our bodies. And thus dressed, we worked in the summer. It would get very hot, 30 degrees C (86F), and dressed as we were to stop the bugs, the heat became a great torture. Today, women's pants are an unremarkable article of clothing, but in the camp setting 40 or 50 years ago, just wearing normal pants would have been such a blessing. Consequently, after release, I sewed my first dress out of 2 flour sacks, and it felt so civilized! Later in the exile years more standard clothing did become available for purchase.

Further into my exile I got to work in the restaurant for a half a year. It felt so great to be protected against the heavy work and insects. But this came to an end; as an exiled political prisoner, I had to go back and continue lumbering in the forest. At the job site it was permitted to have food breaks, and soon my job was as the camp lunch cook. I fed the horsemen, those workers who carted the logs from the worksite to the riverbank, utilizing horses. It seems unbelievable that one can cook soup in the middle of the forest, even at temperatures of -25 or -30 C (-20F). One can - I did it. A large pot would be hung between 2 trees, the kind of pot my mother would use to cook "sugar potatoes" years ago. In there we would add snow to the food ingredients we had available to make the soup. The horsemen would devour this hot meal in the freezing cold of winter, with gratitude.

Then, in 1953, news reached us that Stalin had exploded. Forgive me, please, for my harsh remembrances. Humans die, but this bloody animal, disguised as a human, should only explode. Stalin has been the greatest mass murderer of the 20th century. As documented by Aleksandr Solzhenitsyn, Stalin had murdered just Russians alone to the tune of 70 million people. [**NOTE:** *this number has varied widely due to differing definitions, data sources, and researchers, but a more widely accepted number is around 40 million; Mao in China is usually referred to as the greatest murderer of the 20th century, with 70 million victims, although from a much larger population base*]. Even the Kremlin bosses only notified the people of Stalin's death 3 days after they knew of it - they were afraid he would reawaken and then wipe them off the face of the earth.

After much political jockeying and drama, the more liberal Nikita Khrushchev became the ruler of the USSR. We imprisoned souls greeted this news happily. Khrushchev issued a directive that all political prisoners could write a plea, and their cases could get investigated. I wrote my plea. Latvia's highest court, after a 1.5 year time period, notified me that my plea was acknowledged, that I had been wrongly convicted and punished, and that I was officially rehabilitated. This is after 16 torture-plagued years, which stole from me the best years of my life. All those rehabilitated were issued new passports, allowed to travel, and allowed to acquire an apartment in their new place of residence. The workplace where you were arrested had to give you 3 months back-pay, and I did get that from the dairy company in Latvia where my troubles had begun. They were also to pay for the value of items confiscated from me at the time of my arrest. Since my former apartment and all my goods had been plundered at the time of my arrest, I had nothing - no goods at all - to declare, and consequently I got nothing. There was also to be a pension owed me by the state. To determine that value, I had to define the total work I did during the sum of my deportation, prison camp, and rehabilitation years.

Khrushchev quickly changed things for the better and was much appreciated. There were songs written about his goodness. The prison guards started acting in a more moral fashion. He even had Stalin's body removed from the mausoleum. Under Stalin's reign, we never would have gotten out of our slave labors in the forest. During our enslavement period, we would be visited in the camps by traveling performers and agitators sent by the government, whose message was to prepare ourselves to spend a lifetime in those present circumstances, because this was the way it would always be. This also applied to families that had been deported to populate the harsh, underdeveloped parts of Russia, where they built homes, started their lives anew, and too often did not survive. They also were visited by these traveling groups and told to expect to never leave their place of exile, and never to go back to their original home. So, many simply stayed in their new homes even after they were permitted to leave.

9.8 A HUSBAND; RETURN TO SOME NORMALCY; AMERICA!

I also stayed, because during my exile period I met a loving person who later became my husband. Our mutual sadness and our hard lives made us tighter and bound us closely together. If you're really close, dear reader, just by warmly holding hands, it seems that the hardness of life gets a bit easier. My husband had also suffered through 10 years in the labor camps of Kolyma. That is the infamous gold mining area in the far northeast of Russia, where almost all who were sent there, died there. He stayed alive only by circumstance, having a special skill set that got him a position as an accountant. His journey included prison and torture and other pressures to force him to sign a confession. For 8 days and nights he was held alone in a cement box to force a confession to the lies to which the authorities were confronting him with. My husband was also rehabilitated about the same time as I was, and we met on a transit.

*[**NOTE:** Rita only briefly mentions her husband, but it seems to have been a very loving and important relationship. We do not have his name, but other relatives thought that he had been a senior officer - perhaps a General - of the Polish Army, or possibly a Russian military leader, and enslaved in the Gulag by the Soviets. But he had survived. His primary place of imprisonment, Kolyma, was special for all the wrong reasons. It was called the Auschwitz of the Gulag...].*

Rita continues: In 1957 (at 51 years of age), my husband and I gave up our work implements, our axes and saws. Holding hands, with our free hand we each carried a pail with household goods and clothes. These were all the possessions we had after 16 years of hard labor. We experienced peace and lightness in our hearts. Finally, we were leaving the forests and all the insects that had plagued us for so long.

We settled and lived in the western part of Siberia in a big village on the shores of Lake Baikal. Soon we found work and had a small apartment. Let me tell you about the scenic Lake Baikal. It is the largest lake in Eurasia, with very clear clean water. It is 700 km (420 miles) long and 73 km (45 miles) wide, and very deep. Because of the depth, the hydrobiology didn't diversify, and it is thought that Baikal's waters are connected to a large underground water system. 336 rivers flow into it, but only one river flows out of it, the Angara. On this river there are 2 major power plants, at Irkutsk and Bratsk. Lake Baikal is also the only lake that has a very tasty and famous fish, the Omul. *[**NOTE:** Lake Baikal is a geographic splendor. Measured by volume, it is by far the world's largest lake, and alone contains 20% of the world's freshwater. It's maximum depth is 5387 feet, also by far the* *record. It has its own ecosystem with unique animals such as freshwater seals, and produces its own weather systems. It is a place of fascination, mystery, and majesty, and Rita's memoirs show great appreciation of the splendors of the area. She appears to have found a little bit of joy there after a life of toil and sadness.]*

Rita continues: After a few years we moved into the city. In 1968, my dear husband died. To lessen my sorrow, I communicated with my relatives who lived in the US and Canada, and they invited me to visit them. With major help from my brother Kondis Jaunzemis, and after delays and complications, I was finally granted visiting rights in the US for three months. After spending time with my relatives I did not wish to return to the Soviet Union and asked for asylum in the US, which was granted. Finally, after the events of June 14, 1941, I was reunited with my Latvian family, people who would not harm me…they were my relatives.

There were not many Latvians who did not have someone they knew well sent to Siberia during the 1941 June deportations - fathers, mothers, husbands, wives, brothers, sisters, and children. I had such a family, and fortunately we were all able to find out what had happened to all our members. For years there had been no contact possible for either party to know of their loved ones' destiny, what the conditions were like in the places in which they found themselves, and how their Motherland's culture was destroyed. I hope my story will help the families who lost loved ones in Siberia to understand how the deported suffered, and how their suffering finally ended. Even worse than my imprisonment and the circumstances of other deported families, as I was told by survivors, was the fate of prisoners sent to the extreme Gulag camps such as Vorkuta, Kolyma/Magadan and others. From these camps, few returned alive. The extremely hard labor, starvation rations, and the nine months of cold snowy weather too often killed them. It was cold enough with temperatures of -70 C (-94 F) that the ground never thawed, with permafrost everywhere. In the Magadan/Kolyma area especially, conditions were simply unbearable, and it was so far North that it remained dark much of the time. I raise my clasped hands in thanks to God that I received his blessing by not having been sent there.

The human language has not yet produced the words that can fully express the torture and human suffering that people endured in prisons, slave camps and psychiatric hospitals. My slavery years were very long and hard. At the beginning of my enslavement, I was still young (34 years old, having been born on August 23, 1906). Faith and the understanding of God's triumph, mercy and love, were not divulged to me to a sufficient degree to quell my doubts, and I started questioning God's will. In the worst times, not having the Cross to lean on made everything worse. There was no one to argue with or pray to for mercy, or from where to gain some understanding of the unbearable burden. Now I believe deeply in an Almighty God. He guarded over me and gave me the strength to overcome all my suffering in those most difficult times of my life.

My dear fellow countrymen, please always remember the many thousands of our Latvians under Soviet rule who suffered in jails, prison camps, psychiatric hospitals, and died in tormented conditions, and are dying even today. *[NOTE: Rita wrote these words prior to Latvia's latest independence in 1991].* Those Latvians were our Nation's sons and daughters. Their lives ended but there are no monuments erected in their memory, there were no proper burials in a cemetery, no headstones, no crosses, nothing. So in remembrance of June 14, 1941 we should go to church on that date and honor those people, have a service in their remembrance, ask for God's blessing, and bring flowers to be placed on the alter. You Latvians who reached freedom - you are in debt to those countrymen who suffered and still suffer, who died in great agony and still die, and be thankful that you did not experience the slavery of the Soviet Union. Remain a Latvian, honoring those who suffered and keeping them in your hearts and thoughts with your deeds.

CHAPTER 10

FAMILY SIRAKS/POMMERS

A fter the long detour illustrating what happened to those countrymen
and relatives who stayed in Latvia, let me now return to the rest of
my family history as it unfolded in America after the flight out of Europe.

10.1 1950s: BUFFALO NY

To review, Mom and I were living in Buffalo when Aleks visited us,
beginning a courtship while still working in Connecticut. With both feeling the time pressure of their shattered lives, in short order he moved to
Buffalo and they married on February 27 1955. Immediately a new and
much improved chapter began in our lives. It seems that the remainder of
the 1950s were relatively good years for our new family, with a few exceptions. We were financially viable. Our expenses were small, with total thrift
being the guiding principle. The economy was strong enough that Aleks
had steady employment at the NY Central Railroad. Our two bedroom
upstairs apartment was affordable, partly because inner city Buffalo was
transitioning to being a minority ghetto. Mom had a goiter attack; it was
removed and she stopped working at the Gerber sausage plant, never to
work at a company again. She also had her final miscarriage, losing Aleks'
potential son. This pregnancy had been a troubled one, and Mom told
the physician that things did not feel right. He listened and observed and
assured her that all was okay - and then she lost my half-brother. Although

I was too young to have a sense of loss, I do clearly remember the pain and bitterness that Aleks and Anna felt. Aleks especially was angry and bitter, feeling that the incident was another example of the unfairness of life and its poor treatment of the second-class citizens of the world. Through all this, the newlyweds had the relief and joy of finding a sense of newfound security, a sense of love and sharing, together. Their happiness had to be heightened by the contrast to their recent, separate lives - it is only by living through especially low valleys that one can experience exceptional highs. Although I have no specific memory, I must have strongly felt the comforting warmth of these times.

We were part of a small Latvian community in the Buffalo area, so there was a sense of social normalcy. The center of this Latvian community was the Latvian Evangelical Lutheran Church, which we attended weekly and in which Mom and Aleks had been wed. Space was rented from a larger congregation for the weekly services, but the Pastor was a Latvian immigrant who had fled like the rest of us. His name was Rev. Vejins (pronounced Vay'-insh, meaning "Wind"), and he was a wonderful man, the embodiment of what a pastor should be. He took great care of the spiritual needs of his congregation that had suffered so much and lost everything. Being around him gave me a sense of being near holiness, and although our interchanges were few, I remember him with extreme fondness.

Our extended family, Uncle Arturs, Aunt Elza, Kitija, Inara, Olita, and Grandma Berta were also in the greater Buffalo area. They provided a family and social anchor of great importance. Aleks had no relatives in the US, and Mom's side had the Jaunzemis family in Niagara Falls plus a few other more distant relatives a few hours away in Canada. Arturs and Elza both worked - he in a box company, she at the bushel factory - while the three daughters continued with school. With a personal mortgage-type loan from the wonderful Miller family of Colden, they built a four bedroom, one bath house in the fields of Orchard Park, New York, now a trendy suburb of Buffalo. My family would often go there on weekends and special occasions, and these expeditions gave me a wonderful sense of family and some sense of social security. The home, at 718 Chestnut Ridge Road, still exists, and it will be ever in my heart. My aunt and uncle were wonderful to me, and my three cousins were (and are) such loving souls. I don't know if they have ever realized how much their affection meant to me. Such warm memories!

Grandma Berta also lived there, and I remained close to her. When I would spend some extended time at the house, especially during summer vacation, I would share her upstairs bedroom and her bed. I remember waking in the morning and seeing her sitting next to me, silently braiding her silver hair, and smiling at me. To entertain me while all the others were gone, she taught me some card games. We would play, and she would cheat in such a manner that I could catch her, but she would win, always with a big smile to let me know that it was just a fun game. My anger and frustration at this behavior was quite intense, perhaps too intense, but she did teach me some lessons about the ways of the world, which I think have helped me navigate life. Bottom line, I was very fond of Grandma.

Later in 1955 Grandma got very sick with liver cancer. We had all gathered at the house one evening when the end was expected, and the end came. She was in great pain and from that perspective her passing was a blessing. Everyone, but especially Anna and Arturs, were broken hearted. Perhaps the depth of suffering that this, or any small family experiences, does tend to heighten the feelings for one another - and they were deep. I also recall this as my first experience of an intense emotional low. A bit prior to Grandma's passing, I sat alone next to her, asking her how she felt. Through the fog of pain she replied "it hurts everywhere", and then drifted off. These final words and impressions of seeing Grandma near death deeply disturbed my young mind, and for the first and only time in my life I had vivid and frightening nightmares, and could not sleep alone in my bed for a bit.

My life seemed good during this time. I had a new father and I was very happy about that. This consciously made me normal, like other kids.

My mother was visibly more relaxed, with the new husband and provider in the house able to share her load and lighten her burdens. We had the Studebaker and the gift of mobility, with day trips to area parks, Niagara Falls, and visiting the relatives in Orchard Park. I was doing very well in school, despite being relatively new to English, and it was recommended to Mom that I skip second grade. Wisely, she refused. During this time I learned to love school, and to really appreciate my teachers who were so helpful and kind to me. Also at this time began a lifelong love of reading, with strong encouragement from Anna and Aleks. Here I also had my first non-family friends, including my buddy Norman; Denise Lenihan, my first "wife"(!) from a first grade kids' ceremony; and Jane, who lived around the corner from us. The downside was a case of scarlet fever; the realization that my vision was extremely poor (20/400?), soon corrected by lenses; and my first and last whipping with a belt by Aleks for a misconstrued fun roughhousing event in the snow with other friends. I never forgot or forgave Aleks for this event, and I think it produced a slight wariness of my stepfather that lasted a lifetime. But bottom line, this was a good and happy time for our small family.

10.2 1950s - 1960s: ROCHESTER, EAST ROCHESTER

Things soon changed again. Aleks' railroad job moved to Rochester New York, and we followed. I began fourth grade at Number 19 School. We lived in a downstairs apartment on Hawley Street in the city's 19th Ward, very close to where my future wife, Sue Galloway, was growing up. Later on we discovered that some of my fourth grade classmates had become lifelong friends of Sue's - especially Steve O'Neil (deceased around 2014) - who is forever notable for giving me the nickname "Indy". Bless him!

The move to Rochester cut into our social circle of Latvian friends and relatives. We would visit the Buffalo area relatives periodically, which we all really enjoyed, but my folks never established any real connection with the small Rochester Latvian community and church. This was the beginning of the lifelong retreat from normal socialization for Aleks and Anna. I believe that this was the way Aleks wanted to live, and Anna went along with it willingly, wanting to keep her new husband happy and wanting to preserve peace in the family. This may have also been the beginning of the growth of Aleks' mental difficulties, or perhaps the result of them. These issues grew to be quite severe by the end of his life, resulting in paranoia, plots by neighbors against him, and occasional verbal outbursts and rants that increasingly threatened to get physical, but never did. It did keep me on edge, however, since one never knew when an outburst might happen.

The other side of the story must also be mentioned to give some balance to Aleks' life. He was a good, hard-working man with a profound sense of right and wrong, and a deep-seated hatred of injustice. He worked tirelessly to provide for his new wife and stepson. Anna and Aleks had the closest loving relationship I have ever seen - they absolutely cherished one another. It was more like being two cells of a single organism rather than two close organisms. They found peace in each others presence, and quiet joy. But this closeness also pulled them from society and made for an insular existence.

In the summer of 1956 we moved again, this time to East Rochester, a village of 10,000 people with a major New York Central Railroad facility, the "Car Shops". ER was actually America's first planned community, with grid of streets (tree names in one direction, presidents' names in the other), and designed around several industries. Biggest of these was the New York Central Railroad Car Shops, and the other was the Aeolian Piano Works. This was a middle-class town with a predominant Italian population, reflected in the strength of St. Jerome's Catholic Church, a powerful influence in the Village.

We moved into a small second story apartment on E. Elm St. It was a short walk to work for Aleks, and the town was pleasant and generally good to us. Here I met my first local friends and schoolmates - Frank,

Marcia, Jane, Dave, and later Tom, Greg, Zeb, Stan, Lenny, Brian, Lynn and others - plus other classmates with whom I still meet annually to play golf. I entered the fifth grade here, blessed with a wonderful and welcoming teacher, Mrs. Quenell, and stayed in the ER system until graduation from high school. There were many great teachers and coaches who influenced my life in a good way.

Mom and Aleks made several other moves in East Rochester. Each was closer to the Car Shops and the main line of the New York Central Railroad tracks, with consequently cheaper rent. Every apartment was upstairs, with a single bedroom. After E. Elm St., we moved to W. Chestnut St., and there we happened to be next-door to Frank, a talented basketball player several years my senior. Frank ultimately became a basketball star at Rochester's elite McQuade Catholic High School. His back yard hoop gave me a place to play a sport I loved, and I learned it all there.

Aleks was too busy to participate in any way in sports with his step-son, plus he had no sports background, having led a hard life of work on the farm, then the armies, then as a refugee, and so on. In a sense, his childhood had been stolen from him and he never got it back. Apparently he had played some soccer in his own elementary school years, and perhaps in some pickup games as a soldier, but that was sadly it. So he was ill-equipped to guide anyone in athletics, but was always a supporter for the role of sports in my life. I often wonder if Aleks would have been a great athlete under different circumstances. He was about 5'7" and weighed 200 pounds at his prime, but thick, large-boned, and exceedingly well muscled. His fingers were of enormous girth, probably twice the size of mine, and he was famous for his sheer strength which he would never brag about but which would be evident when he would casually pick up some heavy object that others could not budge. Once, in a fit of joy, he and I raced around a loop in nearby Powder Mill Park. I was probably in eighth grade, a fast runner, and in good shape - and he won! We will never know what he might have become athletically, but I can imagine him as a feared football linebacker, unable to be blocked, of legendary strength and stamina, and a quiet leader by example. Again, how sad that life dealt him a hard hand and denied him many joyful pursuits.

After Chestnut Street, we moved to 114 E. Maple St., directly next to the main line railroad tracks, with trains often rumbling and whistling through, all of which took some getting used to. A year or two later, after our monthly rent was jacked up by $5, we moved next door to 112 E. Maple St., again a small second story apartment with our usual floor plan of a kitchen, bathroom, bedroom and living room whose pullout couch was my bed until I graduated college and went off on my own.

All through this time Aleks worked as a machinist or machinist's helper primarily in the Car Shops. There were periods of unemployment, with forays into other companies for work, but when the the Car Shops called him back, he went. During the stretches of unemployment, the mood in our home was tense. I remember not wanting to go home from elementary school, and even hiding in bushes near the Elm St. apartment to wait until Aleks left for work on the 4 PM through 11 PM shift. When I saw him leave, I would get up out of my hiding place and go home to my loving Mother. There was never any openly physical or even verbal violence, but Aleks was always on edge during his unemployed times and I did not want to be near him. Again, our relationship had this as a component until he died, along with many good times. In his defense, life pressures were so hard on him - he would always be the most productive worker but seemed to be let go early because he was newer, could not linguistically argue his case, and was not of Italian heritage in a railroad union seemingly dominated by Italians who were often relatives. A profound sense of unfairness permeated Aleks' life, based on his stacked experiences; he strongly resented the injustice for himself and his family, but more importantly, for all mankind. There was an anger always brewing under the surface. Yet, we had to financially survive, and the pressure was on him to overcome these feelings and play the hand he had been dealt the best he could.

Mom during the late 1950s was still sickly - perhaps from the goiter removal, and possibly the effects of menopause. Despite this, she started to contribute to the family larder by taking in laundry for ironing. This activity slowly expanded to cleaning houses of wealthier area residents, and then doing some babysitting. Her marketing was done by word-of-mouth, and she was much appreciated by her clients. Her work was also excellent - she and Aleks were simply outstanding workers, and I think (hope?) some of that rubbed off on me. What a great gift!

Our primary entertainment during the late 1950s through early 1960s was fishing. This became a passion for Aleks and he was a relatively relaxed and happy person while so engaged. We started on some small ponds, extensions of Lake Ontario, places like Buck Pond, Cranberry and Long Ponds. The primary catch was sunfish and yellow perch, with an occasional northern pike, largemouth bass or walleye. Here began my love for freshwater fishing - although there were plenty of times that I would have strongly preferred doing something else with my friends - and my first exposure to boating. We would occasionally rent a rowboat to increase our fishing range, and started branching out to larger waters such as Sodas Bay of Lake Ontario and Conesus Lake, and this increased the catch. Although the sport was fun, we were also after the meat. Nothing caught was ever thrown away, and all was consumed. Nearby, at Irondequoit Creek in Powder Mill Park, trout were stocked for opening day on April 1, and we would often go there and catch our limit of 10 trout each. Mom would join us and especially enjoyed seeing Aleks being happy and me also having a good time. I did always hope that no one I knew would ever see my mother while fishing, because it was a source of private embarrassment for me. But fishing like this was a healthy source of recreation, a money-saving source of protein, and a family activity that we could enjoy together. Aleks built a portable smokehouse and we would set it up in Powder Mill Park and smoke our catch in it, to the great delight of our relatives who would get some of the bounty. Mom also made delicious fried/baked fish meals that everybody enjoyed, and our children still remember fondly.

10.3 THE SMALL-TRIBE IMMIGRANT EXPERIENCE

I want to add some thoughts about the immigrant experience as seen through my eyes, which became very apparent to me in the time-frame I have been presenting. This is the perspective of a young boy without siblings, without a larger immigrant community to which one could attach, relative poverty, and parents who looked, acted, and spoke in a foreign manner. Take this as a small addition to the breath of the immigrant experience, so common throughout world history; please do not take my remembrances as a plea for pity. I actually was quite happy with my surroundings and had a decent life, but was very conscious of that which I am about to describe.

Let me start with my name, Indulis Pommers. The last name worked, but the first was a source of torture, even after I became "Indy" in the fourth grade. In school, the first roll call with any new teacher was highly embarrassing. Names would be read off until the middle of the "P's", and then the teacher would pause. I would feel the flush of embarrassment, a redness traveling up my body. To this day, that feeling is well-remembered and highly unpleasant. Next, there would be some questioning mispronunciations of "Indulis". The class would smile and look at me, as I gave the correct pronunciation. Then it would be over. Unlike now, those were times when foreign names really stuck out, but even now, I would think that immigrants with strange names would understand this experience. Related to this, and cited earlier in this book, was the embarrassment of my birthplace, Bad Rothenfelde, Germany. Though the name was rarely mentioned publicly, to me it translated internally as "Bad Rotten Field", and I hated it!

Another downer was living in a one bedroom apartment, from fifth grade through college, in a middle class town where this was very unusual. I slept on the fold out couch in the living room. Fine, but I never, ever had any friends come over. I hid the lack of the personal bedroom totally - I believe no one ever knew. One particular incident surrounding the subject is still seared in my memory. In the summer after my freshman year of high school I broke my right ankle while playing basketball outdoors with classmates Tom and John. They came over to our apartment to check up on me. At the time I was laying on the couch in the living room with my ankle in a cast, elevated. As my mother announced their arrival, I was filled with dread. Would they notice that I had no bedroom, and tell everyone else? Would they notice that there was no TV or telephone? Of course, my fears were exaggerated and proved to be groundless as I discovered many years later when questioning one of these visitors. But having spartan living quarters is a common immigrant experience, and many children have probably reacted to it the same way that I did. My way of dealing with the small apartments was to indulge in fantasy and imagination. The weekend newspaper we would occasionally get had a house blueprint as a feature; I would, with great satisfaction, doodle and draw my dream home based on these plans. I also played a game when in the car where I owned every 10th house that we passed, yielding some great dwellings that were "mine".

But… no phone, no TV until my junior year in high school. I specifically remember an eighth-grade assignment to write about your favorite TV show. My essay was about the Robert Q. Lewis radio show, which my peers didn't know existed. Again, it felt odd and out of place, although I remember defending it as a great show that my peers had regrettably missed. Regarding the telephone - if friends would say "I'll call you", I would always give an excuse and tell them I would call them. Two blocks away was a public phone at Woods Drugstore, where I would drop a dime and talk like regular people. I believe no one knew the truth.

Or… when there were parent conferences at school. My Mother would go. I would be a mess the day before, and the day after. The thought of my loving Mom, sitting there with unshaven legs in the European-style, speaking very broken English, working, to my great embarrassment, as a housecleaner and launderess, among the parents of my classmates - how would they treat her? What would they say to their children about the weird lady? Was her son also different? Would my classmates look at me strangely the next day?

Or dress - or habits - or spending money - or knowledge of dining etiquette - the antenna were always up, looking around to see what was "right" behavior, and quickly imitating it.

Perhaps, dear reader, this strikes you as overly sensitive, and perhaps I am…but this was my world. I hope that sharing these experiences will cast more light on the immigrant experience of children, especially those of small and unheard-of tribes. Yet this can also be the source of certain strengths, which may have eventually served me well. Absolutely no regrets!

10.4 1960s - 1970s: SOME PARENTAL PEACE

Now back to Anna and Aleks. After I left home for college in 1964, they continued their lives as usual. Aleks got long term employment at Fannon Metal Parts Company on Jefferson Road in Henrietta, New York after the RR Car Shops closed. He was a machinist, and was highly respected by his peers and management. It was a very good work experience. Mom continued to iron clothes, clean houses and babysit for her customers. Around 1971, with some help from my wife Sue and me, they bought a small house on 379 West Lake Road on Conesus Lake, an area called Sleggs Landing. It was a small house, with one bedroom, a living room, kitchen, a bath with a pit toilet, a glassed-in porch, and a basement. The water supply was pumped directly from the lake. Being right on the water, with their own dock, it was perfect for them. Since leaving Latvia, this was their first house! They loved it there, and did a lot of fishing from their 15 foot boat. When they moved to the lake, Mom stopped work, being in her 60's. In a few years Aleks also retired. They lovingly improve the property, using Aleks' skills as a natural born engineer. They added a flush toilet, created a rudimentary bedroom in the basement, along with other improvements. Their boat was upgraded to a dual hull, 50 hp, 16 foot boat named "L and

A", for our children Lauren and Amy. These were probably the best years of their lives. Sue and I had moved back into the Rochester area from Albany, and we would visit them frequently and enjoy the lake - boating, swimming, fishing. Our children also have fond memories of this time. In 1979 we moved out of the area to go to Boston, and the frequency of visiting obviously dropped.

Besides the aging process and its various infirmities, the only other downside was that Aleks' paranoia began to grow. For example, although they got along well with their neighbors, Aleks confided to me that neighbor John was sneaking over at night and pouring hot water on Aleks' tomato plants, as part of some scheme to claim some of Aleks' property. Understand that the properties were perhaps 20 feet apart, so the landgrab might have been for a 2 foot strip, hardly worth the effort! When I asked Aleks if he had actually witnessed these nocturnal activities, he said no, but that there could be no other explanation. This got my attention.

10.5 1980s - 2000s: GOOD TIMES, BAD TIMES, END TIMES

In 1984 Sue and I were planning to buy a lake home on Lake Winnipesaukee, a huge New Hampshire lake several hours north of our Acton, Massachusetts home. By then, as their only child, I was quite worried about having aging parents so far away, especially since their physical and mental ailments were growing. So, without giving it too much thought, I asked if Anna and Aleks would like to permanently move into such a lake house, participate in the costs, and be able to see our family more frequently. The answer came back as an immediate and strong "yes", but also without a lot of reflection. We were surprised by the speed of events, but proceeded to buy a larger house and the folks moved in.

At first, they loved their new home and much enjoyed the grandchildren's visits. They found acceptable physicians, chose the new food markets they preferred, and established good relationships with their neighbors. Aleks discovered how to fish the Lake, and soon had great success in both winter and summer. The fishing was actually better then in Conesus Lake, with more species, and larger sizes. The scenery and the side roads of the area were also beautiful, with more mountains, lakes and islands. Initially, the move seem to be working out really well.

Soon the troubles started. Aleks' paranoia became rapidly worse. I have heard that this is common when a change of scenery occurs to compromised individuals. In response, we expanded the house and created an apartment for them, so there was more privacy and distance; this also failed. Periodically, without warning, Aleks would explode with rage about something that we could not understand. One example was an outburst about a Christmas card my mother-in-law, Kay Galloway, had sent years ago to them. Aleks thought it was a cheap card and intended as an insult to them. Other times he would express that loving extended family members who would come to visit at the Lake would be insulting to him, behaviors that no one else ever saw. Another time, he was very angry about how our children had rubbed the sleeve of the wool shirt that he was wearing and exclaimed that "your shirt feels rough". He brought this up several years after the incident as being an insult to him. Aleks also started complaining about the lake and the fishing. Several times I had to send the family into the safety of the car and then back out of the lake house, with Aleks threateningly walking towards me, to escape back to Boston. These rides home were horrible, and rides back to the lake the next time were worse. Upon arrival "the next time", serious confusion would set in. Aleks would be a wonderful host, asking why we had not come earlier, etc. When told of the difficult incidences in the prior meeting, there would be a quizzical reaction of not understanding. Later, in a conversation with a psychologist friend, it was explained to me that people with Aleks' condition often have no memory of these outbursts. This would explain things, but I was not aware of it at the time. Also during this time Aleks was under a doctor's care and was given antipsychotic medicines. But as is often the case, he stopped taking them.

Things simply could not continue as they were. I feared for the safety of my family, a position that caused great internal agony. We had to confront the situation head-on, and did so. Anna and Alex had to leave. I made many trips back to New York and finally bought them a house on the same side of Conesus Lake as before, and they moved back in 1988. With less contact, relations became more peaceful, although periodic outbursts perhaps once a year would happen, but since I was typically the only member of my family there, the outbursts were less worrisome.

Life again seem to normalize for Anna and Aleks in their new/old environment. They had a nice and larger house on the same side of their familiar lake; they now had a garage, which Alex always wanted and which the first Conesus Lake house lacked; they had their same boat back in familiar waters; they had their few but familiar friends, and some new terrific neighbors who cared and looked out for them. We also visited periodically and made sure that our children would see both sets of grandparents.

Now aging began to take it serious toll. Mom had emotional trauma, well controlled but clearly there, about her husband's strange behavior and its consequences. Many years prior she had suffered a pulmonary embolism, and in the process of injecting a dye into her foot to track blood clots, the top of her foot had been chemically burned to the bone. A skin graft was performed and somewhat healed, but all this impaired her locomotion drastically and the slowdown over the years contributed significantly to her physical decline. In her mid-80s she started getting stomach complications, resulting in a diagnosis of a stomach tumor and perhaps cancer. One time, at age 86 in 2001, she was hospitalized with stomach bleeding issues and the prognosis was not good. I visited her in Highland Hospital in Rochester and had what we both thought to be our final conversation. This was actually a beautiful moment - the deepest, most loving conversation the two of us ever had. Then she rallied, and lived for more than another year!

On July 9, 2002, she went back into the hospital with additional intestinal bleeding. At 3 AM the morning of July 10, I got the call that she had died of a heart attack. My sadness for this wonderful Mother who was everything to me during the early years was profound, but it was dwarfed by the anguish that overwhelmed Aleks. I also realized that in her last year Mom was trying to leave me a present. She was teaching her son how to pass into that final stage, with grace and nobility.

While Mom's medical history at the end was grim, and not helped by some loss of vision due to macular degeneration, those years back on Conesus Lake from 1987 to 2003 were, I think, fairly happy times. She was with her Aleks, and they were both secure in there legendary love for each other. Mom was performing her comfortable routines as mistress of the house - cooking, cleaning, provisioning. She could attend her flowers and vegetables, fish a bit, and enjoy the Lake and Aleks' love of it. Her brother Arturs, sister-in-law Elza, best friend and niece Kitija and her family were close enough for easy visiting. Other friends and neighbors - few but loyal - were nearby. We would visit, and she could enjoy her two granddaughters and revel in the mutual love. Despite a hard life, she ended up a satisfied person.

Aleks also had an illness to deal with. In 1999 he had a heart attack, was hospitalized for weeks, and was on a ventilator for too long. Nurses attending him said he wouldn't make it. I had just lost my job at Unica and had time to stay with Anna and help them through this trauma. This was especially important since Mom had never learned how to drive. We were both by Aleks' side frequently and our bonding grew even stronger. Aleks had a pacemaker implanted and made a remarkable recovery - with no rehabilitation clinic required! We had been told to plan on a month or more of rehab, but in typical Aleks fashion he proved be strong as a bull and absolutely astounded the doctors. The first day he was allowed to walk, after weeks on his back, much of it comatose, he was climbing stairs, to everyone's utter amazement. While all this was going on, his non-Parkinson's hand tremors continue to worsen, to the point that eating and drinking became difficult, along with all the other tasks of life that require steady hands. Prostate cancer also paid him a second visit, and the radiation treatments left him with an internal scarring that would periodically leave him unable to urinate, resulting in emergencies with a horrible "drilling" cure. When Anna passed on, he was deeply wounded and lost. I stayed with him but could not invite him to live with us - fearful that an episode of paranoia might put my family in danger. We tried to get him to move near us in Massachusetts, but he refused. The next plan of having his Latvian nieces, who had visited them earlier, move in with him fell through because of immigration restrictions. These nieces then invited him to move back to Latvia and stay with them, which he happily accepted.

10.6 FULL CIRCLE: BACK TO LATVIA

I took Aleks to Kennedy Airport in New York City for his flight to Riga, Latvia, late in 2002. This also became an adventurous trip. His urethra had closed up the day before departure, and he had it drilled open. At 3 AM of the morning before we left - his last night on his beloved Conesus Lake - he started urinating blood, spraying all over the bathroom. It was as if the Lake was punishing him for leaving! I urged him to cancel the trip, but he was insistent on going. So we went - and at JFK, after passing the security and check-in line, we last saw each other. He turned, smiled, waved, and was gone forever.

We ended up on good terms, which is a blessing. One does not want to have unresolved grudges to carry indefinitely. He appreciated the help my family gave him in his latter, lonely stages; and we tried to acknowledge the debilitating illnesses he had, their effects on him, and his sincere efforts to be a good person, stepfather and grand stepfather. We were both at peace.

In Latvia, Aleks lived with his two nieces, neither of whom had families, in Plavinas, a small town on the Daugava River 50 miles east of Riga and 50 miles south of Gulbene. I was wary of the situation and had warned the sisters of his periodic odd behavior, but they were thrilled to have him. He took sufficient money with him for all of them to live comfortably. During phone calls with him, he seemed satisfied. He did some fishing in the River and enjoyed simply being in Latvia. Later I was told by the nieces that he did have a few episodes of paranoid rage, and they rented a small house for him close to the River and their apartment in Plavinas, and that this arrangement worked well. Unfortunately, his urinary tract difficulties continued and he was hospitalized for a while, and recovered. Then came a comedic/tragic stretch. Aleks always loved cars but explicitly planned to not drive in Latvia. A year prior to Anna's passing he had bought a late model Toyota Corolla, and absolutely loved the car. After he left for Latvia, I had driven this car to our home in Massachusetts and parked it there until Aleks decided what he wanted to do with it. Soon he decided. He wanted it shipped to Latvia!

With great trepidation, I made the arrangements for the shipment. It started with the drive to the Port of Newark, New Jersey, delivering it to the shipping company. After several weeks, it was shipped to Riga. Upon arrival, Aleks was notified and the sisters took him to the Port's import office to claim the car. When they arrived at the building, Aleks sat down in the waiting area on the first floor, while the sisters went upstairs to do the paperwork. When they came back down, they found Aleks - dead. The irony of this is gruesomely humorous and obviously tragic: the excitement of getting his beloved car back may have killed him! More ironic is the two sisters telling me that Aleks would never have received a driver's license in Latvia - so the whole purpose of shipping the car was doomed to failure. I wish I had known.

The date of Aleks' passing was November 6, 2003. I'm glad it was quick and merciful, and that he did not have to struggle with pain for an extended period. He only lasted for 16 months after Mom's passing, which is not a surprise since one cannot live long with half of yourself missing. I have also learned since this time that relationships continue to evolve after someone has passed; I had always thought that the state of a relationship would be frozen at the passing, but I have seen Aleks more clearly and in a better light since his departure.

He deserved better. But the story continues. Since I was now the titular owner of the car, only I could claim it. Notification arrived that the storage charges were about $80 per day. I immediately flew to Latvia, hoping to sell the car there or give it to relatives, but legal complications totally closed this door. So arrangements had to be made to ship it back to New Jersey - again, costing thousands of dollars - where eventually I picked it up and dragged it back to our home in Massachusetts. To complete this strange tale, I then sold the car to in-laws at a very attractive price. The young lady who drove it within about a week completely totaled the car. Fortunately, no one was hurt. So ends the story of the world's most expensive and well-travelled Toyota Corolla!

During this trip to Latvia, I stayed for a few days with Aleks' nieces in their Riga apartment, where they had lived throughout their working years. This was the typical two room plus a bathroom high-rise Soviet apartment, somewhat scary with cold-eyed Russian man with hard stares hanging about, some drunk, with urine smells in the hallway, no elevators, et cetera. But I got to know the sisters, learned of their hard lives as children of an enemy of the people, with their dad having been executed by the Communists. The sisters were extremely pleasant, highly intelligent, but always scared. When they left me alone in their apartment, they first gave severe warnings that I not open the door if anyone knocked. They were deeply concerned that there might be an attempt to rob the rich American relative that had been noticed. All their lives they had kept their heads low. Totalitarian states squeeze the joy out of people and leave them permanently altered, and scared to the bone. They fully realized what an all powerful state can do, and has done, to its citizens.

Anna had wanted to be buried next to Aleks. He had taken her ashes with him to Latvia (interestingly, Mom had refused to visit Latvia while alive), and he was also cremated. He wanted to sleep eternally in his home soil, so burial for both of them had to be in Latvia. The sisters insisted on making the arrangements, and acquired a plot in the locality of Indrani, in the "Visagala Kapi" (cemetery) about 20 miles away from Plavinas, and perhaps 30 miles from Gulbene. Their mother - Aleks' sister, Milda - was already buried there. Since Aleks had died in the fall and the ground was already frozen, the funeral was to be in the spring.

That date was set for April 2004. I had offered to help in any and all ways, naturally feeling that burying my family was my responsibility, but the sisters insisted that they would do all the arrangements. So the plot, the headstone, the minister, and a small remembrance lunch was all planned by them.

The burial was sobering and touching. In attendance were the sisters; a Lutheran minister; Anita (the grandniece of Aleks from Gulbene); my cousins Ievina and Maija; second cousin Ineta (Maija's daughter) and her husband at the time, Ugis; and Aina and Vilis from Gulbene (Aunt Elza's direct family, and also distant relatives of mine, a wonderful helpful and hospitable couple who serve as my hosts when I visit Gulbene). This tiny procession laid Anna and Aleks to rest, together, in the place they both wanted. It was was a tearful, reflective time for me. Reviewing their lives, and the star-crossed journey back to their birth and burial country, fills one with sadness and other feelings - perhaps anger? - over the unfairness of life and the cruelty of mankind…as well as the strength and beauty of love. All these thoughts mixed together and seethed through me at that time.

Things then got strange at the funeral lunch. One of the sisters had a scary, massive headache. I had brought with me some pictures of Aleks and Anna in their happy times and wanted to pass them around to the guests, but the hosts insisted that does not be done. I relented, but was confused, then hurt and quietly angry. The lunch proceeded in a lighthearted manner, with reflections on the good times Aleks and Anna had together, ending with deep and sincere thank you's and goodbyes till the next time, and I left for Massachusetts. The sisters who had done so much for Aleks near the end of his life and beyond were quiet, tense, and seemingly closed off from the rest of us. It was very awkward for the guests.

After I got home, I called the sisters several times to thank them for their efforts and make sure that they were okay, that their needs were being met. I was again received with coldness, quietness, virtually no conversation, and almost hostility. The contrast between this behavior and their behavior during the time I stayed with them after Aleks's death could not have been more striking. At first they had luxuriated in our new relationship, exclaiming it was a bright light in their lives, and a blessing from the otherwise dismal events of their time with Aleks when he joined them in Latvia. But at the end, there were one-word answers to open questions, long silences, and sullenness. This was a highly upsetting mystery. I polled the other attendees of the ceremony and all had noticed the obvious behaviors, and no one had any insight. I have ended up with a theory which I shall keep to myself out of respect for all that the sisters had done, and all they had lived through. But let me mention that they certainly were highly targeted victims of a brutal political system, and this has to have enormous downstream effects, however hidden those may be at times. I feel very sad for them.

CHAPTER 11

EPILOGUE

Since much of the reason for this book was to present a family history, here's the rest of our story.

11.1 FAMILY GALLOWAY

My wife Susan's parents were Donald E. Galloway and Mary Kathryn (Gunther) Galloway. Don was the youngest of 7, and his siblings were named Harold, Jim, Fred, Ethel, Chuck, and Karl. Fred, Jim's twin, died around age 3, but Sue and I knew some of these aunts and uncles quite well, and have stayed in touch particularly with Jim and Annie Galloway - Jim and Helen Galloway's two children - and Hal Galloway, now deceased, Harold and Alice's only child. They all lived in the Rochester, NY area.

Sue's paternal grandfather, Charles, worked for the railroad, and very much enjoyed a drink with his Irish friends and was a poor provider. Around 1953 he probably had a stroke, and died. His wife, Dora, Sue's paternal grandmother, kept the family together - and it wasn't easy. Everybody in the family worked from a young age to make ends meet and all the siblings ended up as successful people. Their innate intelligence, street smarts, and motivation to succeed and escape from their poverty helped make them successful.

Don used to tell the story of working his first job, delivering groceries after school. He saved his money and bought a bed for him himself, because he had none. When he got it home, his mother promptly confiscated it and gave it to older brother Harold, who was working full-time and was perceived to need it more. Characteristically, Don did not tell this tale bitterly, as many would have. Instead, it was told humorously and with a drawn lesson: life isn't always fair, but keep working and you'll end up on top.

Sue's mom, always known as Kay, was one of two siblings born to Irene (Wilson) and Alfred Gunther. Father Alfred had a checkered employment career and moved by himself to Detroit, where the marriage functionally dissolved. It is thought that he started another family there. Mother Irene Gunther was a street smart, tough, intelligent and attractive lady who raised her two daughters on her own. Kay's younger sister, Margaret, married Lynn Bruening, a special guy that we were privileged to know, and they had two children, Margie and Bobby. Bobby died with a heart ailment at the age of 26, and mother Margaret had a fatal heart attack at 48. Margie is the only remaining member of the family, and the only relative of Sue's from her mother's side. We are fond of Margie, her husband Don Greene and their children to this day.

Kay grew up poor but proud, and retained a quiet dignity and loving disposition her entire life. She and Don raised two children, Sue and Donald. Donnie was born on October 12 1942, during World War II. Father Don was drafted into the army within a year of Donnie's birth - fortunately, stationed stateside, not in a foreign foxhole - and so Kay raised young Donnie alone in his early years. Young Don had a great mind for math, and displayed a very independent, headstrong streak. He took on various jobs after graduation from West High School in Rochester, and ended up being part of father Don's business, a distributorship for Beltone Electronics, the world leader in hearing aids and accessories. Relations with father Don were not easy. Don the elder was a headstrong, dominating and somewhat intimidating personality - as was Donnie the younger! So they worked together for years, but with conflict. Ultimately, it all ended up well. Younger Don became a great, dutiful son in the last years of his parents' lives, and a great friend to me and a great brother to Sue. His wife, Carol, remains a good friend to this day, and they had a wonderful marriage that produced two sons, Dan and Brian.

Donnie inherited the hearing aid business in 2005 after his father's passing, and he and Carol were planning to move from Rochester to Arizona, near to son Brian and his family. Brian is a member of the border patrol protecting our southern flank. Then tragedy struck. While visiting son Dan in New York City, Don experienced what he thought was serious indigestion. While waiting in their hotel room for his family to bring in a take out dinner, he died of a massive heart attack on August 20, 2006, at the age of 63.

Carol moved to Green Valley, Arizona, near Tucson. She seems content there, is near her son Brian, his wife and granddaughter. Her oldest son Dan, a successful banker living in Charlotte North Carolina, the headquarters of his employer, Bank of America, has two sons, is remarried, and visits his mother often in Arizona.

But back to Kay and Don, Sue's parents. After their marriage on August 18,1934, Don worked in sales at Rochester Gas & Electric. Then he moved into the electronics field with television, a rapidly emerging market, as his focus. He was drafted in World War II but spent his time stateside as an electronics expert. Upon returning home in 1945 Don was determined to stay in some branch of electronics, so in 1948 he became a distributor for Beltone, a prominent hearing aid manufacturer. He played an outsized role in this industry for his lifetime, being President of the National Association, and even being a member of President Nixon's Council on Aging. Kay and Don had daughter Susan in 1947, which rounded out their family, and they moved from an apartment on Flint Street in Rochester to a nice home on 440 Wellington Avenue in Rochester's 19th Ward. Kay worked in their office in the Sibley Tower Building, and raised the children. These were the traditional roles of the times - the father as main provider, the mother helping out economically whenever possible, but primarily raising the children and managing the household. It worked for Don and Kay, and their lives were satisfying.

Don was also involved local politics, and became an alderman of Rochester's 19th Ward. He knew many politicians, did many good works, and used his public exposure the best that he could to enhance the Beltone business. Don was a businessman to the core, and not really a politician. The lessons of his early life were never lost, and he worked diligently, seven days a week, until he was hospitalized at age 96 and died at 97 of cancer. I have never known a more dedicated, hard worker, and I give Don great credit for teaching me about hard work and perseverance during the short time I worked for him. These lessons, plus my first-time exposure to the high level business skills that Dan possessed, were absolutely critical to my future business endeavors.

The Galloways moved to the beautiful Georgetown condominium complex in Fairport, New York in 1973. Don continued work, and Kay ran the household. Because of Don's outsized personality, Kay had to take a secondary role in many decisions and maintained a quieter persona, but basically they were both happy.

Kay had a hip replacement in the late 1980s, a major surgery at the time. Later she had lung cancer and a lobe was removed. She remained quietly cheerful and dignified throughout all these procedures. In 2000 she went into a nursing home, and despite all her hopes and plans to the contrary, never came out. She died on March 19, 2003 at age 92. Characteristically, she hung on while we children were at her bedside, and as soon as we left, she passed. That was the final loving act of a lovely lady.

After Kay's passing, Don lived on alone at the Georgetown condo through 2004. At one point he developed severe stomach aches and drove himself to the hospital. He was diagnosed with sepsis, needed immediate surgery, and never really recovered. He had had colon cancer in 1972, and had a colostomy bag for 30 years - never complaining, always staying positive; but complications in that area final resulted in the surgery just mentioned, followed by an additional diagnosis of cancer in multiple sites, including his bones. Don want to a nursing home in Penfield New York, and died at age 97 with Sue next to him on May 22, 2005.

11.2 SUE: EARLY YEARS; GUARDIAN ANGEL STRIKES AGAIN!

Now on to my dear wife Sue. She was born in Rochester General Hospital on 3/25/47, in the middle of the year's biggest snowstorm - which in Rochester, a prime snow-effect geography, is a really big deal. Her younger years were pleasant, with the strong mother and father, an older brother somewhat distant from her due to the age gap, and aunts, uncles and cousins with whom to share the holidays. Dad's business was doing well and they were financially in good shape. The family bought a small cottage in Sodus Point, New York, directly across the street from the Sodus Bay Country Club, overlooking this beautiful Lake Ontario bay. Many good summers were spent here.

Sue was a good student through grade school and at West High School, where her father had also attended. She had close friends and an active social life. Upon graduation, she first attended Adelphi University in Long Island, but was not happy there since a large part of the student body were commuters. Next came a transfer to Nazareth College in Rochester for her sophomore year, followed by the final transfer to the State University of New York at Geneseo for two years. Speech pathology was the major, and Geneseo had a world renowned program in that area, headed by the distinguished Dr. Starbuck. Ironically, Sue developed a voice issue - Spasmodic Dysphonia - in her early 50s, a neurological condition managed with botox injections.

In early May 1966, following her year at Adelphi, Sue and I met. The circumstances make for another intriguing story featuring fate in the leading role. We were both back in the Rochester area following the school year (Sue's freshman year, my sophomore year), and attended a dance featuring a popular local band, Wilmer Alexander Jr. and the Dukes. Toward the end of the evening, in a burst of courage, I asked an exotic beauty - Sue! - for a dance. She accepted, we had fun and got along, and I asked for and received her phone number. The next weekend I met her parents as I picked her up on our first date, which we both enjoyed. The following week, I again asked Sue for a date, but she could not accept because brother Don's marriage to Carol was happening that weekend. So I went out with my buddy Stan to another Dukes dance, being held at Bristol Mountain Ski Center on June 5/6, 1966. The plan was to spend the night at Stan's parents' cottage on the southeast end of Canandaigua Lake, not far from Bristol Mountain. We never made it. Stan's 1957 MGA sports car - two-seater, convertible, no seatbelts - missed a curve in Bristol Center, in front of the church, and plowed into a vineyard replete with stakes, wires and vines. I was thrown out on impact.

On the next morning, June 6, I woke up in Canandaigua Hospital, with no memory of the accident (and I still have none). The big concern was the possible brain bleed, along with lesser injuries of a serious concussion and facial and body lacerations that had been stitched up upon my arrival in the hospital. That morning, when I came to, the first memories began. I was being wheeled somewhere and caught a reflection of a swollen, discolored, lacerated and stitched up face in a mirror. At first, I had no recognition of what I was seeing, and then it dawned on me like a thunderbolt - that this was me! Although I was frightening to behold, the big picture was quite good. The feared brain involvement did not materialize, and I was released to go home in a few days and continued treatment with our family doctor.

Needless to say, my appearance extinguished all confidence with the opposite sex. I planned to simply not call Sue and just end the one date relationship then and there. She should not be expected to date someone who looked like me.

A week or so later I had to go into downtown Rochester to a photography studio to have pictures taken for insurance purposes. When my mother and I went into the waiting room, who should be sitting there but Sue's mother! She did not recognize me - I was better but nowhere near my pre-accident self. I whispered Kay's identity to my Mom, and she said "go say hello". I at first refused, but she nudged me and repeated her words. So I went over to Kay and reintroduced myself and Kay said the magic words, "You ought to give Susie a call". I believe that is a direct quote. So I did, Sue accepted my call, and we began to date again after I had healed a bit more.

Was this mere circumstance - or fate - or the invisible hand of God's will - or again the work of my Guardian Angel, Arnolds? I'm not sure, though others have strong opinions about these possibilities. The Rochester area is large, with 1,000,000+ people, and Sue lived in the western part of the city while I was in the east. As the birthplace of Eastman Kodak Company, Rochester offered a choice of many photographic studios. Timing had to be perfect; there was an overlap of only several minutes in the waiting room between Kay picking up the wedding photos and Mom's and my arrival. So the odds of meeting at exactly the same place at exactly the same time, brought together for entirely different reasons, were infinitesimally small...but it happened, and everyone's life changed because of that chance meeting. We have been in love for 50+ years!

Sue and I continued dating through college. I graduated in 1968, joined VISTA (Volunteers in Service to America) and was stationed in the Ozark Mountains of Arkansas. Sue graduated in 1969, and, probably in May - thoughtlessly living little time for planning - I asked for her hand in marriage by phone. On June 27, 1969 we were married back home and immediately drove back to Arkansas to finish my VISTA commitment.

11.3 INDULIS' STORY, CONTINUED

I attended East Rochester High School from 1960 - 1964, did well as a student and athlete, and started getting some pride in myself. Upon graduation with a 90 average, I won a Regents Scholarship and a small local scholarship. ER was a great school for me from a number of perspectives, with outstanding teachers and coaches, and I have maintained relationships from that time to this day. Too much time was also spent surreptitiously in Ely's Pool Hall, where some street-smarts were etched into me. In high school athletics, I applied some God-given gifts of speed and leaping ability - I could dunk a basketball at 5'8" - as a member of some great basketball teams, undefeated for years, and in track, I won titles in the long jump with a personal best of 22'2". Besides my own vanity, I mention this because jumping is genetic; if any of my descendants display this trait, they can trace it back a bit and blame me, as I wish I could blame some ancestor who achieved local fame by jumping haystacks and streams.

At the State University of New York at Buffalo my record was subpar. I was drifting and on my own, did not study hard, ending up with a B average. Starting in Chemistry, I soon began switching majors and ended up in Geography, primarily due to the influence of a great teacher. Basically I followed my heart, with the romance of foreign places trumping any concept of obtaining a major which might point me toward a more direct career. It has all worked out, but there were many mistakes made by an unguided, unsophisticated kid - me. My college track career also ended early, with a slow-healing heel injury that stopped me cold. There was also a 2 year stint in Air Force ROTC that I did not appreciate at the time but that ultimately gave me valuable insight about those who serve.

Sue and I dated during the last half of college, and immediately after graduation in 1968, I began my service in VISTA (Volunteers in Service to America). This choice was partially due to my need to do something socially relevant in those fast changing times, and partially to gain a one year deferment from being drafted. It was the height of the Vietnam War and college grads were being sent there in droves.

For VISTA, I trained six weeks at the University of Oklahoma and nearby environs. There was a strong civil rights aspect to the training, and our Nation was undergoing a trauma while properly straightening out the relationship between the races. Racism against black Americans was still baked into our culture at that time, and conditions and opportunities for minorities were quite horrible. Universities and students played a leading role in calling for change, and acted on the need through organizations such as VISTA.

I was trained to be a "community organizer" - just like Pres. Obama in his early career! As part of the training, I lived with a black family in a semi-rural ghetto in Chickasha, Oklahoma, for three weeks. It was an interesting experience, and having been somewhat poor and an outsider myself, I could relate.

After the six weeks of training in ways to right racial wrongs, I was assigned as a VISTA volunteer to Newton County, Arkansas, deep in the Ozark Mountains... an entirely white geography! No prior volunteer had lasted the one-year tour of duty there, and five of us - three males and two females, were sent there to serve. Three volunteers soon quit, and a fellow volunteer, Bob, and I did serve out our full tours. We ended up doing mostly service work -taking people to hospitals etc., and did set up a wood-cutting business where unemployed youth cut timber, the primary winter fuel, with some of it being given to the poor, and the rest being sold. Most of the efforts, unfortunately, could be described as failures. The lesson is that poverty is caused by a variety of variables, with solutions that are complex and difficult, and with truths that are often unpleasant to acknowledge.

Just prior to enrolling in VISTA, I had asked Sue for an engagement. About three-fourths of the way through my tour, we arranged to get married on June 27, 1969. We headed back for Arkansas later that night after the ceremony and reception. Our Volkswagen was loaded and dragged a small U-Haul trailer full of our life's possessions, and we headed back to finish my tour at VISTA, which ended in August 1969.

We have been happily together ever since!

11.4 SUE, INDY...PLUS LAUREN AND AMY

We moved back to Rochester and soon had our first apartment, an upstairs unit on Rundel Park. Sue had a job in a temporary placement office and then at the Board of Cooperative Educational Services, and I was a groundskeeper at Oak Hill Country Club, where many US Opens were played. Then, in 1971, we headed to Albany, New York. Sue had a full-time job at the Northeast New York Speech and Hearing Center and started on a Masters degree in Speech Pathology at the State University of New York at Albany. I attended the Albany Law School of Union University. After one semester, I resigned and got a job as a "communications consultant "- i.e. sales - for the New York Telephone Company. It was during my physical for the NY Tel job that a spine issue was revealed, resulting in a 4F deferment from the draft. With Vietnam now in our rearview mirror, we upgraded our small apartment at 91 Shaker Ln., Albany, by building a new three bedroom, one bath, one car garage ranch house on a lot in East Greenbush, just across the Hudson River.

Time out for a cute related story: in 2016 I ended up in the Anne Arundel Medical Center in Annapolis, Maryland with some complications following large-intestine surgery. While being prepared for some tests, the nurse and I began conversing, leading to the discovery that we had both once lived in the Albany, New York area. I asked her which town she lived in - she replied East Greenbush - I responded that we had also lived there - and then she said that she grew up at 37 Tamarack Ln., which was directly across the street from our first house at 36 Tamarack Ln! Although Sue and I had moved out of the area several years before the nurse's family bought this house, we knew common neighbors, and she was good friends with the people who had bought our house. To add to the coincidence, our daughter Amy had been the transplant coordinator for a few months at Georgetown Hospital before resuming her former position in inten-sive care - and the nurse that replaced Amy as the new transplant team coordinator at Georgetown was this same nurse! What are the odds of these two coincidences happening between our families?

Now, back to our story. After building the house and having some income, it was time to have children. Our first daughter, Lauren Marie Pommers, was born at Albany Medical Center on September 1, 1972, and her first home was on Tamarack Lane. All three of us were comfortable and the extended family was thrilled with our new arrival.

After Sue got her first Masters degree, we moved. I became enamored of being part of a successful family business - my father-in-law Don Galloway's Beltone franchise - and he welcomed me. We moved back to Rochester in 1974 to a three bedroom, bath and a half, single car garage, split level located at the top of the steep driveway at 38 Farmview Drive in rural West Walworth, New York. It was served by the excellent Penfield School District. Sue got a job at the Al Siegel Center, a great speech and hearing clinic. The plan was to have a second child, and this did happen very soon. Amy Beth Pommers was born on June 26, 1975, another beautiful child, and our family was complete. We did have a major scare during this time when Amy, at the age of 2, got viral meningitis and had a severely weakened leg, but she soon recovered with no continuing problems.

My career at Beltone was a decidedly mixed bag. Father-in-law Don taught me well in the fundamentals of business, which came as a shock to me, but for which I will ever be grateful. However, I was not motivated and was not a great addition to the team. Consequently, in 1976, I was hired by MDSI, and this CAD/CAM (Computer Aided Design and Manufacturing) Company was my first exposure to computers and software. The district manager who hired me, Steve, I looked up to and remember gratefully to this day. This was also the beginning of a lifetime friendship with Aaron, a great businessman, intelligent, hard-working and street smart. Aaron also had the DP experience in Germany, plus the US immigrant experience, and we've always been able to complete each others' sentences.

In 1979 I was promoted by MDSI to Boston, and we moved to 606 Old Stone Brook in the Nagog Woods condo development in Acton, Massachusetts. This was home until 1991. Nagog was a terrific place, with a pool, tennis courts, a clubhouse, and with people just like us with children like ours. There are still many deep friendships from those days, with people like Pam and Jack, Marty and Patty, Jay and Roe, Howie and Ronna, Bob, and others.

Sue got a job in Medford as a speech and hearing therapist at a small private preschool. It was a long commute and a half-time job, so she kept looking. Around 1980 she got a position as a speech and language therapist in the Concord Massachusetts School District, at the Thoreau School in West Concord. Sue's work was prized there, and she stayed in the District until her retirement in 2006, giving a lot but learning even more. Her final job there was as a Special Education Team Chairperson for out-of-district placements, and as the Preschool Coordinator/Team Chair. Many children and families were helped by Sue's efforts, and many lifelong friendships were formed, especially with Ina and Ron.

My work life became spotty. Notice a trend? I left MDSI in 1981 and soon joined a small competitor, Encode, in the same CAD/CAM space. In 1982, following a reorganization at Encode, I got a new position at another CAD/CAM start up, Cadlinc (aka Cimlinc Inc.). This company was funded by the famous Palo Alto, California venture firm of Kleiner Perkins; it was to be a fast growth company but it ultimately just missed going public, becoming "the living dead" in venture capital terms. I had some stock which became worthless, got exposure to people like John Doerr, the famous Dean of the VC world, but, most importantly, I caught the startup bug. In 1984 I was fired after an open dispute with a Cadlinc VP. Despite this ugly termination, there were many valuable lessons, among them being that in the startup world success is quite rare, difficult, and noisy; and that failure is common, easy, and silent. Looking for something I could grow, I soon joined a small software company in Concord that had developed a simulation software program (ACSL®). As VP of Sales, I staffed up, got results, and started a new subsidiary called MGA Inc. of which I was part owner and president.

The function of this new entity was to plan and execute the marketing and selling tasks of new technical software products, using and refining our prior successful techniques. Many software products were launched. One of these, Matlab®, became a world leading, serious winner. By 1991 Matlab was a renowned, successful product, and the parent company was bigger than we were. After heavy negotiations and offers to combine companies, I left and used the proceeds of the transaction to start another new company, Amber Technologies. The charter was to be the same as for MGA Inc. - to monetize new technical software.

Amber at first grew quickly, and then floundered when certain software products fell behind the fast-moving times. In 1994-1995 things were very unpleasant, with expensive lawsuits and almost total loss of the income stream. I was a mess - could not eat or sleep - and shrink from 200 pounds to 165. At the very lowest point, I drove home midday and tearfully pleaded for my deceased Father and siblings to help me, that it was unfair for them to have abandoned me. Perhaps my pleas were heard and answered because soon thereafter I spotted an ad for a large data set analysis software program from a Boston-based company; my impression was that this could be a good fit. That small company, Unica, did need our services and we began to work together. Ultimately we merged the companies and I served as president. The core product was software and services employing pattern recognition in large data sets, with artificial intelligence and machine learning attributes. We focused this product to the CRM (Customer Relationship Management) space, to better predict future customer behavior and needs based on analysis of their past activities. In retrospect, Unica was a very early pioneer and thought leader in what is now an exploding market. Upon acquiring venture funding around 1999-2000, it was time for me to leave. The company went public on NASDAQ in 2005 - with a decent return for the money I had put into the start-up phase - and was purchased by IBM in 2010. I thus had the sweet pleasure of helping build, with talented partners, a Company from nothing to a valuation of $.5B. Perhaps my Guardian Angel had a hand in this?

While I was business-adventuring, sometimes without income, Sue was drawing a steady paycheck and important benefits like medical insurance. Any successes were our successes. Although we had to focus on making a living, much of our time was spent raising our kids and performing all the typical parental tasks. We gave them a good start on life, on which they have nicely built.

Daughter #1, Lauren, graduated from the University of Vermont with an IT/Business degree, and later earned a Masters in Education to pursue her interest in reading instruction. She married Matthew, a star football player and great student at Middlebury College, followed by a highly successful career as an investment banker. Their children are Maya and Nina, bright children with exceptional talents.

Daughter #2, Amy, graduated from Villanova University with a BS in Nursing and has worked in Intensive Care hospital units for years, witnessing hair-raising events and saving countless lives. She met husband Sean, a great swimmer and student, at Villanova, and he went on to become a very successful Dentist. They have 3 children, Caitlin, Anna, and Matthew, who are also all bright children with exceptional talents.

We are not biased!

Sue and I are blessed to have these daughters and their families in our lives. They are all caring people who make the world a better place. We often thank the fates for each of them and hope that their odysseys continue on their wonderful vectors, and that their disappointments are few and far between. We take comfort in the sense that our Guardian Angel watches over us all.

To complete our story, in 1991 we built a new home at 8 Larch Rd in Acton, and lived there until 2007. After Unica went public in 2005, I fully retired while Sue kept on for a year. We started searching for a home in a warmer place, yet near the children. In 2006 we bought our present home, on South River Landing Rd. in Edgewater, Maryland, and moved in 2007. This home overlooks the South River, has a community boat pier that houses our boat - "Aleksandra", a 34 foot power boat - and is simply a great place to live. Daughter Lauren and family are thousands of miles away, but Daughter Amy and her family are only an hour's drive. Our lives are spent boating, traveling, golfing, being with friends from our community and the Annapolis Yacht Club, and enjoying our children and their families.

No regrets - its been a great life…and maybe we got some angelic help?

CHAPTER 12

REFLECTIONS

What might be learned through this search through my family's past, especially through those tumultuous times when trapped between Hitler and Stalin, between Nazism and Communism? The chilling events that my research screamed at me was overwhelming; the early roots began only 40 miles away from my family, at the Russian border, but soon engulfed my ancestral nation and people. Becoming immersed in the stories of the millions of innocents, their living agonies and silent deaths, makes one ponder about the human condition, and inspired some scatter-gun thoughts.

An inescapable reflection has been the acknowledgement, forced on me, of the heavy hand and consequent importance of Fate. It is amazing how the intersection of person, place and time can affect so much in a life; where seemingly random events coalesce to form full pictures, for good and bad. We all want control of our lives, and we do have some control. Yet often large events simply appear, and sweep past our illusions of control - and what happens simply happens. The power, mystery and majesty of Fate and its religious overtones is breathtaking. And yes, there just might be guardian angels!

Another lesson increasingly hammered home was the importance of context to enhanced understanding. Events are best measured and labeled from the perspective of the human condition, drawn from the broadest possible examples, and not from a theoretical perfection. My readings, so often revealing the darkness that visited so many, helped in this regard. Those tougher issues of American life can often be better dealt with by appreciation of what so many other world citizens have survived - so this has been a gift to me, and perhaps to my readers - while not denying the very real traumas that all humans can face. The rough histories that my family lived through are not uncommon, and put lesser problems of modern life in their proper place.

A sad reflection is the acknowledgment of man's cruelty to man. History reveals that it breaks out on a continual basis, and so its roots must always be around, just sometimes in the shadows. The cruelties are often justified by the perpetrators, typically saying that it's to make the future better - or accelerate a righteous dream - or perhaps it's simply Darwinian, with competition determining that the strongest survive. All we can do is publicize the crimes and try to avoid them in our own lives and political systems, if we have a choice.

The power of religion lit up my exploration of history. Though only possessing a weak classic religious gene myself, the deep human need for religion and its consequences is profound. Those who best survived the horrors I have documented were believers; when atheistic governing systems tried to take over, they always targeted the religious structures early, because they feared their power; and after extinguishing religion, the new atheistic rulers would de facto replace it…with themselves!

Ask! If you want to know that great novel of your family history, and as you age, you will - ask before it's too late. I thought I inquired a lot, but now I realize the gaps in knowledge that I yearn to fill - but it's too late. Ask!

Finally, a lesson drawn from my exploration involves political governance. The difficulties my family experienced and the absolute horrors of their Neighborhood, lasting decades and totally defining hundreds of millions of lives, have a common root cause - bad governments. Certain choices, despite good intentions to "make things better", can have nightmarish consequences. Generally, the Capitalist economic system and its connected political system, Democracy, appear by any rational examination and measure to be superior to alternatives, although not perfect. A good proof is that people flee toward Capitalism systems, if allowed.

In contrast, Socialism, broadly defined, with its tendency to slide left toward the Communist economic system, too often has Dictatorship as its connected political system. While the Socialist systems aim to right wrongs, and have certainly had some historic success, their cure is almost universally worse than the disease. Witness the proofs: poverty and inequality grow; re-education and slaughter of the citizenry becomes too common; and most tellingly, citizens try to leave, taking existential risks to get away, but are fenced in. This evidence is clear in the examples of Russia, all the nations of Eastern Europe, much of South America, China, North Korea, Cuba, Venezuela, and many others, including Nazi Germany (yes, "Nazi" means "National Socialism").

Why is this? What so commonly connects Dictatorship to "Socialist" societies? I believe that the major culprit is the concentration of power, which seems to be an inevitability. When a ruling group gets to make all the choices - economic, political, cultural , religious etc. - tremendous power accrues, and attracts those who seek power as their primary focus. Hitler, Stalin, Mao, Maduro, PolPot, Castro etc., again, are not accidents. Once in power, these folks do not want to give it up. They believe that they reflect absolute truth and superior moral righteousness. So they might change the constitution to maintain power - "the job is not yet done!" - and they arrest or eliminate anyone not bowing to them. Furthermore, having murdered their way to the top, they soon realize that they have created serious enemies, and maintaining power becomes a very personal, existential act. Anyone offering alternatives is labeled an enemy of the state, and it becomes a moral act to beat sense into them, or perhaps eliminate them entirely - all to make the world a better place! When people compete for this dizzying level of power, the worst person wins. The one willing to first pull the trigger on the rivals triumphs.

In brief contrast, Capitalism/Democracy tends to disperse power. Citizens can generally make their own choices, within certain limits imposed by popular mandate. There must always be an element of socially responsible behavior and resource sharing, but just where this line gets drawn is key to the political drama, with an incorrect placement becoming all too often catastrophic. The distinction between these competing systems of governance is clear. There is no perfection in any system created by humans, but there is better or worse. Support better!

Free citizens must stay alert to the steps that lead to totalitarianism and its profound consequences. So beware of the fanning of class warfare, whether ethnic, economic or national; bookburning; politicalization of the judiciary, security, and government workers; compromised media; vote manipulation; de-arming of the citizenry; false narratives of history; politicized education; thought crimes; squelching of dissenting thought; mocking of religion; and re-defining language. Educate yourself on how the Nazis, Soviet, Chinese, North Korean and many other Communist and Socialist nations acquired and maintained power. Avoid the steps they took. If not, the results can be truly horrifying.

We in the free West live in a good place at a good time, under economic and political systems that generally deliver the greatest good for the greatest number, all in sharp contrast to competing systems that sound good but have a dismal record. Realize this, defend it with word and deed, cherish it, and thank those who have sacrificed to keep it.

So this story ends. My family survived through all the curveballs life threw at them, and the next generation thrived. Our ancestors were a strong group, toughened by their history, the offspring of hardy souls who always did what they had to do to make things better for their children. May we all inherit the courage and resilience they displayed.

ACKNOWLEDGEMENTS

Primary encouragement and motivation were provided by my patient wife, Sue, who had to deal with the funks that occur while her mate was marinating in some difficult subjects. Thanks, Hon! I love you for this and so many other reasons. Daughters Lauren and Amy provided additional motivation to get our family story out to them and the next generations. Cousins Kitty, Inara and Lee were especially supportive information sources, with Kitty the elder deserving special accolade for her vivid recollections. Thanks also to relatives Andris, Vilnis and Maris, and boating friend and author, Ward Anderson.

Discussions and interviews with my Latvian family obviously gave me much of the personal family history material recounted here. Mom was the biggest contributor - she should be smiling down from heaven, happy that her stories are out - and Stepfather Aleks contributed greatly, though in a terse manner. Uncle Arturs and Aunt Elza, along with their 3 daughters mentioned earlier, shared their knowledge and filled in many dates and gaps in the narrative. In Latvia, cousins Ievina and Maija were a fountain of knowledge, shared with joy; cousin Ineta and husband Agris often changed their plans to become wise tour guides imparting both general historic information and family specifics; and in the hometown of Gulbene, my relatives Aina and Vilis and their daughter Daiga plus others of their family have always been most welcoming while providing deep knowledge of history of the country and locale. Aleks' grandniece Anita, from Gulbene, was a huge source of Siraks family history. All my informants are very bright, curious and interesting people, and I hope that their traits will flow downstream - and so far, so good. My profound thanks goes out to all.

Although it's too late, our cousin Rita Jaunzemis deserves accolades for her memoir, published here. Her suffering in the Gulag should not be forgotten. Kudos to Cousins Andris and Vilnis for retaining this document all these years, and sharing it.

The non-interview body of the narrative comes from numerous sources: hundreds of books, newspaper and magazine articles; on-line articles and studies, especially Latvian Government data freely available to all; more recently, an explosion of relevant YouTube videos; and museum visits, especially the Museum of Occupation and the Corner House Museum, both in Riga, and other Museums in different countries including Ireland and the Czech Republic, which gave overview and insight into the Communist ways.

Books were a source of information, with many of them listed below, but several books deserve special mention. Melanija Vanaga's book "Suddenly, A Criminal: *Sixteen Years In Siberia*" (translated by Marata Voitkus-Lukins, FriesenPress 2015) gave specific information very relevant to my family history, so I summarized a few of her pages to better explain the times and places. Aleksandr Solzhenitsyn's entire body of work is heroic, especially since published under extreme duress. His "One Day In The Life Of Ivan Denisovich" opened the gate to expose the hidden conditions in the USSR, and deeply affected me. Authors Varlam Shalamov, Eugenia Ginzburg and Anne Applebaum deserve special highlighting, but there are many others, both observers and victims, who have helped reveal the conditions surrounding my family story. I applaud them all.

SUGGESTED READINGS

The books listed below are a partial list of readings that influenced the flavor and facts of this effort. I want to thank the authors for their insights, but more importantly pay tribute to those writers who survived the grimmest times, yet had the courage to write about their experiences. This was often done during times when their political culture wanted to stop them by cancelling their works...or even their lives...to hide the truth.

Alexievich "Secondhand Time"

Allaback "Alexander Solzhenitsyn"

Ambrose "D Day"

Anderson "Flight From Ukraine"

Amster/Asbell "Transit Point Moscow"

Apinis "Latvia - Country, Nation, State"

Applebaum "Gulag"

Applebaum "Iron Curtain"

Applebaum "Red Famine"

Avedon "In Exile From the Land of Snows"

Bankovics "Driven West, Taken East"

Beevor "Stalingrad"

Benton "Baltic Countdown"

Binyon "Life in Russia"

Bissell "Chasing the Sea"

Blosfelds "Stormtrooper on the Eastern Front"

Bonsfield "The Rough Guide to the Baltic States"

Browder "Red Notice"

Bukovsky "To Build a Castle"

Bullock "Hitler"

Burg/Feifer "Solzhenitsyn"

Buruma "Year Zero: A History of 1945"

Buttar "Between Giants"

Butterfield "China"

Chang/Halliday "Mao"

Charles River Editors "Siberia and the Gulag"

Conquest "Harvest of Sorrow"

Cox "The Soviet Takeover of Latvia"

Crankshaw "Putting Up with the Russians"

Davies "Heart of Europe"

Davies "Mission to Moscow"

Dirlam "Beyond Siberia"

Djilas "Conversations With Stalin"

Doder "Shadows and Whispers"

Dolgun/Watson "An American in the Gulag"

Dolot "Execution by Hunger"

Dreiser "Dreiser Looks at Russia"

Duffey "Red Storm on the Reich"

Dwyer "Between Two Tyrannies"

Egremont "Forgotten Land"

Eksteins "Walking Since Daybreak"

Fatland "The Border"

Figes "Natasha's Dance"

Figes "Revolutionary Russia 1891-1991"

Figes "The Whisperers"

Frazier "Travels in Siberia"

Fritz "Frontsoldaten"

Garrels "Putin's Country"

Ginzburg "Journey Into the Whirlwind"

Ginsburg "Within the Whirlwind"

Grant "In the Time of Famine"

Grazzini "Solzhenitsyn"

Greene "Midnight in Siberia"

Grossman "Life and Fate"

Hanson "The Second World Wars"

Howe "The Koreans"

Hyde "Stalin"

Irbitis "Of Struggle and Flight"

Ji Li Jiang "Red Scarf Girl"

Kaiser "Russia"

Kaplikis "Exile From Latvia"

Kapuscinski "Imperium"

Karski "Story of a Secret State"

Keenan "Russia and the West"

Klemme "The Inside Story of UNRRA"

Klose "Russia and the Russians"

Koestler "Darkness at Noon"

Konengsberger "Along the Roads of the New Russia"

Korotich/Porter "The New Soviet Journalism"

Kostov/Whiting "The Gulag Rats"

Kovaly "Under a Cruel Star"

Kowalski "Hell on Earth"

Kramer "A Journey to the Russian Heartland"

Kubica "The Gulag Trail"

Kruschev "Kruschev Remembers"

Kuhn/Kuhn "Russia on Our Minds"

Lebedev "Oblivion"

Lee "Russian Journal"

Levchenko "On the Wrong Side"

Lewis "Red Pawn"

Lewis "Soviet Union"

Lowe "Savage Continent"

Manvell/Fraenkel "Heinrich Himmler"

Martin "Winter Dreams"

McCormick/Burton "Lenin's Harem"

Medvedev "All Stalin's Men"

Milosz "The Captive Mind"

Montefiore "Stalin"

Moorhouse "Berlin at War"

Nagorski "Reluctant Farewell"

Napjus "Ada and Andrius"

Nekipelov "Institute of Fools"

Nekrich "The Punished Peoples"

Nesaule "A Woman in Amber"

Newby "The Big Red Train Ride"

Olson "Citizens of London"

Penkovsky "The Penkovsky Papers"

Pezzino "Three Small Pebbles"

Plakans "The Latvians: A Short History"

Polansky "Molotov's Magic Lantern"

Pond "From Yaroslavsky Station"

Punga/Hough "Guide to Latvia"

Ramsdell "A Train to Potovka"

Ratushinskaya "Grey is the Color of Hope"

Raven/Raven "Driving the Trans-Siberian"

Reid "Leningrad: The Epic Siege of WWII 1941-1945"

Rohan "Siberian Odyssey"

Rupert "A Hidden World"

Ryan "Last Words: Surviving the Holocaust"

Rybarczyk "Neighbors From Hell"

Salisbury "Russia"

Schecter "An American Family in Moscow"

Schlagel "Moscow, 1937"

Schneider "The German Comedy"

Sejna "We Will Bury You"

Sepetys "Between Shades of Gray"

Sepetys "Salt to the Sea"

Sereny "Into That Darkness"

Shalamov "Sketches of the Criminal World"

Shalamov "Kolyma Stories"

Shevchenko "Breaking Moscow"

Shifrin "The First Guidebook to Prisons and Concentration Camps of the Soviet Union"

Shipler "Russia"

Shirer "The Nightmare Years"

Smith "The New Russians"

Smith "The Russians"

Snyder "Bloodlands"

Solzhenitsyn "Cancer Ward"

Solzhenitsyn "Lenin in Zurich"

Solzhenitsyn "One day in the Life of Ivan Denisovich"

Solzhenitsyn "The First Circle"

Solzhenitsyn "The Gulag Archipelago" Books 1, 2, 3

Suvarov "The Liberators"

Svencs "The Latvian Legion (1943-1945)"

Tanner "Ticket to Latvia"

Taubman "Kruschev"

Taubman "Moscow Spring"

Taurins "Between Two Tyrannies"

Taylor "River of No Reprieve"

Tesson "Berezina"

Thubron "Among the Russians"

Thubron "Behind the Wall"

Thubron "In Siberia"

Thubron "Shadow of the Silk Road"

Thubron "The Lost Heart of Asia"

Tobien "Dancing Under the Red Star"

Toland "Adolph Hitler"

Tzouliadis "The Forsaken"

Vanaga "Suddenly, a Criminal"

Veedam/Wall "Sailing to Freedom"

Vellutini "Stories From My Life"

Verzemnieks "Among the Living and the Dead"

Vilka "Caur Sirdi Plustosa Dzive"

Weschler "A Miracle, a Universe"

Willis "Klass"

Wren "The End of the Line"

Wyman "DP's"

Yakovlev "A Century of Violence in Soviet Russia"

Zarina "The Red Fog"

Zgustova "Dressed for a Dance in the Snow"